Reverends
JAMES KILLGALLON,
GERARD WEBER
and
LEONARD ZIEGMANN

Life in Christ

Revised Edition

Life in Christ • *233 E. Erie Street* • *Chicago, Illinois 60611*

NIHIL OBSTAT
   Rev. Msgr. James K. Lafferty
   Censor Librorum

IMPRIMATUR
† Most Rev. Frank H. Greteman D.D.
   Bishop of Sioux City

March 19, 1976

First Edition July 1958
1,250,000 copies in print.
Second Edition
First printing Sept. 1976–35,000
Second printing Nov. 1976–65,000
Third printing May 1978–50,000
Fourth printing May 1979–75,000
Printed in the U.S.A.

Foundation for Adult Catechetical Teaching Aids

Library of Congress Catalogue No. 76-26451
ISBN No. 0-914070-08-8

Introduction

GOD, OUR FATHER, has spoken to us, revealing to us the meaning and purpose of our life. He sent his Son, Jesus Christ, to redeem us and to teach us the truths by which we are to live as children of God.

The study of a catechism is a study of the teachings of our Savior, Jesus Christ. The more diligence and thoroughness we bring to such a study the better we shall know the life-giving truths which Christ came to teach us.

But mere study will enable us to know only the *teachings* of Jesus Christ. It is not enough to know his teachings. We must know Jesus Christ himself. We must know him and love him and, by living according to his teachings and his example, strive to become more and more like him. It is only by being united to Christ, his Son, and by loving him and all men in him that we can be pleasing to our heavenly Father.

While studying the teachings of Jesus Christ, therefore, we must pray to him. We must pray for help to understand those teachings, and we must make an effort to apply to our daily life the truths we are coming to know. We must also enter into the prayer-life of the Church, in which we re-live every year the life of Christ and pray to the Father through Christ.

One of the chief aims of this catechism is to help those who study it to become familiar with the inspired word of God, the Holy Scriptures. The many scriptural references and texts which are contained herein are meant to be studied in connection with the lessons in which they appear. Such a study, the authors believe, is really necessary for a truly effective use of *Life in Christ*.

3

For this reason those who use this catechism should have their own copy of the New Testament, in order that they might read and study it in connection with the lessons.

An attempt has been made, too, to introduce prospective converts gradually to the liturgical life of the Church and to the private devotional practices which are part of the life of the Church.

At the end of most of the lessons there is a suggested practice. In the first half of the catechism these practices are mostly concerned with learning and saying certain prayers and with the reading of Scripture, particularly the New Testament By using these practices the will as well as the intellect will be brought into use right at the outset.

When *Life in Christ* made its appearance in 1958 it was seen as something of a new approach to catechetics. The last eighteen years have brought about many changes—new knowledge, new insights, new approaches that could not have been foreseen, much less incorporated into a catechism in 1958.

There have been many requests from many quarters for a revision of *Life in Christ*. The authors hesitated because of the problem of updating the work in the areas of theology and Scripture.

Monsignor Leonard M. Ziegmann was one of those who was interested in a revision, so interested, in fact, that he volunteered to undertake the task himself. This new edition is the result of his work. It is a revision that updates the canon law and liturgy in *Life in Christ*. Both Monsignor Ziegmann and the original authors realize that a thorough revision—a new treatment of Scripture and theology would be impossible without a total re-thinking and re-writing which would result in a completely different book.

Here, then, is a revision which we believe will serve to bring *Life in Christ* up to date as much as possible while retaining the form and content of the original text.

CONTENTS

part IV : GROWTH IN THE DIVINE LIFE

part V : THE COMMANDMENTS OF GOD

Prayers—*Our Father, Hail Mary, Act of Contrition, page 18; Morning Offering, 24; Glory Be to the Father, 30; Apostles' Creed, 111; Grace before and after meals, 153; Come, Holy Spirit, 174; Act of Faith, Act of Hope, Act of Love, Prayer of St. Francis, 230.*

section **1** **Happiness**

In times past, God spoke in fragmentary and varied ways to our fathers through the prophets; in this, the final age, he has spoken to us through his Son, whom he has made heir of all things and through whom he first created the universe. This Son is the reflection of the Father's glory, the exact representation of the Father's being, and he sustains all things by his powerful word. When he had cleansed us from our sins, he took his seat at the right hand of the Majesty in heaven—
HEB. 1:1–3.

SOME two thousand years ago there lived one whose influence on the world is unique in history. He did not live in one of the great centers of civilization, but in a remote corner of the world. He was not born with the material advantages that wealth and social position can give; he was born in a stable. He did not have a long career, nor one which carried him into many countries; his life span was only thirty-three years; his activity was confined to an area of a few hundred miles. His life did not end on a note of triumph; he suffered the shameful death of crucifixion.

Yet today, twenty centuries later, this man is worshiped by hundreds of millions in every country of the world as the Savior of mankind. Through the centuries since his death millions have gladly renounced all that the human heart holds dear, home, family, riches and friends, to carry his name to other corners of the earth. He is loved throughout the word as no other man has been loved. His cross, once a symbol of a criminal death, is now displayed triumphantly atop churches throughout the world, a

7

symbol of hope and love. His teachings have humanized and ennobled men and nations.

What is it that makes Jesus Christ unique among all the men in history? What is it that accounts for the influence he has had and still has on the world? The answer is, of course, that Jesus Christ was not merely a great teacher and religious leader; he is the Son of God. He is the Redeemer promised by God, who brought salvation to the human race, who ransomed man by his death on the cross.

Jesus Christ is a true man. He is the mediator between man and God. No man can come to the Father except through him. Jesus Christ is also God. His teachings, therefore, are the word of God revealed to man.

Jesus Christ is "the way, and the truth, and the life"—JOHN 14:6. It is by union with *him* that men receive the life of grace. It is through the acceptance of *his* teachings that men find salvation. It is by submission to *his* rule that men find the freedom of the sons of God.

Jesus said to his disciples, "Know that I am with you always, until the end of the world"—MATT. 28:20. Although he ascended into heaven, and we can no longer see and hear him as did his mother and his contemporaries, Jesus in his great love for us remains with us in his Church. He continues to give life and truth and guidance to those who are joined to him.

1. Does Jesus Christ promise happiness to those who love him?

Yes. Jesus Christ promises eternal happiness to those who love him.

2. Does Jesus Christ promise us happiness in this life?

Yes, Christ promises us happiness in this life, but not the kind of happiness the world seeks.

Peace is my farewell to you,
my peace is my gift to you,
I do not give it to you as the world gives peace.
Do not be distressed or fearful—JOHN 14:27.

8

3. How does the happiness which Christ promises differ from that which the world seeks?

The kind of happiness which Christ promises in this life comes from loving God and being loved by God, and from the expectation of eternal happiness in heaven. Christ does not promise us pleasure or wealth. Rather, he tells us that it is only through suffering and self-denial that we can attain joy and peace of soul in this life.

Do not lay up for yourselves an earthly treasure. Moths and rust corrode; thieves break in and steal.

Make it your practice instead to store up heavenly treasure, which neither moths nor rust corrode nor thieves break in and steal. Remember, where your treasure is, there your heart is also—MATT. 6:19—21.

4. In what words did Christ tell us how to attain happiness in this life?

In the Sermon on the Mount Christ said:

How blest are the poor in spirit:
the reign of God is theirs.
Blest too are the sorrowing; they shall
be consoled.
[Blest are the lowly; they shall inherit
the land.]
Blest are they who hunger and thirst
for holiness; they shall have their fill.
Blest are they who show mercy;
mercy shall be theirs.
Blest are the single-hearted
for they shall see God.
Blest too the peacemakers; they shall
be called sons of God.
Blest are those persecuted for holiness'
sake; the reign of God is theirs—MATT. 5:3—10.

a. Christ here is promising happiness. The word blest means happy.

9

b. The reward promised in each of these Beatitudes is primarily heaven. But if we live according to the plan of Christ we shall have a foretaste of the happiness of heaven in this life.

c. Christ tells us that we will be happy by doing for his sake the very things which we think will make us unhappy.

d. Christ tells us that we must not set our hearts on money, whereas most men want even more money than they have.

e. Christ tells us that we must forgive our enemies and love them, whereas most men want to "get even with" or at least avoid those who hurt them.

f. Christ tells us that we must avoid all sin, that we must be willing to take a lower place, that we must suffer for him, etc. These are things which are distasteful to us and which we think would make us unhappy. But the Lord says just the opposite.

5. How is it possible for us to live according to these high standards set by Christ?

Christ has not only *told* us how to live; he has *shown* us by his example. What is more, he gives us all the help we need to follow his example. If we love Christ and try to follow his example we shall receive the strength he promised when he said, "I am the vine, you are the branches. He who lives in me and I in him, will produce abundantly, for apart from me you can do nothing"—JOHN 15:5.

Practice

▲ The greatest thing that Catholics do and the greatest expression of our unity is the worship we give to God in the Mass.

One who is taking instructions in order to be received into the Church should begin at once the practice of assisting at Mass on Sundays and Holydays of obligation.

You should stand, sit, and kneel with the rest of the congregation whenever you attend Mass. You may join in the singing and praying the various responses. You may not receive Holy Communion until you are admitted to full communion with the Church.

"Lord," said Thomas, "we do not know where you are going. How can we know the way?" Jesus told him:

> *"I am the way, and the truth, and*
> *the life;*
>
> *no one comes to the Father but*
> *through me.*
>
> *If you really knew me, you would*
> *know my Father also.*
>
> *From this point on you know him;*
> *you have seen him."*

"Lord," Philip said to him, "show us the Father and that will be enough for us."

"Philip," Jesus replied, "after I have been with you all this time, you still do not know me?

> *"Whoever has seen me has seen the Father.*
>
> *How can you say, 'Show us the Father?'*
>
> *Do you not believe that I am in the Father*
> *and the Father is in me?*
>
> *The words I speak are not spoken*
> *of myself;*
>
> *it is the Father who lives in me ac-*
> *complishing his works.*
>
> *Believe me that I am in the Father*
> *and the Father is in me,*
> *or else, believe because of the works I do"–*
> JOHN 14:5–11.

JESUS tells us that God is his Father. He tells us that God is also our Father. This is Christ's great message. God is not a remote power, who rules the universe from afar. He is our loving

11

Father, who sent his Son into the world in order that he might share his life with us.

God wants to unite us to himself. Therefore we must know him. We must know him not merely by observing the world about us, the work of his hands, but by hearing what he has told us of himself.

1. Who is God?

God is the Father of all men. He calls all men, regardless of their race, color or social condition, to unite themselves with him.

2. Why is God called the Father of all men?

God is the Father of all men because:

a. He has created all men.

> *God created man in his image;*
> *in the divine image he created him;*
> *male and female he created them*—GEN. 1:27.

b He provides for the needs of his children.

> *He said to his disciples: "That is why I warn you, Do not be concerned for your life, what you are to eat, or for your body, what you are to wear. Life is more important than food and the body more than clothing. Consider the ravens: they do not sow, they do not reap, they have neither cellar nor barn—yet God feeds them. How much more important you are than the birds! Which of you by worrying can add a moment to his life-span? If the smallest things are beyond your power, why be anxious about the rest?*
> *"Or take the lilies: they do not spin, they do not weave; but I tell you, Solomon in all his splendor was not arrayed like any one of them. If God clothes in such splendor the grass of the field, which grows today and is thrown on the fire tomorrow, how much more will he provide for you, O weak in faith! It is not for you to be in search of what you are to eat or drink. Stop worrying. The unbelievers of this world are always running after these things. Your Father knows that you need such*

12

things. Seek out instead his kingship over you and the rest will follow in turn' – LUKE 12:22–31.

c. He loves men so much that he sent his Son to save them.

Yes, God so loved the world that he gave his only Son, that whoever believes in him may not die but may have eternal life. God did not send the Son into the world to condemn the world, but that the world might be saved through him – JOHN 3:16–17.

d. He has shared his life with men.

See what love the Father has bestowed on us in letting us be called children of God! Yet that is what we are. The reason the world does not recognize us is that it never recognized the Son. Dearly beloved, we are God's children now; what we shall later be has not yet come to light. We know that when it comes to light we shall be like him, for we shall see him as he is. Everyone who has this hope based on him keeps himself pure, as he is pure – 1 JOHN 3:1–3.

3. How do we know that God exists?

We know that God exists because the world in which we live proclaims his existence.

The wrath of God is being revealed from heaven against the irreligious and perverse spirit of men who, in this perversity of theirs, hinder the truth. In fact, whatever can be known about God is clear to them; he himself made it so. Since the creation of the world, invisible realities, God's eternal power and divinity, have become visible, recognized through the things he has made – ROM. 1:18–20.

a. The world about us gives witness to the existence of a supreme being. Everywhere in nature we find order and design. To try to explain order and design as the result of chance is foolish. Order and design are clearly the result of an intelligence at work. No one would ever seriously maintain that a watch simply came into being, that the metal out of which it is made happened to form itself into the shape of a watch, that the numerals on the face of the watch *just happened* to form themselves

13

in the sequence of one to twelve and locate themselves in mathematical precision just so far from one another as to allow the hands of the watch to move (again by chance) precisely this fraction of an inch every minute. Even if one allowed millions of years for all this to have happened one could not reasonably claim that anything as orderly and complex as a watch was produced by blind chance.

If this is true of a watch, what is to be said about the earth, the planets, the solar system, the universe itself? Everywhere in nature there is order and design. Everywhere we find the "laws of nature." Only a living, intelligent being could have designed the universe. This being we call God.

b. We also know that God exists because he has told us so.

In times past, God spoke in fragmentary and varied ways to our fathers through the prophets: in this, the final age, he has spoken to us through his Son, whom he made heir of all things and through whom he first created the universe–HEB. 1:1–2.

When God spoke to Moses, commanding him to lead his people out of Egypt and into the promised land he told Moses his name: *"I Am."*

"But," said Moses to God, "when I go to the Israelites and say to them, 'the God of your fathers has sent me to you,' if they ask me, 'What is his name?' what am I to tell them?" God replied, "I am who am." Then he added, "This is what you shall tell the Israelites: 'I AM sent me to you'"–EX. 3:13–15.

4. What has God told us about himself?

Speaking through men whom he inspired, God has told us:

a. **God is love.**

We have come to know and believe in the love God has for us. God is love, and he who abides in love abides in God, and God in him–1 JOHN 4:16.

God is all good. He created the world in order to show forth his glory and to share his happiness with the beings he created.

14

Holy, holy, holy is the LORD of hosts! . . .All the earth is filled with his glory!–IS. 6:3.

He shares his life with men.

. . .he has bestowed on us the great and precious things he promised, so that through these you who have fled a world corrupted by lust might become sharers of the divine nature–2 PET. 1:4.

He loves all men and wills that all men be saved.

. . .With age-old love I have loved you; so I have kept my mercy toward you–JER. 31:3.

Yes, God so loved the world that he gave his only Son, that whoever believes in him may not die but may have eternal life. God did not send the Son into the world to condemn the world, but that the world might be saved through him–JOHN 3:16–17.

. . .for he wants all men to be saved and come to know the truth–1 TIM. 2:4.

He is all-merciful, ready to forgive any sinner who repents.

Merciful and gracious is the LORD, slow to anger and abounding in kindness. For as the heavens are high above the earth, so surpassing is his kindness toward those who fear him. But the kindness of the LORD is from eternity to eternity toward those who fear him, and his justice toward children's children–
PS. 103:8, 11, 17.

I tell you, there will likewise be more joy in heaven over one repentant sinner than over ninety-nine righteous people who have no need to repent–LUKE 15:7.

b. **God is all knowing.**

Nothing is concealed from him; all lies bare and exposed to the eyes of him to whom we must render an account–HEB. 4:13.

He plumbs the depths and penetrates the heart;
their innermost being he understands.

The Most High possesses all knowledge, and sees from of
old the things that are to come:

He makes known the past and the future, and reveals
the deepest secrets.

No understanding does he lack; no single thing
escapes him–SIR. 42:18–20.

c. God is just.

A faithful God, without deceit how just and upright
he is!–DEUT. 32:4.

Eternal life to those who strive for glory, honor, and im-
mortality by patiently doing right; wrath and fury to
those who selfishly disobey the truth and obey wicked-
ness–ROM. 2:7–8.

d. God is infinite.

There is no limit to his life.

Great is the LORD and highly to be praised.–PS. 145:3.

Your throne stands firm from of old; from everlasting
you are, O LORD–PS. 93:2.

e. God is unchangeable.

Every worthwhile gift, every genuine benefit comes from
above, descending from the Father of the heavenly lumi-
naries, who cannot change and who is never shadowed
over–JAS. 1:17.

f. God is eternal.

He had no beginning and will have no end.

Before the mountains were begotten and the earth and
the world were brought forth, from everlasting to ever-
lasting you are God. . . For a thousand years in your
sight are as yesterday, now that it is past, or as a watch
of the night–PS. 90:2–4.

. . .before Abraham came to be, I AM–JOHN 8:58.

The Lord shall reign forever and ever–EX. 15:18.

g. **God is all-powerful.**

. . .O LORD, great are you and glorious, wonderful in power and unsurpassable. Let your every creature serve you; for you spoke, and they were made, You sent forth your spirit, and they were created; no one can resist your word–JUD. 16:13–14.

h. **God is everywhere.**

Where can I go from your spirit? from your presence where can I flee?

If I go up to the heavens, you are there; if I sink to the nether world, you are present there.

If I take the wings of the dawn, if I settle at the farthest limits of the sea,

Even there your hand shall guide me, and your right hand hold me fast.

If I say, "Surely the darkness shall hide me, and night shall be my light"–

For you darkness itself is not dark, and night shines as the day. [Darkness and light are the same.] –
PS. 138:7–12.

i. **God is a spirit.**

He is the one limitless, almightly, all-knowing spirit. He does not need anything or anyone outside of himself. He depends on nothing and on no one, but all things depend on him. Yet God cares for and sustains all the things which he has created. And he calls all men to become his adopted children.

Practice

▲ Now that we have learned God is more properly a Father we should begin to use the prayer which Jesus gave us which best describes our relationship with Him.

Two other prayers which Catholics use frequently are the "Hail Mary" and the "Act of Contrition." You should use these prayers daily as part of your own personal prayer.

In the Name of the Father, and of the Son, and of the Holy Spirit. Amen.

Our Father, who art in heaven, hallowed by thy name, thy kingdom come, thy will be done on earth as it is in heaven. Give us this day our daily bread and forgive us our trespasses as we forgive those who trespass against us and lead us not into temptation, but deliver us from evil. Amen.

Hail Mary, full of grace, the Lord is with thee. Blessed are thou among women, and blessed is the fruit of thy womb, Jesus. Holy Mary, Mother of God, pray for us sinners now and at the hour of our death. Amen.

My God, I am sorry for my sins with all my heart. In choosing to do wrong and failing to do good, I have sinned against you whom I should love above all things. I firmly intend, with your help, to do penance, to sin no more, and to avoid whatever leads me to sin. Our Savior Jesus Christ suffered and died for us. In his name, my God, have mercy.

† † †

section **3**   The Gift of Life

*A certain Pharisee named Nicodemus, a member of the
Jewish Sanhedrin, came to him at night. "Rabbi," he said,
"we know you are a teacher come from God, for no man can
perform signs and wonders such as you perform, unless God
is with him." Jesus gave him this answer: "I solemnly assure
you, no one can see the reign of God unless he is begotten
from above."*

*"How can a man be born again once he is old?" retorted
Nicodemus. "Can he return to his mother's womb and be
born over again?" Jesus replied: "I solemnly assure you, no
one can enter into God's kingdom without being begotten
of water and Spirit. . . . Yes, God so loved the world that he
gave his only Son, that whoever believes in him may not die
but may have eternal life. God did not send the Son into the
world to condemn the world, but that the world might be
saved through him."–JOHN 3:1–17.*

WE can appreciate the astonishment of Nicodemus, hearing
these words for the first time. "I solemnly assure you, no one can
enter into God's kingdom without being begotten of water and
Spirit." This rebirth demands the giving of a new kind of life,
the life to which Christ referred when he said, "I came that they
may have life, and have it more abundantly." It is the divine life,
that gift of God which makes men share in the very life of God.

No wonder, then, that Jesus Christ sums up his whole work of
redemption by speaking of re-birth and a new kind of life. No
wonder, too, that without an understanding of this new life we
should never be able to see in proper focus the great realities
which God has revealed to us, or to appreciate the wonderful destiny that is ours.

19

1. What does Jesus mean when he says that we must be "born again"?

Jesus means that in order to achieve the supernatural destiny for which God has created us we must receive a new kind of life, a supernatural life, which is a created share in the life of God.

This is the life to which Jesus referred when he said:

. . .I came that they might have life and have it to the full–JOHN 10:10.

I am the vine, you are the branches. He who lives in me and I in him, will produce abundantly, for apart from me you can do nothing. A man who does not live in me is like a withered, rejected branch, picked up to be thrown in the fire and burnt–JOHN 15:5–6.

. . .I am the way, and the truth, and the life–JOHN 14:6.

I am the bread of life. Your ancestors ate manna in the desert, but they died. This is the bread that comes down from heaven for a man to eat and never die. I myself am the living bread come down from heaven. If anyone eats this bread he shall live forever; the bread I will give is my flesh, for the life of the world–JOHN 6:48–51.

If only you recognized God's gift, and who it is that is asking you for a drink, you would have asked him instead, and he would have given you living water. . . . Everyone who drinks this water will be thirsty again. But whoever drinks the water I give him will never be thirsty; no, the water I give shall become a fountain within him, leaping up to provide eternal life–JOHN 4:10–15.

2. What is this supernatural destiny for which God has intended us?

God intends that after death we share his own happiness in a heaven which is not natural to human beings or to any other creatures, but to God alone.

3. How can we live in a heaven which is natural to God alone?

We could not live in heaven just as we are, with merely our human life. To live in heaven it is necessary to have a share in the life of God. We have no right whatever to such a gift. But since God wants to share his happiness with us he has willed to share his life with us.

4. What is this share in the life of God called?

This share in the life of God is called the *divine life* or *sanctifying grace.*

"Grace" means a free gift, something to which we have no right. We have a right to our human life because we were created as human beings. Human life is *natural* to us. But to share God's life is something which is totally *above* man. For this reason sanctifying grace is also called *super*-natural life. It is called "*sanctifying*" because it makes us like God, our Father, who is holiness itself.

5. In what way does the divine life make us like God?

The divine life makes us "sharers of the Divine Nature" (2 PET. 1:4) because it empowers us to live as God lives, that is, to know God as he knows himself and to love him as he loves himself.

6. Do we have any idea of the life of God?

The life of God is the deepest of all mysteries. God is ". . . the King of Kings and Lord of Lords; who alone has immortality and dwells in unapproachable light, whom no human being has seen or can see. . ."–1 TIM. 6:15–16. However, we have a hint as to the life of God in our own life. We know and love in our own limited way. God knows and loves without limit. His life consists in knowing and loving himself, the highest truth and the greatest good.

7. How shall we know and love God when we share his life in heaven?

In heaven, because we shall be united to God, we shall know and love him as he knows and loves himself. God will fill our minds with himself, dazzling, immeasurable truth, and our wills with himself, goodness so inexhaustible that all created love is

21

but his shadow, in a fulfillment of love which is beyond all power of imagination.

8. Does the divine life make us divine?

The divine life makes us divine in the sense that we share God's life. It does not make us divine in the sense that we become God or "part of God." Such an idea would be absurd. Even in heaven, seeing and loving God face to face, we shall never lose our identity, our individuality, or our complete dependence on God.

9. How does the divine life make us adopted children of God?

St. John tells us,

See what love the Father has bestowed on us in letting us be called children of God! Yet that is what we are. The reason the world does not recognize us is that it never recognized the Son. Dearly beloved, we are God's children now; what we shall later be has not yet come to light. We know that when it comes to light we shall be like him, for we shall see him as he is. Everyone who has this hope based on him keeps himself pure, as he is pure—1 JOHN 3:1—3.

By nature we are creatures of God, the work of his hands. When we receive the divine life we live with the life of God and take on an inner resemblance to him. Our relationship with God becomes then not merely that of creature and creator but that of child and Father.

This divine adoption is much more thorough and real than human adoption. When a married couple adopt a child they merely go through a legal process. No internal change takes place in the child they adopt; they must choose a being who is already like them, who has the same kind of nature. But when God adopts us as his children he actually transforms us internally. We take on an inner likeness to him because we share his life.

10. What is the greatest gift which comes with the gift of the divine life?

22

The greatest gift which comes with the divine life is *God himself.* Grace is mysterious and therefore difficult to explain in human terms. But when we do have grace, or the divine life, God does live with us.

> *. . .Anyone who loves me will be true to my word, and my Father will love him; we will come to him and make our dwelling place with him*—JOHN 14:23.

11. Why does God come and dwell within us?

God comes and dwells within us to begin, in an incomplete way, the possession of him which we will have in heaven.

12. What is actual grace?

Actual grace is help from God. It is light for our minds and strength for our wills. It is the kind of grace for which we should constantly pray because we constantly need it.

Often the thought comes to us, "I ought to pray more," "I should try to correct this fault in my character," "I should help this man." Often, too, we suddenly see a truth about God, our-selves, and our relation to God a little more clearly. These promptings and enlightenments are not accidental, trivial occur-rences. They are sent by God. They are actual graces. God sends us these actual graces in order that we might perform actions which will merit for us an increase of the divine life. One who has lost the divine life through mortal sin cannot repent unless God gives him actual graces which will enable him to do so.

Practice

▲ God is always offering us actual graces. We should strive to realize how completely we depend on them and to cooperate with them at all times. To this end prayer is a necessity, prayer for ourselves and for others. We should pray for more and more actual grace. Without it we are helpless.

We should strive to realize how much we depend on God and to acquire a sense of his continual presence. God himself will give us this realization if we pray for it. One type of prayer which is well suited to give us a sense of the continual presence of God and to unite us with him throughout the day is an offering of ourselves made to God in the morning and renewed frequently during the day.

We may make this offering in our own words immediately upon rising. Or we may use this formula.

O Jesus, through the Immaculate Heart of Mary, I offer you all my prayers, works, joys and sufferings of this day, for all the intentions of your Sacred Heart, in union with the Holy Sacrifice of the Mass throughout the world, in reparation for my sins, for the intentions of all our associates, and for the general intention recommended this month.

GOD, OUR FATHER, shows forth his beauty, his power and his majesty in the world he created. He gave his children a wonderful world in which to live. God's original plan was beautifully simple. He gave man the gift of divine life at the instant he created him, and placed him in the world in order that he might prepare for heaven. We were to be born in possession of the divine life and were to keep it always. There was to be no disorder, no sickness, no death, provided man remained faithful to God and did not rebel against him by sinning. But, Adam, the head of our race, failed God and us, his descendants. He sinned and thereby lost his and our most precious possession, the divine life, which makes us children of God.

The story of God's creation of the world and of our first parents, of their elevation to the divine life and of their rebellion against God is told in the first book of the Bible, the book of Genesis.

In the beginning, when God created the heavens and the earth, the earth was a formless wasteland, and darkness covered the abyss, while a mighty wind swept over the waters.

Then God said, "Let there be light," and there was light. God saw how good the light was. God then separated the light from the darkness. God called the light "day," and the darkness he called "night." Thus evening came, and morning followed—the first day.

Then God said, "Let there be a dome in the middle of the waters, to separate one body of water from the other." And so it happened: God made the dome, and it separated the water above the dome from the water below it. God called the dome "the sky." Evening came, and morning followed—the second day.

Then God said, "Let the water under the sky be gathered

25

into a single basin, so that the dry land may appear." And so it happened: the water under the sky was gathered into its basin, and the dry land appeared. God called the dry land "the earth," and the basin of the water he called "the sea." God saw how good it was. Then God said, "Let the earth bring forth vegetation: every kind of plant that bears seed and every kind of fruit tree on earth that bears fruit with its seed in it." And so it happened: the earth brought forth every kind of plant that bears seed and every kind of fruit tree on earth that bears fruit with its seeds in it. God saw how good it was. Evening came, and morning followed— the third day.

Then God said: "Let there be lights in the dome of the sky, to separate day from night. Let them mark the fixed times the days and the years, and serve as luminaries in the dome of the sky, to shed light upon the earth." And so it happened: God made the two great lights, the greater one to govern the day, and the lesser one to govern the night; and he made the stars. God set them in the dome of the sky, to shed light upon the earth, to govern the day and the night, and to separate the light from the darkness. God saw how good it was. Evening came, and morning followed—the fourth day.

Then God said, "Let the water teem with an abundance of living creatures, and on the earth let birds fly beneath the dome of the sky." And so it happened:

God created the great sea monsters and all kinds of swimming creatures with which the water teems, and all kinds of winged birds. God saw how good it was, and God blessed them, saying, "Be fertile, multiply, and fill the water of the seas; and let the birds multiply on the earth." Evening came, and morning followed—the fifth day.

Then God said, "Let the earth bring forth all kinds of living creatures: cattle, creeping things, and wild animals of all kinds." And so it happened: God made all kinds of wild animals, all kinds of cattle, and all kinds of creeping things of the earth. God saw how good it was.

Then God said: "Let us make man in our image, after our likeness. Let them have dominion over the fish of the sea, the birds of the air, and the cattle, and over all the wild *animals and all the creatures that crawl on the ground."*

God created man in his image; in the divine image he cre-
ated him; male and female he created them.

God blessed them, saying: "Be fertile and multiply; fill
the earth and subdue it. Have dominion over the fish of the
sea, the birds of the air, and all the living things that move on
the earth." God also said: "See, I give you every seed-bear-
ing plant all over the earth and every tree that has seed-bear-
ing fruit on it to be your food; and to all the animals of the
land, all the birds of the air, and all the living creatures that
crawl on the ground, I give all the green plants for food."
And so it happened. God looked at everything he had made,
and he found it very good. Evening came, and morning fol-
lowed—the sixth day.

Thus the heavens and the earth and all their array were
completed. Since on the seventh day God was finished with
the work he had been doing, he rested on the seventh day
from all the work he had undertaken. So God blessed the
seventh day and made it holy, because on it he rested from all
the work he had done in creation—GEN. 1:1–31, 2:1–3.

THE STORY of creation as it is given in the Bible was based
on the oral traditions of the people. It was written with these
people in mind. It is, of course, inspired by God. It is not, however, a scientific account. We must not expect in it answers to
scientific questions. It is up to human learning and research,
guided by the teachings of the Church, to determine, for example,
the age of the earth and the question of evolution. The Bible was
not intended to answer such questions.

1. What does this Biblical account of creation teach?

This account teaches certain important religious truths:

a. There is only *one* God.

b. God is the creator of everything, even of the sun, moon
and the stars (which some of the neighboring peoples worshipped
as gods).

c. God created everything effortlessly, merely by his word.

d. All things created by God are good.

27

e. God has given man dominion over the things on this earth.

2. Does this account teach us that the world was made in six days?

No. The six days are a purely literary device, i.e., a manner of speaking which made it easier for the audience to understand and remember.

Thus God is described as creating "places" on the first three days and the inhabitants of these "places" on the second three days. The "work" of the first and the fourth day is described as the separation of light and darkness on the one hand, and on the other the creation of the heavenly bodies which regulate light and darkness. The "work" of the second and fifth days is described as the separation of the waters on the one hand (the Jews thought that there were waters above the sky and under the earth) and on the other the creation of the fish which live in the waters and the birds which live in the air separating the waters.

The "work" of the third and sixth days is described as the creation of the earth and plant life and of animals and man.

3. Why did the author use this literary device?

a. If the author had known what science now knows about the origin of the world and had stated this information in scientific terms, the people would have been bewildered and would not have understood his religious message.

b. The author wished to stress the holiness of the Sabbath day, which the Jews were already bound to observe. So he represented God as working six days and resting on the seventh (the Sabbath).

4. Does this account rule out evolution?

This account of creation reveals that God is the creator of all things. The manner in which creation took place is not revealed in the Bible. Modern science teaches us the evolution of plant and animal life. As long as this teaching does not exclude God as the creator and director of the process of evolution, it does not contradict revelation.

5. What is the meaning of the word create?

To create means to make something out of nothing. Human beings can make things, using materials which already exist, but the power to create belongs only to God.

Creation means more than making something out of nothing. When God creates something he also keeps it in existence. If he did not, it would return to nothing.

6. Was it necessary that God create?

No. God is absolutely free. He need not have created anything. God has no need of anything outside of himself.

7. Why, then, did God create?

God created in order to manifest himself and to share his goodness with the beings he created. He has shared his existence with the whole of creation, which mirrors him in various degrees of clarity.

The heavens declare the glory of God, and the firmament proclaims his handiwork–PS. 19:2.

He has created images of himself in the spiritual world, angels and men; and in his infinite goodness he has willed to give to angels and men as an utterly free and undeserved gift a share in his nature, the divine life.

8. What are angels?

Angels are spiritual beings created by God. They, like human beings, are created in the image of God, more clearly in God's image than man because they are completely spiritual, having no need of bodies or of anything material.

9. How do angels differ from God?

Angels are creatures, i.e., they were created by God; they depend absolutely upon God's sustaining hand for their existence and activity. Although of a higher nature than man, they, too, are limited beings.

10. What is the story of the elevation and fall of the angels?

At the moment he created them God gave the divine life to the angels. Since they are beings with free will they, too, had to prove their fidelity to God before being admitted to heaven. A vast multitude of the angels rebelled against God and fixed their powerful wills forever on evil. These evil spirits live now in hell and are called "devils."

The angels who remained faithful to God enjoy the vision of God in heaven.

11. Do angels play any part in our lives?

Yes. Our guardian angels protect and help us. The devils tempt us and try to lead us into sin. Satan, the leader of the devils, tempted Eve to sin and to lead Adam into sin.

Practice

▲ In the Mass, at the conclusion of the Eucharistic Prayer a beautiful scene is presented to us; all God's creation is gathered around the cross of Christ, who by his death has redeemed the world and drawn all things to himself:

Through him, with him, in him, in the unity of the Holy Spirit, all glory and honor is yours, almighty Father, forever and ever.

Everything in the world was created to give glory to God. We, the greatest of all his earthly creatures, must praise him with our minds, our hearts, our whole being. The worship of God is our first, our most important and our most exalted function.

The Church worships God, above all, in the Mass. Strive to realize when you assist at Mass that you are worshipping God in the highest possible way.

Make your own the short prayer of praise which the Church uses so often:

Glory be to the Father and to the Son and to the Holy Spirit, as it was in the beginning, is now, and ever shall be, world without end. Amen.

30

I. The Creation of Man

The creation of man is described twice in the Book of Genesis, in the first chapter and again in the second.

Then God said: "Let us make man in our image, after our likeness. Let them have dominion over the fish of the sea, the birds of the air, and the cattle, and over all the wild animals and all the creatures that crawl on the ground."

God created man in his image; in the divine image he created him; male and female he created them – GEN. 1:26–28.

The LORD God formed man out of the clay of the ground and blew into his nostrils the breath of life, and so man became a living being – GEN. 2:7.

The LORD God said: "It is not good for the man to be alone. I will make a suitable partner for him."

So the LORD God cast a deep sleep on the man, and while he was asleep, he took out one of his ribs and closed up its place with flesh. The LORD God then built up into a woman the rib that he had taken from the man. When he brought her to the man, the man said:

"This one, at last, is bone of my bones
and flesh of my flesh;
This one shall be called 'woman,'
for out of 'her man' this one has been taken."

That is why a man leaves his father and mother and clings to his wife, and the two of them become one body – GEN. 2:18, 21–24.

Jesus Christ, when he came to bring men the divine life, was restoring something which had been lost. God, in creating man, exalted human nature by giving mankind the divine life of sanctifying grace. Then by a great tragedy which occurred at the very beginning of the human race, man lost the divine life and the means of attaining heaven. Jesus, therefore, chose to share in our humanity in order that we might come to share in his divinity, i.e., might receive from him the divine life, which had been lost in the sin of Adam. Through Jesus, God has made our restoration to the divine life more wonderful than the original gift. "I came that they might have life and have it to the full"— JOHN 10:10.

1. What are the main points which God teaches us in this account of the creation of man?

The main points which God teaches us here are these:

a. God has a special love and care for man, above all the beings he created;

b. woman shares the same nature with man. The two sexes therefore compliment each other and are interdependent, and they are of equal dignity in the sight of God;

c. the soul of man was created directly by God.

2. Could the origin of man's body be explained by the theory of evolution?

The Bible does not give us the answer to this question. The theory of the evolution of man's body could fit into the story as we have it in the Bible, provided of course, that we understand by evolution a process directed by God, not by chance.

Revelation makes it very clear, however, that the *souls* of Adam and Eve were created directly by God, as is the soul of every human being.

3. What is man?

Man is a creature with a material body and a spiritual soul, made by God in his likeness.

All creatures reflect God in the sense that each mirrors in its own limited way the boundless reality and beauty of God. Man, because he has a spiritual soul, has dominion over the other earthly creatures and is a more perfect image of God than anything else on this earth.

> *When I behold your heavens, the work of your fingers,*
>   *the moon and the stars which you set in place—*
> *What is man that you should be mindful of him,*
>   *or the son of man that you should care for him?*
> *You have made him little less than the angels,*
>   *and crowned him with glory and honor.*
> *You have given him rule over the works of your hands,*
>   *putting all things under his feet:*
> *All sheep and oxen,*
>   *yes, and the beasts of the field,*
> *The birds of the air, the fishes of the sea,*
>   *and whatever swims the paths of the seas—PS. 8:4—9*

4. Has the soul a life of its own?

Yes. The soul is a living thing. Without the soul the body would not have life. But the soul, even after it leaves the body, will live forever. Since it has not any parts it cannot "fall apart" or die. It would cease to live only if God were to destroy it.

After death human souls are separated from their bodies, but they are not angels. God has created us as men and has revealed that at the end of the world our souls and bodies will be reunited. We shall always be men.

II. The Gift of the Divine Life and Its Loss by Our First Parents

> *Now the serpent was the most cunning of all the animals that the LORD God had made. The serpent asked the woman, "Did God really tell you not to eat from any of the trees in the garden?" The woman answered the serpent: "We may eat of the fruit of the trees in the garden; it is only about the fruit of the tree in the middle of the garden that God said, 'You shall not eat it or even touch it, lest you die.'"*
>
> *But the serpent said to the woman: "You certainly will not die! No, God knows well that the moment you eat of it you will be like gods who know what is good and what is*

33

bad." The woman saw that the tree was good for food, pleasing to the eyes, and desirable for gaining wisdom. So she took some of its fruit and ate it; and she also gave some to her husband, who was with her, and he ate it. Then the eyes of both of them were opened, and they realized that they were naked; so they sewed fig leaves together and made loincloths for themselves.

When they heard the sound of the LORD God moving about in the garden at the breezy time of the day, the man and his wife hid themselves from the LORD God among the trees of the garden. The LORD God then called to the man and asked him, "Where are you?" He answered, "I heard you in the garden; but I was afraid, because I was naked, so I hid myself." Then he asked, "Who told you that you were naked? You have eaten, then, from the tree of which I had forbidden you to eat!" The man replied, "The woman whom you put here with me—she gave me fruit from the tree, and so I ate it." The LORD God then asked the woman, "Why did you do such a thing?" The woman answered, "The serpent tricked me into it, so I ate it."

Then the LORD God said to the serpent: "Because you have done this, you shall be banned from all the animals and from all the wild creatures; On your belly shall you crawl, and dirt shall you eat all the days of your life. I will put enmity between you and the woman, and between your offspring and hers; he will strike at your head, while you strike at his heel."

To the woman he said: "I will intensify the pangs of your childbearing; in pain shall you bring forth children. Yet your urge shall be for your husband, and he shall be your master."

To the man he said: "Because you listened to your wife and ate from the tree of which I had forbidden you to eat, "Cursed be the ground because of you! In toil shall you eat its yield all the days of your life. Thorns and thistles shall it bring forth to you, as you eat of the plants of the field. By the sweat of your face shall you get bread to eat, Until you return to the ground, from which you were taken; For you are dirt, and to dirt you shall return."

The man called his wife Eve, because she became the mother of all the living–GEN. 3:1–20.

Here, in terms of the earthly paradise, the tree of life, the serpent and the tree of knowledge of good and evil God reveals to us the story of his gift of the divine life and its loss through Adam. Our first parents were to pass on the divine life to their descendants. But first they had to prove their fidelity to God. Instead of remaining faithful, they listened to the suggestion of the evil spirit, deliberately turned their wills against God and lost the divine life, with tragic results for themselves and their descendants.

1. What was the greatest gift God gave to our first parents?

The greatest among the many gifts God gave mankind was the gift of divine life or sanctifying grace. Thus our first parents enjoyed a close friendship with God.

2. What was the sin which our first parents committed?

The exact nature of the sin has not been clearly revealed to us. From the figures of the tree of the knowledge of good and evil and the words of the tempter, ". . .your eyes will be opened and you will be like gods who know what is good and what is bad"–GEN. 3:5, it appears to have been a sin of pride, a refusal to acknowledge their complete dependence on God. This sin of our first parents is called original sin.

3. How were Adam and Eve affected by their sin?

Therefore, just as through one man sin entered the world and with sin death, death thus coming to all men inasmuch as all sinned–ROM. 5:12.

By far the most tragic consequence was their loss of the divine life. But they also lost other gifts. Although the union of spirit and matter is in itself one in which there would naturally be some conflict, there was no such conflict in the case of our first parents. Adam and Eve had received a special gift, a harmony between body and soul which is not natural to man. All the inclinations of the body were under the perfect control of the soul; all the powers of the soul were oriented to God. By their sin our first parents lost this special gift. They suffered disharmony within themselves. Their bodies were no longer completely subject to their souls; their souls no longer oriented to God. They became subject, too, to sickness, suffering and death.

4. How are we affected by the sin of Adam?

Because of the sin of Adam we come into the world deprived of the divine life and subject to death, sickness and the inclination to sin.

> *We know that the law is spiritual, whereas I am weak flesh sold into the slavery of sin. I cannot even understand my own actions. I do not do what I want to do but what I hate. When I act against my own will, by that very fact I agree that the law is good. This indicates that it is not I who do it but sin which resides in me. I know that no good dwells in me, that is, in my flesh; the desire to do right is there but not the power. What happens is that I do, not the good I will to do, but the evil I do not intend* – ROM. 7:14–19.

Original sin—the fact that we come into the world without the divine life—must not be confused with actual or personal sin, which we ourselves commit. Actual sin may be either *mortal* or *venial.* Mortal sin is an offense against God which is so serious that it destroys our divine life and breaks our friendship with God. Venial sin is an offense against God which does not destroy the divine life, but which weakens our will and paves the way for mortal sin.

5. What was God's response to the sin of Adam and Eve?

God did not restore the lesser gifts, such as freedom from death. But what is much more important, he promised that his own Son would become man in order to redeem us and restore the divine life.

When the Son of God became man he took the name Jesus, which means savior.

6. What did Jesus mean when he said that he came that we might have "life more abundantly"?

Since God has become man we have been honored and exalted more than the angels. We have Jesus Christ as our head, teaching us and sanctifying us through the Church. We have the sacraments, through which the divine life flows into our souls. We eat and drink the body and blood of Christ in the Eucharist. We have the Mass, the re-offering of Christ's death, in which we now have a part.

We have as our mother and model the greatest of all God's creatures, the only human person who was conceived without original sin, Mary, the Mother of God.

Despite the tragic sin of Adam and the struggle for salvation in which we must now engage, despite the suffering and evil which are in the world as a consequence of that sin, the Church still exults in a most striking and beautiful song, which is sung in the Easter Vigil service.

> *Father, how wonderful your care of us! How boundless your merciful love! To ransom a slave you gave away your Son. O happy fault, O necessary sin of Adam, which gained for us so great a Redeemer!*

Practice

▲ Because of the sin of Adam we have inclinations which will lead us into sin unless we keep them in check. We all have tendencies towards pride and selfishness. Even our natural desires, good in themselves, can easily get out of hand and cause us to go to excess.

We are weak. We must, therefore, from time to time, strengthen ourselves by denying ourselves even legitimate pleasures. The Church helps us to do them by strongly urging us to forego meat on Fridays and to fast at certain times.

section **6**   **The Preparation for the Redeemer**

So Paul arose, motioned to them for silence, and began: "Fellow Israelites and you others who reverence our God, listen to what I have to say! The God of the people Israel once chose our fathers. He made this people great during their sojourn in the land of Egypt, and with an outstretched arm he led them out of it. For forty years he put up with them in the desert: then he destroyed seven nations in the land of Canaan to give them that country as their heritage at the end of some four hundred and fifty years. Later on he set up judges to rule them until the time of the prophet Samuel.

"When they asked for a king, God gave them Saul son of Kish, of the tribe of Benjamin, who ruled for forty years.

"Then God removed him and raised up David as their king; on his behalf God testified, 'I have found David son of Jesse to be a man after my own heart who will fulfill my every wish.'

"According to his promise, God has brought forth from this man's descendants Jesus, a savior for Israel"–ACTS 13:16–23.

THOUSANDS of years elapsed between the sin of Adam and Eve and the coming of Christ. During that time men fell deeper and deeper into sin and drifted farther and farther from the idea of the one true God. A great part of the world worshipped idols and had so debased religion that vice was sometimes considered virtue. Yet God had not abandoned men. Immediately after the fall of Adam he promised a redeemer. Throughout all the centuries which elapsed as man floundered in sin and unbelief, God's providence was still at work. Then, in his own time, God began the immediate preparation for the coming of his Son into the world.

1. How did God begin the immediate preparation for the coming of Christ?

About 2,000 B.C. God began the immediate preparation for the coming of Christ when he said to Abraham:

Go forth from the land of your kinsfolk and from your father's house to a land that I will show you. I will make of you a great nation, and I will bless you; I will make your name great, so that you will be a blessing. I will bless those who bless you and curse those who curse you. All the communities of the earth shall find blessing in you— GEN. 12:1–3.

2. Who was Abraham?

Abraham was the founder of the Jews,* the people whom God chose as his own, the people to whom God spoke through the prophets in the Old Testament.

3. What was the importance of the Jews in the plan of God?

The Jews were the people through whom God kept alive belief in the one true God during the centuries before Christ. God's ancient revelation was given to the Jews. It was they who preserved it and handed it down. When the Son of God became man he chose to be born a Jew.

The Jews, therefore, are our spiritual ancestors. Christianity is the Jewish religion brought to its fulfillment in Christ and opened up to the whole world.

4. Who was Moses?

Moses was the great leader and law-giver whom God chose to

---

*The chosen people were not called "Jews" until later in their history. For the purpose of simplification, however, the word "Jews" will be used throughout these lessons.

lead the Jews out of captivity in Egypt into the land he had promised them. It was to Moses that God gave the Ten Commandments on Mount Sinai when he entered into his covenant with the Jews.

5. What is the Old Testament?

The Old Testament is the collection of the sacred books of the Jews which tell the story of their relationship with God. It is usually classified as forty-five books, which vary in length and literary form: twenty-one books of history, eighteen books of prophecy and seven books of wisdom literature.

These books are to be understood in the light of the literary style and of the mentality of the times in which they were written. Recent archeological studies have in many cases indicated the geographical and historical reliability of the Old Testament, where it has been attacked. The books were written by many authors over a long period of time. The traditions of the Jews recounted in the first five books certainly go back to the time of Moses (1,400–1,200 B.C.), while the story of the Machabees, told in the last two books, was written about 100 B.C.

6. Why is this collection of books called the Old Testament?

These books are called a TESTAMENT because they are an account of the covenant (agreement) entered into by God with his chosen people through Moses on Mount Sinai. This testament, or covenant, is called OLD to distinguish it from the NEW one which God entered into with all men through Christ on Mount Calvary.

The prophet Jeremias foretold the transition from the old to the new testament five hundred years before the birth of Christ.

The days are coming, says the LORD, when I will make a new covenant with the house of Israel and the house of Judah. It will not be like the covenant I made with their fathers the day I took them by the hand to lead them forth from the land of Egypt; for they broke my covenant and

40

I had to show myself their master, says the LORD. But this
is the covenant which I will make with the house of Israel
after those days, says the LORD. I will place my law within
them, and write it upon their hearts; I will be their God, and
they shall be my people. No longer will they have need to
teach their friends and kinsmen how to know the LORD.
All, from least to greatest, shall know me, says the LORD,
for I will forgive their evildoing and remember their sin no
more–JER. 31:31–34.

7. What kind of history is recorded in the Old Testament?

The Old Testament is a theological history of God's dealing
with his chosen people. Consequently, it is an interpretative history and does not intend to give a thorough account of all the
secular events.

a. The Old Testament is the history of God's kingdom on
earth. The Jews were God's people. He was their king, who exercised his authority through the prophets, judges and kings. God
separated the Jews from all other people and promised them large
families, good harvests, peace and his continual presence and protection if they were faithful to him. He threatened them with
war, famine, plague and exile if they were unfaithful. The Jews
frequently turned from God. In each case God chastised them,
forgave them and accepted them again as his chosen people.

b. The Old Testament tells the story of only one people,
the Jews. Other people are mentioned only incidentally. It does
not give a complete history of even that people, but treats of only
those events which have direct bearing on the plan of God. There
are gaps of hundreds of years in the narrative, and only men who
have a direct relationship to Christ figure prominently in it.

c. The Old Testament is centered on the coming of the
Messiah. It tells of the historical events leading up to his coming.
It records the prophecies which he was to fulfill.

8. What is a prophet?

A prophet is a man sent by God to tell the people the will of
God and to bring them his message. The prophets of the Old

Testament strove continually to keep the Jews faithful to God; they reminded them of his promises to them, of his past benefits and of their future glory if they remained faithful to him. Some of the prophets also foretold future events such as the destruction of the kingdom of Israel. Many of the prophets spoke of the coming of the Messiah and of his kingdom.

> *The word of the LORD came to me thus:*
> *Before I formed you in the womb I knew you,*
>   *before you were born I dedicated you,*
>   *a prophet to the nations I appointed you.*
> *"Ah, LORD GOD!" I said,*
>   *"I know not how to speak; I am too young."*
> *But the LORD answered me,*
> *Say not, "I am too young."*
>   *To whomever I send you, you shall go;*
>   *whatever I command you, you shall speak*–JER. 1:4–7.

9. What things were foretold by prophets concerning Christ and his kingdom?

Many individual traits of the person, character, kingdom and rule of the Messiah were foretold by the prophets. These facts were revealed over a long period of time and were never gathered into one picture in any book of the Old Testament. Many of the prophecies were obscure. Most likely the prophets themselves did not understand exactly how their prophecies would be fulfilled. In fact, various prophecies seemed to contradict one another. One group showed a victorious king ruling in justice over a peaceful people, while another group foretold the humiliation, the rejection, the suffering and the violent death of the Messiah. Many of the prophecies were not clearly understood until after Christ came and by his life and actions fulfilled them, even those which had seemed to be contradictory.

> *After Jesus' birth in Bethlehem of Judea during the reign of King Herod, astrologers from the east arrived one day in Jerusalem inquiring, "Where is the newborn king of the Jews? We observed his star at its rising and have come to pay him homage." At this news King Herod became greatly*

disturbed, and with him all Jerusalem. Summoning all of the chief priests and scribes of the people, he inquired of them where the Messiah was to be born. "In Bethlehem of Judea," they informed him. "Here is what the prophet has written:

'And you, Bethlehem, land of Judah, are by no means least among the princes of Judah, since from you shall come a ruler who is to shepherd my people Israel'"–
MATT. 2:1–6 cf. MICH. 5:2.

When they had crucified him, they divided his clothes among them by casting lots–MATT. 27:35.

they divided my garments among them, and for my vesture they cast lots–PS. 22:19.

Liturgy

Every year the Church re-lives the period of preparation for the coming of Christ during the season of Advent. Throughout this liturgical season, which extends for about a month, beginning four Sundays before Christmas, the mood is one of longing and expectation. The Gloria is omitted, and violet vestments are used at Mass; the Masses and offices of the season express the need for redemption, our longing for the Savior.

The liturgy of Advent admonishes us to do penance for our sins and to purify our hearts for the coming of Christ at Christmas. But underneath is the note of joy and hope; our deliverance is almost at hand; he is coming!

Practice

▲ We should become acquainted with the Old Testament. It is important, first of all, because it is the word of God. It is a great source from which we can gain a deeper appreciation of the greatness and the goodness of God, his providence, and his love for us. It contains a wealth of inspiring thoughts and stories.

The Old Testament is important, too, for a fuller understanding of the New Testament. Christianity has its roots in the Old Testament. In order to understand Christianity more fully one must know and understand its background, which is the Jewish religion. Both are based on belief in the same God and his *one* plan for mankind.

It would not be wise, however, to approach the Old Testament without any preparation and to try to read it from cover to cover. It would be less difficult to read certain selections first.

Read some part of the Old Testament. Suggestions:

> Some of the Psalms
> The Book of Job
> Parts of the Books of Proverbs, Wisdom and
>   Ecclesiasticus (Sirach).

† † †

section **7** **Jesus Christ, the God-Man**

All that the Father gives me shall come to me; no one who comes will I ever reject, because it is not to do my own will that I have come down from heaven, but to do the will of him who sent me. It is the will of him who sent me that I should lose nothing of what he has given me; rather, that I should raise it up on the last day. Indeed, this is the will of my Father, that everyone who looks upon the Son and believes in him shall have eternal life. Him I will raise up on the last day—JOHN 6:37–40.

WHEN, "in the fullness of time," God sent the long promised Redeemer, he sent not merely a man empowered to teach and act in him name, but his only-begotten Son. Jesus Christ is no mere man; he is God become man that he might be the mediator between God and man.

44

Jesus Christ expressed the threefold office he holds as the God-Man in his words, "I am the way and the truth and the life."

Jesus is the life—our priest, who redeemed us by his death on the cross, who shares with us his divine life.

Jesus is the truth—our teacher, who reveals to us by word and example the eternal truths of the kingdom of heaven.

Jesus is the way—our king, who came to draw all men to himself in a spiritual kingdom, begun here on earth in his Church and to be completed in his everlasting kingdom in heaven.

It is as man that the Son of God fulfills these three offices. It was as man that he first revealed himself to men. Later he openly proclaimed and proved his divinity. But first he won the love and trust of men by showing them his humanity.

In studying the life of Christ, therefore, we shall approach the God-Man as he revealed himself, through his human nature.

1. Who is the mother of Jesus?

The Blessed Virgin Mary is the mother of Jesus.

2. How did the Blessed Virgin become the mother of Jesus?

We read in St. Luke's Gospel:

> In the sixth month, the angel Gabriel was sent from God to a town of Galilee named Nazareth, to a virgin betrothed to a man named Joseph, of the house of David. The virgin's name was Mary.
>
> Upon arriving, the angel said to her: "Rejoice, O highly favored daughter! The LORD is with you. Blessed are you among women." She was deeply troubled by his words, and wondered what his greeting meant. The angel went on to say to her: "Do not fear, Mary. You have found favor with God. You shall conceive and bear a son and give him the name Jesus. Great will be his dignity and he will be called Son of the Most High. The LORD GOD will give him the throne of David his father. He will rule over the house of Jacob forever and his reign will be without end."
>
> Mary said to the angel, "How can this be since I do not know man?" The angel answered her: "The Holy Spirit will

come upon you and the power of the Most High will over-
shadow you; hence, the holy offspring to be born will be
called Son of God. Know that Elizabeth your kinswoman
has conceived a son in her old age; she who was thought bo
be sterile is now in her sixth month, for nothing is impossible with God."

Mary said: "I am the servant of the Lord. Let it be
done to me as you say." With that the angel left her—
LUKE 1:26—38.

3. Why did the angel greet Mary, "Rejoice, O highly favored daughter!"?

The angel greeted Mary thus because, destined to be the
mother of God, she was the most highly privileged of all God's
creatures. She is the only human person who was preserved immaculate from all stain of original sin at the first moment of her
conception. Moreover, so perfectly did she cooperate with God
that she is the holiest of all his creatures. Throughout all her life
she was never guilty of the slightest sin.

4. What is meant by the words, "The Holy Spirit will come upon you, the power of the Most High will overshadow you"?

These words mean that Jesus was conceived in the womb of
Mary miraculously, without the aid of a human father.

5. Why was Jesus born of a virgin?

Jesus was born of a virgin because his Father willed it. It
would have been possible for Christ to have had a human father;
but it was eminently fitting that his mother be a virgin and his
conception miraculous. Throughout the centuries of preparation
for the coming of Christ, God had worked wonders in the conception of his servants who prepared the way for the coming of
his Son. Abraham received a son from Sarah only when she was
old and past the child-bearing period. Elizabeth, who had been
sterile, miraculously, in her old age, conceived John the Baptist,
the precursor of Christ. An even greater miracle should mark the
conception and birth of the Redeemer himself. He should have
no earthly father. He is God's own Son. It was fitting too, that

the womb which bore the Son of God should not thereafter bear a mere human child. Mary, the Mother of God and the Spouse of the Holy Spirit, remained a virgin after the birth of Christ.

6. Who was St. Joseph?

St. Joseph was the husband of Mary and the foster father of Jesus.

7. Who are the "brothers of Jesus" mentioned in the Bible?

They are not brothers, but relatives. The word brother was commonly used at that time to express blood relationship. The word first-born, too, does not imply that there were any other children. It is a technical term referring to the first-born male, who had to be offered to God under Jewish law—cf. EX. 13:2.

8. What is the story of the birth of Christ?

We read in St. Luke's Gospel:

In those days Caesar Augustus published a decree ordering a census of the whole world. This first census took place while Quirinius was governor of Syria. Everyone went to register, each to his own town. And so Joseph went from the town of Nazareth to Galilee to Judea, to David's town of Bethlehem—because he was of the house and lineage of David—to register with Mary, his espoused wife, who was with child.

While they were there the days of her confinement were completed. She gave birth to her first-born son and wrapped him in swaddling clothes and laid him in a manger, because there was no room for them in the place where travelers lodged—LUKE 2:1–7.

9. Where did Jesus live most of his life?

After his birth in Bethlehem and an exile in Egypt (to escape King Herod, who sought to kill him) Jesus lived in the little town of Nazareth until he was about thirty years of age.

10. Why did Jesus spend thirty years in a hidden life?

He did so in order to give us an example of the perfect

human life. Most men cannot imitate Christ in his life of preaching and teaching. But all men can imitate him in the quiet family life of Nazareth.

11. Did Jesus feel and act as other men do?

Yes. In becoming man he took to himself all that belongs to human nature, sin and ignorance alone excepted.

12. What are some of the incidents in the Gospels which show us the humanity of Jesus?

Throughout his boyhood the behavior of Jesus was that of a normal boy, so much so that when as a man he proclaimed himself to be the Messiah the people of his own town refused to believe him—cf. LUKE 4:16–30.

There was only one unusual episode in the boyhood of Jesus, his teaching in the temple at the age of twelve—cf. LUKE 2:42–51.

He felt hunger, thirst, fatigue—cf. LUKE 4:2; JOHN 19:28; JOHN 4:6.

He was fond of children—cf. MARK 10:13–16.

He felt sorrow and wept—cf. JOHN 11:32–36; LUKE 19:41–44.

He knew loneliness—cf. MATT. 26:37–46.

He enjoyed human companionship—cf. JOHN 2:1–12.

He visited the homes of his friends—cf. LUKE 19:1–10.

He felt keenly the betrayal of Judas and the denial of Peter —cf. LUKE 22:39–62.

He experienced the agony of his passion and death. The very anticipation of it caused him such mental suffering that he sweat blood—cf. LUKE 22:41–44.

The tender love of Jesus for all men is evident continually throughout the Gospels. In no place is it so beautifully shown as in his discourse to the apostles which St. John relates in his narration of the Last Supper. This discourse and prayer of Christ for his apostles runs through four chapters of St. John's Gospel —cf. JOHN 14–17.

13. When did Jesus begin his public life?

Jesus began his public life when he was about thirty years of age. At that time he left Nazareth and went about preaching, teaching and working miracles.

Liturgy

Christmas in the liturgy begins with Mass at midnight. There are three different Masses for Christmas, the midnight Mass, the Mass at dawn and the Mass later in the morning. At the midnight Mass the emphasis is on the eternal generation of the Word of God before all time:

. . . Before the daystar, like the dew, I have begotten you— PS. 110:3.

But the Gospel, even at this first Mass on Christmas, gives us St. Luke's wondrous account of the birth of our Savior in Bethlehem.

In the dawn Mass the emphasis is on Christ as the light of the world.

In the third Mass once again the emphasis is on the divinity of our Lord. God has sent his Son into the world to save all men. All who hear him and follow him will be made sons of God.

During the octave of Christmas we celebrate the feasts of St. Stephen, the first Christian martyr, St. John the Evangelist, the Holy Innocents, St. Thomas of Canterbury and St. Sylvester. The octave day of Christmas is the feast of the Solemnity of Mary, New Year's Day.

On the great feast of the Epiphany, twelve days after Christmas, we celebrate the manifestation of Christ to the gentiles. This manifestation is epitomized in the persons of the three Wise Men, who came from the East to pay homage to the Christ Child.

Devotion

We worship Jesus Christ even in his human nature, because that human nature belongs to the Second Divine Person, the eternal Word of God. One of the ways in which we worship Christ in his human nature is through devotion to the Sacred Heart of Jesus. The heart of Jesus is taken as a symbol of his manhood and of the infinite love of Christ and the mercy he has for sinners.

The first Friday of every month is set aside for special devotion to the Sacred Heart of Jesus. The Church encourages all to receive Holy Communion on these first Fridays. Our Lord has promised that whoever does so for nine consecutive first Fridays will not die without receiving whatever help is necessary for his salvation.

Devotion to the Sacred Heart of Jesus is one of the best means of acquiring a deeper love of our Lord.

The feast of the Sacred Heart is celebrated on the Friday following the second Sunday after Pentecost.

✝   ✝   ✝

section **8**   **Jesus Christ, Supreme Teacher**

He addressed them at length in parables, speaking in this fashion: "One day a farmer went out sowing. Part of what he sowed landed on a footpath, where birds came and ate it up. Part of it fell on rocky ground, where it had little soil. It sprouted at once since the soil had no depth, but when the sun rose and scorched it, it began to wither for lack of roots. Again, part of the seed fell among thorns, which grew up and choked it. Part of it, finally, landed on good soil and yielded grain a hundred- or sixty- or thirtyfold. . .

"Mark well, then, the parable of the sower. The seed along the path is the man who hears the message about God's reign without understanding it. The evil one approaches him to steal away what was sown in his mind. The seed that

50

fell on patches of rock is the man who hears the message and at first receives it with joy. But he has no roots, so he lasts only for a time. When some setback or persecution involving the message occurs, he soon falters. What was sown among briers is the man who hears the message, but then worldly anxiety and the lure of money choke it off. Such a one produces no yield. But what was sown on good soil is the man who hears the message and takes it in. He it is who bears a yield of a hundred- or sixty- or thirtyfold."–MATT. 13:3–8; 18–23.

CHRIST WAS SENT into the world by his Father to tell fallen men of God's saving love for them and of the coming of the kingdom. It was to the Jews that he preached because it was to the Jews that God had promised the Redeemer. Our Lord spent the three years of his public life seeking out the people to tell them of his kingdom.

He preached in the towns and in the country, in the streets and on the hillsides, in the temple and in the homes of the people. When his life had but a day to run our Lord summed up his teaching of the word of his Father thus:

I have made your name known to those you gave me out of the world.

These men you gave me were yours; they have kept your word.

Now they realize that all that you gave me comes from you.

I entrusted to them the message you entrusted to me, and they received it.

They have known that in truth I came from you, they have believed it was you who sent me–JOHN 17:6–8.

Our Lord was a courageous teacher. He did not modify his doctrine to please the leaders of the people or the people themselves. He knew that many of his words would fall upon deaf ears, but he also knew that those who received his words with joy "would yield fruit a hundredfold" and would carry his message to the ends of the earth.

1. What did our Lord teach the people?

Our Lord taught the people that salvation and redemption were at hand and that the kingdom of God was come. St. Mark says that he was heralding the joyful tidings of God's kingdom—cf. MARK 1:14. St. Matthew says that he went about preaching "the good news of the kingdom"—MATT. 4:23.

Jesus *reaffirmed* the teachings of the Old Law, which the Jews had received from God, purging it from the legalistic elements which the Scribes and Pharisees had introduced.

Jesus *fulfilled* the Old Law. He took each part of the old revelation, doctrine, moral law and worship, and brought it to completion in a new, more perfect revelation of doctrine, law and worship.

> *Do not think that I have come to abolish the law and the prophets. I have come, not to abolish them, but to fulfill them*—MATT. 5:17.

In preaching his Gospel Jesus told men of the infinite love of God for them, of the mystery of the Trinity, of his own divinity, of his Church and of the sacraments. All the teachings of the Catholic Church can be traced back to the teachings of Jesus Christ.

2. How did Jesus teach?

Jesus taught in various ways. Some of his teachings, for example, the law of love, he stated simply and directly. Some of his teachings he gave by means of parables, stories such as that of the sower. Although Jesus taught in words which carried great authority and worked miracles which amazed the people, he taught most effectively by his example. St. Augustine, referring to the example of Christ says, "He did not say, 'Learn from Me how to build a world and raise the dead' but 'Learn from me; I am meek and humble of heart.'"

3. What is a parable?

A parable is an illustration of a truth by means of an example or a story. By using parables Jesus was able to present great religious truths in a form which allowed them to be grasped and remembered by all, the unlearned as well as the learned.

For example, Jesus taught

—the necessity for good works, in the parable of the barren fig tree—cf. LUKE 13:6—9.

—the virtues of humility and contrition, in the parable of the Pharisee and the publican—cf. LUKE 18:9—14;

—the necessity of being prepared for death at any moment, the need of being in possession of the divine life at all times, by the parables of the wise and foolish virgins—cf. MATT. 25:1—13 and the marriage of the king's son—cf. MATT. 22:1—14;

—the necessity of forgiving one's enemies by the parable of the unmerciful servant—cf. MATT. 18:23—35;

—the necessity of loving one's neighbor, by the parable of the good Samaritan—cf. LUKE 10:30—37;

—the love and mercy of God, by the parable of the prodigal son—cf. LUKE 15:11—32.

4. What are some of the doctrines which our Lord taught by his example as well as by his words?

Our Lord exemplified all his teachings in his life, particularly those on the love of God and one's neighbor, prayer, submission to the will of God and poverty.

5. How did Jesus teach love?

Jesus taught:

You have heard the commandment, "You shall love your countryman but hate your enemy." My command to you is: love your enemies, pray for your persecutors. This will prove that you are sons of your heavenly Father, for his sun rises on the bad and the good, he rains on the just and the unjust. If you love those who love you, what merit is there in that? Do not tax collectors do as much? And if you greet your brothers only, what is so praiseworthy about that? Do not pagans do as much? In a word, you must be made perfect as your heavenly Father is perfect—MATT. 5:43—48.

He exemplified this teaching by freely laying down his own life for all men.

There is no greater love than this: to lay down one's life for one's friends–JOHN 15:13.

On the cross he prayed for those who crucified him, ". . . Father, forgive them, they do not know what they are doing" –LUKE 23:34.

Most of his miracles were worked out of compassion for the sick and the suffering.

The cure of the centurion's servant–cf. MATT. 8:5–13.

The raising from the dead of Jairus' daughter–cf. MATT. 9:18–26, the widow's son–cf. LUKE 7:11–16, and of Lazarus–cf. JOHN 11:1–44.

The cure of the paralytic at the pool of Bethsaida–cf. JOHN 5:1–9.

The cure of the man who had been born blind–cf. JOHN 9:1–38.

6. How did Jesus teach prayer?

Jesus taught the true spirit of prayer, insisting on sincerity and simplicity, and denouncing hypocrisy and wordiness in prayer–cf. MATT. 6:5–9.

The whole life of Jesus was lived in constant union with his Father. All his actions were in perfect accord with the will of the Father. His whole life, therefore, was one continual prayer.

But Jesus also spent long periods absorbed in prayer. The Gospels frequently state that he spent the whole night in prayer.

He prefaced his public life by retiring to the desert, where he spent forty days and nights in prayer and fasting–cf. LUKE 4:1–2.

When he was about to choose his disciples, Jesus spent the whole night in prayer–cf. LUKE 6:12.

A great many of his miracles were preceded by prayer, e.g., the healing of the deaf mute–cf. MARK 7:34; the raising of Lazarus from the dead–cf. JOHN 11:41; the multiplication of the loaves—MATT. 14:19.

He began his passion with prayer at the Last Supper—cf. JOHN 17, entire chapter.

He prayed during his agony in the garden—cf. MATT. 26:36 —44.

He prayed as he hung on the cross—cf. LUKE 23:34, 46.

7. How did Jesus teach perfect submission to the will of God?

Jesus said: ". . .I do nothing by myself. I say only what the Father has taught me. The One who sent me is with me. He has not deserted me since I always do what pleases him"—JOHN 8:28—29.

The outstanding characteristic of Jesus is his total, unreserved surrender to the will of God, his mighty burning love for his Father. No other man has ever so completely fulfilled the first commandment of the law, "You shall love the Lord your God with all your heart, with all your soul, with all your strength. . ."

The first recorded words of Jesus, then a boy of twelve, were, "Did you not know I had to be in my Father's house?"— LUKE 2:49. These words he spoke to Mary and Joseph to explain why he had remained in Jerusalem. Yet, having uttered these words, he went down to Nazareth and "was obedient to them"—LUKE 2:51, because such was the will of his Father.

Every action of Jesus' was dictated by his love for his Father. In the anguish he endured in contemplating the sufferings and death he was about to undergo he prayed, "My Father, if it is possible, let this cup pass me by. Still, let it be as you would have it, not as I—"MATT. 26:39.

8. How did Jesus teach poverty and detachment?

Jesus taught:

I warn you, then: do not worry about your livelihood, what you are to eat or drink or use for clothing. Is not life more than food? Is not the body more valuable than clothes?

Look at the birds in the sky. They do not sow or reap, they gather nothing into barns; yet your heavenly Father

*feeds them. Are not you more important than they? Which
of you by worrying can add a moment to his life-span?*

*As for clothes, why be concerned? Learn a lesson from
the way the wild flowers grow. They do not work; they
do not spin. Yet I assure you, not even Solomon in all his
splendor was arrayed like one of these. If God can clothe in
such splendor the grass of the field, which blooms today and
is thrown on the fire tomorrow, will he not provide much
more for you, O weak in faith!*

*Stop worrying, then, over questions like, 'What are we to
eat, or what are we to drink, or what are we to wear?'*

*The unbelievers are always running after these things.
Your heavenly Father knows all that you need. Seek first
his kingship over you, his way of holiness, and all these
things will be given you besides. Enough, then, of worrying
about tomorrow. Let tomorrow take care of itself. Today
has troubles enough of its own*–MATT. 6:25–34.

*Do not lay up for yourselves an earthly treasure. Moths
and rust corrode; thieves break in and steal.*

*Make it your practice instead to store up heavenly
treasure, which neither moths nor rust corrode nor thieves
break in and steal. Remember, where your treasure is, there
your heart is also*–MATT. 6:19–21.

He exemplified this teaching by his own complete detach-
ment:

He was born in a stable.

He worked as a carpenter in the tiny town of Nazareth.

During the three years of his public life, he had no home
and no possessions. He said of himself:

*The foxes have lairs, the birds in the sky have nests, but the
Son of Man has nowhere to lay his head*–MATT. 8:20.

He had special love and concern for the poor.

He chose as his apostles, for the most part, men of little
means, and required that they give up all things in following
him.

Practice

▲ Christ still teaches his doctrines to the world. Now he does so through his Church. One of the most effective ways in which our Lord teaches us today is through the liturgy of the Church.

Remind yourself that it is Christ who is teaching you as you listen to the reading of the scripture lessons and to the homily at Mass.

Read with care the parables of our Lord which are mentioned in question 3 of this lesson. Try to understand the lesson Christ is teaching in these parables, and make an application to yourself.

† † †

section **9** **Christ's Great Teaching, the Blessed Trinity**

Yet I tell you the sober truth:
It is much better for you that I go.
If I fail to go,
the Paraclete will never come to you,
whereas if I go,
I will send him to you.
When he comes,
he will prove the world wrong
about sin,
about justice,
about condemnation.
About sin—
in that they refuse to believe in me;
about justice—
from the fact that I go to the Father

and you can see me no more;
about condemnation—
for the prince of this world has been condemned.
   I have much more to tell you,
but you cannot bear it now.
When he comes, however,
being the Spirit of truth
he will guide you to all truth.
He will not speak on his own, but will speak
only what he hears,
and will announce to you the things to come.
In doing this he will give glory to me,
because he will have received from me
what he will announce to you.
All that the Father has belongs to me—JOHN 16:7—14.

JESUS CHRIST has revealed to us the secrets of the kingdom of heaven. In the greatest of his teachings he has revealed to us the secret of God himself. He has told us of the inmost life of God, the deepest of all mysteries, the mystery of the Blessed Trinity. God, he has told us, is not one Person alone, as we would think, but rather three Persons, Father, Son and Holy Spirit.

All the truths of our faith are mysteries which we cannot fully understand. The Blessed Trinity is the deepest of all mysteries.

Nevertheless God has revealed it to us. He has done so because he wants us to know him as he is, to know as much about him as we can in order that we might in some measure return the boundless love he has for us.

1. How did Jesus teach us of the inmost life of God?

Jesus taught, as indeed the Jews of his time already knew, that there is only one God, one supreme Creator and Law-giver.

But in revealing the inmost life of God, Jesus taught that in the one God there are three distinct Persons, each absolutely equal to each other. He told us the names of these three Divine Persons: Father, Son and Holy Spirit.

58

2. How did Jesus tell us that there are three Divine Persons?

a. Jesus spoke continually of his Father, calling him always by that name. When he drove the money changers from the temple, he said, "Get them out of here! Stop turning my Father's house into a market-place"—JOHN 2:16.

He said to his apostles, "My Father has been glorified in your bearing much fruit and becoming my disciples. As the Father has loved me, so I have loved you. Live on in my love. You will live in my love if you keep my commandments, even as I have kept my Father's commandments, and live in his love"—JOHN 15:8–10.

b. Jesus said that he is the Son, the only-begotten Son of that Father, equal to the Father.

Speaking of himself he said, "Yes, God so loved the world that he gave his only Son, that whoever believes in him may not die but may have eternal life"—JOHN 3:16.

At the Last Supper he prayed to the Father, ". . .Father, the hour has come! Give glory to your Son that your Son may give glory to you, inasmuch as you have given him authority over all mankind, that he may bestow eternal life on those you gave him. (Eternal life is this: to know you, the only true God, and him whom you have sent, Jesus Christ.) I have given you glory on earth by finishing the work you gave me to do. Do you now, Father, give me glory at your side, a glory I had with you before the world began"—JOHN 17:1–5.

He said to his apostles, "All that the Father has belongs to me"—JOHN 16:15.

In response to Philip's words, "Lord, show us the Father," Jesus answered, "Philip, after I have been with you all this time, you still do not know me? Whoever has seen me has seen the Father. How can you say, 'Show us the Father'? Do you not believe that I am in the Father and the Father is in me?"—JOHN 14:8–10.

c. Jesus promised to send a third Divine Person, the equal of himself and the Father.

At the Last Supper he told the apostles, "I will ask the

Father and he will give you another Paraclete to be with you always: the Spirit of truth, whom the world cannot accept, since it does not recognize him. . ."—JOHN 14:16—17.

"the Paraclete, the Holy Spirit whom the Father will send in my name, will instruct you in everything, and remind you of all that I told you"—JOHN 14:26.

"When the Paraclete comes, the Spirit of truth who comes from the Father. . .he will bear witness on my behalf"—JOHN 15:26.

d. When he sent the apostles to preach the Gospel to the whole world Jesus told them to baptize "in the name of the Father, and of the Son and of the Holy Spirit." Here Christ expresses in one short formula the idea of one God (in the name) in three distinct and equal Divine Persons (*of* the Father, and *of* the Son, and *of* the Holy Spirit)—cf. MATT. 28:19.

3. Why is the First Divine Person called the Father?

The First Divine Person is called the Father because it is he who begets the Second Divine Person, the eternal Word, who is ". . .the reflection of the Father's glory, the exact representation of the Father's being"—HEB. 1:3.

4. Why is the Second Divine Person called the Son?

The Second Divine Person is called the Son because he is the perfect image of the Father: "God from God, Light from Light, true God from true God, begotten, not made, one in Being with the Father" (Nicene Creed).

5. Why is the Third Divine Person called the Holy Spirit?

The Third Divine Person is called the Holy Spirit because he is the Person of divine love, breathed forth by the Father and the Son. He is "the Lord, the giver of life, who proceeds from the Father and the Son. With the Father and the Son he is worshipped and glorified. He has spoken through the prophets. . ." (Nicene Creed).

6. How did Jesus teach us to distinguish between the three Persons in God?

a. Jesus spoke of the Father as creator and ruler, because we naturally think of a father in this role. All the time we know it is the three Divine Persons who create and rule.

b. Jesus told us that he, the Second Divine Person, became man and lived and died among men. As God, Jesus is called the Word, the eternal Knowledge of the Father. That is why St. John, speaking of the Second Divine Person, says: "In the beginning was the Word; the Word was in God's presence, and the Word was God. . . . Through him all things came into being, and apart from him nothing came to be. . . . The Word became flesh and made his dwelling among us"—JOHN 1:1–3, 14.

c. Jesus spoke of the Holy Spirit as the one whom he and the Father would send to enlighten and inspire us. We naturally associate works of love and inspiration with the Holy Spirit, since he is Divine Love. All the time we know, however, that it was the three Divine Persons who descended upon the infant Church on Pentecost and who dwell in all who possess the divine life.

7. Do we find any manifestations of the Blessed Trinity in the New Testament?

Yes. When Jesus was baptized by John in the river Jordan:

When all the people were baptized, and Jesus was at prayer after likewise being baptized, the skies opened and the Holy Spirit descended on him in visible form like a dove. A voice from heaven was heard to say: "You are my beloved Son. On you my favor rests"—LUKE 3:21–22.

When Jesus was transfigured before Peter, James and John, the Father spoke from heaven, "This is my Son, my beloved. Listen to him"—MARK 9:7.

On Pentecost the Holy Spirit manifested his coming by the sound of a mighty wind and parted tongues of fire.

When the day of Pentecost came it found them gathered in one place. Suddenly from up in the sky there came a noise like a strong, driving wind which was heard all through the house where they were seated. Tongues as of fire appeared, which parted and came to rest on each of them. All were

filled with the Holy Spirit. They began to express them-
selves in foreign tongues and make bold proclamation as the
Spirit prompted them—ACTS 2:1–4.

8. How do we honor the Blessed Trinity in the liturgy?

The Church usually addresses her prayers to God the Father, through the Son, in union with the Holy Spirit.

On the great feast of Pentecost, fifty days after Easter, we celebrate the coming of the Holy Spirit upon the Church.

We celebrate Trinity Sunday every year on the first Sunday after Pentecost.

9. How may we pray to the Blessed Trinity.

We may pray simply to God, i.e., to the Blessed Trinity.

We may pray to any one of the three Divine Persons.

We may pray as the Church does most often—to the Father, through the Son, in union with the Holy Spirit. Our Lord promised: "...I give you my assurance, whatever you ask the Father, he will give you in my name"—JOHN 16:23.

The equality of the Persons of the Blessed Trinity, their oneness in nature and their distinctness in person is expressed in the Athanasian Creed.

Now this is the Catholic faith: that we worship one God in Trinity, and Trinity in unity; neither confusing the persons nor distinguishing the nature.

The person of the Father is distinct; the person of the Son is distinct; the person of the Holy Spirit is distinct.

Yet the Father and the Son and the Holy Spirit possess one God-head, equal glory and co-eternal majesty.

As the Father is, so is the Son, so also is the Holy Spirit.

The Father is uncreated, the Son is uncreated, The Holy Spirit is uncreated.

The Father is infinite, the Son is infinite, the Holy Spirit is infinite.

The Father is eternal, the Son is eternal, the Holy Spirit is eternal.

Nevertheless there are not three eternals, but one eternal; even as there are not three uncreateds but one uncreated, and one infinite.

So likewise the Father is almighty, the Son is almighty, the Holy Spirit is almighty. And yet they are not three almighties, but one almighty.

So also the Father is God, the Son is God, the Holy Spirit is God. And yet they are not three Gods, but only one God.

So, too, the Father is Lord, the Son is Lord, the Holy Spirit is Lord. And still there are not three Lords, but only one Lord.

For just as we are compelled by Christian truth to profess that each Person is individually Lord and God, so also are we forbidden by the Catholic religion to hold that there are three Gods or Lords.

The Father was made by no one, being neither made nor created nor begotten.

The Son is from the Father only, being neither made nor created, but begotten.

The Holy Spirit is from the Father and the Son, being neither made nor created nor begotten, but proceeding.

Consequently, there is one Father, not three Fathers; there is one Son, not three Sons; there is one Holy Spirit, not three Holy Spirits.

Furthermore, in this Trinity there is no "before" or "after," no "greater" or "less"; for all three Persons are co-eternal and co-equal.

In every respect, therefore, as has already been stated, unity must be worshipped in trinity, and trinity in unity. . . .

Practice

▲ The Blessed Trinity dwells within us because we possess the divine life. We should try to realize this presence of God within us.

St. Paul tells us:

63

You must know that your body is a temple of the Holy Spirit, who is within—the Spirit you have received from God. You are not your own. You have been purchased, and at a price. So glorify God in your body—1 COR. 6:19—20.

We should remember these words wherever we are, at work, at home, at places of amusement. God is within us. We should act accordingly. We should also be anxious to share the presence which is ours with others who do not yet know and love God as we are privileged to.

The sign of the cross is a profession of faith in and an act of adoration of the Blessed Trinity.

Take particular care to realize that you are praying even as you begin your prayers by signing yourself:

In the name of the Father, and of the Son, and of the Holy Spirit. Amen.

† † †

section **10**   **Jesus Christ, High Priest and Redeemer**

Every high priest is taken from among men and made their representative before God, to offer gifts and sacrifices for sins.

He is able to deal patiently with erring sinners, for he himself is beset by weakness and so must make sin offerings for himself as well as for the people. One does not take this honor on his own initiative, but only when called by God as Aaron was. Even Christ did not glorify himself with the office of high priest; he received it from the One who said to him,

"You are my son;
today I have begotten you";

just as he says in another place,

"You are a priest forever,
according to the order of Melchizedek."
In the days when he was in the flesh, he offered prayers
and supplications with loud cries and tears to God, who was
able to save him from death, and he was heard because of his
reverence. Son though he was, he learned obedience from
what he suffered; and when perfected, he became the source
of eternal salvation for all who obey him, designated by God
as high priest according to the order of Melchizedek—HEB.
5:1–10.

IN THESE WORDS St. Paul explains the idea of priesthood (a priest is a mediator between God and man) and emphasizes the fact that Jesus Christ, the God-Man, is the priest of priests. The essential function of a priest is to offer gifts to God in the name of the people and to be the bearer of sacred gifts from God to man. Jesus Christ, the anointed of God, came to offer himself on the cross for the salvation of men. Christ is the mediator between God and man. His sacrifice on the cross is the supreme gift offered to God. Christ, by his death, has made reparation for the sins of men and has made the divine life once more available.

1. What do we mean when we say that Jesus Christ is our high priest?

When we say that Jesus Christ is our high priest we mean that he offered his life as the supreme gift to his Father by dying on the cross for us, and that he brings to us from God all the things which make men holy.

2. What do we mean when we say that Jesus Christ is our Redeemer?

We mean that Christ by the sacrifice of his life on the cross has paid the price for our sins and has made the divine life once more available to us.

3. Does Christ still exercise his office of priest?

Yes, Christ as head of the Church continues to exercise his priesthood. Through the Church Christ offers Mass and administers the sacraments. Therefore we can say that it is Christ who baptizes, Christ who forgives sin, etc.

4. What is the history of the passion and death of Jesus?

Jesus began his passion by eating the Last Supper with his twelve apostles.

At this meal he instituted the Holy Eucharist and ordained the apostles priests:

Then, taking bread and giving thanks, he broke it and gave it to them, saying: "This is my body to be given for you. Do this as a remembrance of me."

He did the same with the cup after eating, saying as he did so: "This cup is the new covenant in my blood, which will be shed for you"–LUKE 22:19–20.

He underwent a night of agony in the garden of Gethsemani:

Then Jesus went with them to a place called Gethsemani. He said to his disciples, "Stay here while I go over there and pray."

He took along Peter and Zebedee's two sons, and began to experience sorrow and distress. Then he said to them, "My heart is nearly broken with sorrow. Remain here and stay awake with me." He advanced a little and fell prostrate in prayer. "My Father, if it is possible, let this cup pass me by. Still, let it be as you would have it, not as I"–MATT. 26:36–39.

He was betrayed by Judas and taken prisoner:

While he was still speaking, Judas, one of the Twelve, arrived accompanied by a great crowd with swords and clubs. They had been sent by the chief priests and elders of the people.

His betrayer had arranged to give them a signal, saying, "The man I shall embrace is the one; take hold of him." He immediately went over to Jesus, said to him, "Peace, Rabbi," and embraced him–MATT. 26:47–49.

He was taken before the high priests, where he professed that he was God:

> . . . *The high priest then said to him: "I order you to tell us under oath before the living God whether you are the Messiah, the Son of God." Jesus answered: "It is you who say it. But I tell you this: Soon you will see the Son of Man seated at the right hand of the Power and coming on the clouds of heaven." At this the high priest tore his robes: "He has blasphemed! What further need have we of witnesses?*
>
> *"Remember, you heard the blasphemy. What is your verdict?" They answered, "He deserves death!"*—MATT. 26:63—66.

He was denied by Peter:

> *All through this, Simon Peter had been standing there warming himself. They said to him, "Are not you a disciple of his?" He denied it and said, "I am not!" "But did I not see you with him in the garden?" insisted one of the high priest's slaves—as it happened, a relative of the man whose ear Peter had severed. Peter denied it again. At that moment a cock began to crow*—JOHN 18:25—27.

He was taken before Pilate, the Roman governor.

He was scourged, mocked, crowned with thorns and condemned to death:

> *Pilate's next move was to take Jesus and have him scourged. The soldiers then wove a crown of thorns and fixed it on his head, throwing around his shoulders a cloak of royal purple.*
>
> *. . . As soon as the chief priests and the temple guards saw him they shouted, "Crucify him! Crucify him!" Pilate said, "Take him and crucify him yourselves; I find no case against him." "We have our law," the Jews responded, "and according to that law he must die because he made himself God's Son."*
>
> *. . . Pilate heard what they were saying, then brought Jesus outside and took a seat on a judge's bench at the place called the Stone Pavement—Gabbatha in Hebrew. (It was the Preparation Day for Passover, and the hour was about noon.) He said to the Jews, "Look at your king!" At*

this they shouted, *"Away with him! Away with him! Crucify him!"* *"What!"* Pilate exclaimed. *"Shall I crucify your king?"* The chief priests replied, *"We have no king but Caesar."* In the end, Pilate handed Jesus over to be crucified*–JOHN 19:1–16.

He was crucified between two thieves:

When they came to Skull Place, as it was called, they crucified him there and the criminals as well, one on his right and the other on his left–LUKE 23:33.

After three hours' agony on the cross he died:

It was now around midday, and darkness came over the whole land until midafternoon with an eclipse of the sun. The curtain in the sanctuary was torn in two. Jesus uttered a loud cry and said,

"Father, into your hands I commend my spirit."
After he said this, he expired–LUKE 23:44–46.

5. Was it necessary for Christ to suffer and die in order to redeem us?

No. It was not absolutely necessary for Christ to suffer and die in order to redeem us. Any action or prayer of Christ would have been of such great value that it could have redeemed any number of worlds. But God decreed that it be by the sufferings and death on the cross that his Son redeem the world.

6. Why did God require the death of his Son?

God required the death of his Son in order to teach us the seriousness of sin and to prove his love for us.

There is no greater love than this: to lay down one's life for one's friends–JOHN 15:13.

a. The passion and death of Christ teaches us, above all, the immense love and mercy of God. If one is ever tempted to doubt the mercy of God, one need only look at a crucifix to be reminded that God's love knows no bounds. The outstretched arms

68

of Jesus on the cross, moreover, illustrate the fact that no one, however great a sinner he be, is excluded from the love and mercy of God.

b. The passion and death of our Lord teaches us the enormity of sin. It was sin which caused Christ to suffer such agony and to die. All the efforts of the world to minimize or to glamorize sin fail before the image of the crucified Savior.

Liturgy

The Church re-lives the Passion and death of Jesus in the liturgy of Holy Week. On Second Passion Sunday, the Sunday before Easter, palms are blessed and distributed. Carrying these palms, we walk in procession singing, "Hosanna to the Son of David," as did the children of Jerusalem at Christ's triumphal entry into the Holy City as he came to begin his Passion. At the Mass which follows the whole story of the Passion and death of Christ is recounted as the Passion of our Lord according to St. Matthew, or St. Mark, or St. Luke. On Holy Thursday evening we celebrate the anniversary of the Last Supper by a Mass which expresses both our joy and gratitude for the great gifts of the Eucharist and the priesthood, and our deep mourning at the Passion of Christ, which began on that night. The service on Good Friday is not a Mass, not the unbloody sacrifice of Christ; it is a service which concentrates, rather, on the bloody death of Christ on the first Good Friday. The service consists of readings, prayers, the reading of the Passion according to St. John, veneration of the cross and Holy Communion. After the services of Good Friday night the Church is empty and silent; the altar is bare. Until the Easter Vigil service on Holy Saturday night we relive the time when the dead body of Christ lay in the tomb.

Devotion

All Catholic churches have a series of fourteen pictures depicting various scenes in the Passion and death of Jesus. These pictures are in sequence, beginning at the front of the church and continuing down one side wall and up the other. They are called "The Way of the Cross" or "The Stations of the Cross." To make the way of the cross or to make the stations, as the practice sometimes is called, all one has to do is to walk from picture to picture meditating on the Passion of Christ. One may "make the stations" privately at any time; the devotion is held publicly in most churches on the Fridays of Lent.

This devotion is one of the most highly blessed devotions in the Church, and one which will give us a deeper realization of the love and mercy of God as well as a greater sorrow for our sins.

Prayers and meditations which can be used in making the way of the cross are to be found in most prayer books or in booklets which can be obtained from pamphlet racks or Catholic book stores.

Practice

▲ Read St. Matthew's account of the Passion of Jesus. It is to be found in chapters 26 and 27 of St. Matthew's Gospel.

† † †

section **11**   The Resurrection of Jesus

. . .and if Christ was not raised, your faith is worthless. You are still in your sins, and those who have fallen asleep in Christ are the deadest of the dead. If our hopes in Christ are limited to this life only, we are the most pitiable of men. But as it is, Christ is now raised from the dead, the first fruits of those who have fallen asleep. Death came through a man; hence the resurrection of the dead comes through a

man also. Just as in Adam all die, so in Christ all will come to life again–1 COR. 15:17–22.

IF JESUS CHRIST had not risen from the dead his life would have been essentially no different from that of any great teacher. He would have been remembered only as a good and wise man who had taught a beautiful doctrine and who had been put to death unjustly. His life would have ended not in apparent failure but in real failure. He would have been conquered by sin; evil would have triumphed over him and destroyed him. He would have shown himself to be a mere man, subject to death as are all men.

But Jesus Christ has risen from the dead. By his resurrection he shows that he is not merely a great teacher but the eternal Son of God. By his resurrection he shows that his life was not a failure but a glorious success. By his resurrection he shows that, far from having been overcome by evil, he is the conqueror of both sin and death.

Finally, Jesus, the first born from the dead, shows us that we too will some day rise from the dead, i.e., our body and soul will be reunited and we will enter into a new form of life called eternal life.

1. Did Jesus Christ claim to be God?

Yes. At his trial the Jews recognized that Jesus was claiming to be the Son of God, the equal of God the Father, and they condemned him to death precisely for making that claim.

We read in St. Matthew's Gospel:

The high priest rose to his feet and addressed him: "Have you no answer to the testimony leveled against you?" But Jesus remained silent. The high priest then said to him: "I order you to tell us under oath before the living God whether you are the Messiah, the Son of God." Jesus answered: "It is you who say it. But I tell you this: Soon you will see the Son of Man seated at the right hand of the Power and coming on the clouds of heaven." At this the high priest tore his robes: "He has blasphemed! What further need have we of witnesses? Remember, you heard the blasphemy. What is your verdict?" They answered, "He deserves death!"–MATT. 26:62–66.

On various other occasions, too, Jesus claimed to be God. For example, he had announced to a paralyzed man that his sins were forgiven. The Pharisees, who had heard him, thought in their hearts, "Who is this man who utters blasphemies? Who can forgive sins but God alone?"—LUKE 5:21. Jesus, giving expression to their thoughts, worked a miracle that all could see showing that he could, indeed, forgive sins, i.e., that he was God.

Jesus even applied to himself the very title for the Almighty, "I am."

> *At this the Jews objected: "You are not yet fifty! How can you have seen Abraham?" Jesus answered them: "I solemnly declare it: before Abraham came to be, I AM"*–JOHN 8:57–58.

2. Is it not possible that Jesus when he said he was the Son of God was merely claiming to be a prophet sent by God?

No. In the first place such a claim would not have been taken as blasphemy. Moreover Jesus called God "my Father" in a way in which no mere man could speak of God. On one occasion he said openly, "My Father and I are one." The Jews thereupon took up stones to cast at him, saying, "You who are only a man are making yourself God"—JOHN 10:33.

In speaking to Philip, Christ said, "Do you not believe that I am in the Father and the Father is in me?"—JOHN 14:10.

And again at the Last Supper he prayed to the Father: "Do you now, Father, give me glory at your side, a glory I had with you before the world began—JOHN 17:5.

3. Does not Jesus at times speak as if he were inferior to the Father and at other times as if he were equal?

Yes. For example, he said, "The Father is greater than I"— JOHN 14:28, and also, "All that the Father has belongs to me— JOHN 16:15.

Jesus Christ is one person. But that one person is both God

and man. At the time of the Incarnation he took a human body and soul. As God, the Second Divine Person, he always existed. The Second Divine Person, therefore, now possesses two natures, a human and a divine. In the Gospels he acts and speaks sometimes in his human nature, i.e., as man, sometimes in his divine nature, i.e., as God. He spoke in his human nature when he said, "The Father is greater than I," in his divine nature when he said, "All things that the Father has are mine."

4. Did Jesus say that he would rise from the dead?

Yes. On many occasions Jesus said that he would rise from the dead.

> At this the Jews responded, "What sign can you show us authorizing you to do these things?" "Destroy this temple," was Jesus' answer, "and in three days I will raise it up." They retorted, "This temple took forty-six years to build, and you are going to 'raise it up in three days'!" Actually he was talking about the temple of his body. Only after Jesus had been raised from the dead did his disciples recall that he had said this, and come to believe the Scripture and the word he had spoken–JOHN 2:18–22.

> Some of the scribes and Pharisees then spoke up, saying, "Teacher, we want to see you work some signs." He answered: "An evil and unfaithful age is eager for a sign! No sign will be given it but that of the prophet Jonah. Just as Jonah spent three days and three nights in the belly of the whale, so will the Son of Man spend three days and three nights in the bowels of the earth"–MATT. 12:38–40.

5. How was Jesus put to death?

In addition to being scourged mercilessly Christ was forced to carry his heavy cross through the city to the place of crucifixion. His condition during this journey was such that his enemies feared that he would die before reaching Calvary. Hence they forced Simon of Cyrene to help carry the cross–cf. MATT. 27:32.

Jesus was nailed to the cross and hung there for three hours. At the moment of his death there was a sign from heaven:

Once again Jesus cried out in a loud voice, and then gave up his spirit.

Suddenly the curtain of the sanctuary was torn in two from top to bottom. The earth quaked, boulders split, tombs opened. Many bodies of saints who had fallen asleep were raised. After Jesus' resurrection they came forth from their tombs and entered the holy city and appeared to many—MATT. 27:50—53.

The Roman soldiers broke the legs of the two thieves who were crucified with Christ in order to hasten their death. But when they came to Jesus they saw that he was already dead; there was no need to break his legs. One of the soldiers, however, took a lance and opened up the side of Christ, piercing his heart—cf. JOHN 19:31—37.

6. What were the circumstances of Christ's burial?

The body of Jesus was placed in a tomb by his friends, and a heavy stone was rolled against the opening to seal the tomb. But the enemies of Christ, taking every precaution, and mindful of our Lord's prediction that he would rise on the third day, placed a guard of soldiers around the tomb—cf. MATT. 27:62—66.

7. What is the story of Christ's Resurrection?

Early Sunday morning several women, followers of Christ, went to the tomb with the intention of anointing the body of Jesus. When they arrived they were amazed to find the stone rolled away and the tomb empty. An angel announced to them that Jesus had risen and instructed them to tell Peter and the other apostles that he would meet them in Galilee—cf. LUKE 24:1—13.

Peter and John, upon hearing the news, ran to the tomb to see for themselves. They, too, found the tomb empty.

8. Did the friends of Christ expect that He would rise from the dead?

No. Despite our Lord's prediction that he would rise on the third day his friends did not expect the resurrection and at first refused to believe that Christ had risen.

Mary Magdelene, seeing the empty tomb, immediately concluded that the body had been stolen. When Christ appeared to her she thought he was the gardener—cf. JOHN 20:1–18.

That evening Christ entered the room where most of the apostles were gathered. Instead of rushing to meet him they cowered in a corner, believing him to be a ghost. Our Lord ate food in order to convince them that he was alive—cf. LUKE 24:36–43.

That same evening Christ appeared to two of his disciples on a road outside of Jerusalem. They had not believed the rumors of the Resurrection either and did not recognize Christ until he had vanished out of their sight—cf. LUKE 24:13–35.

One of the apostles, Thomas, who had not been present the first time Jesus appeared to the others, refused to believe that Christ had risen. He said that unless he could examine the wounds in Christ's body he would not believe. Later Jesus again appeared and insisted that Thomas see for himself—cf. JOHN 20:24–29.

9. What did Christ's Resurrection teach the apostles?

Christ's resurrection taught the apostles that Jesus was not only the promised Messiah but God himself, the eternal Son of God. After the Holy Spirit came upon them on Pentecost they fully understood the fact that Christ was God and grasped the meaning of his death as the act by which he redeemed the world.

10. How is the Resurrection of Christ the source of our hope?

The resurrection of Christ shows us that Christ has conquered sin and death. He conquered sin by his death on the cross. He conquered death by his resurrection. Death is a result of original sin. Christ's victory over death is our pledge that he will raise us up on the last day.

> For if we believe that Jesus died and rose, God will bring forth with him from the dead those also who have fallen asleep believing in him. . . . No, the Lord himself will come down from heaven at the word of command, at the sound of the archangel's voice and God's trumpet; and those who have died in Christ will rise first—1 THESS. 4:14, 16.

11. Where did the soul of Christ go after his death?

After his death the soul of Christ "descended into hell." This means that Christ's soul went where the souls of the just who had died before him were awaiting their entrance into heaven.

12. How long did Jesus remain on earth after his Resurrection?

Jesus remained after his Resurrection for forty days. Then on Ascension Thursday after instructing his apostles to return to Jerusalem to await the coming of the Holy Spirit on Pentecost, he gave them the commission to teach, sanctify and rule in his name and to spread the Church throughout the world. Thereupon he ascended out of their sight into heaven.

13. Will Christ ever return to earth?

At the end of time Christ will come again to judge the living and the dead. Meanwhile, true to his promise, "I will not leave you orphans," he remains in the world in his Church, through which he continues to act in the world. And, although visible only to the eyes of faith, he is present under the appearances of bread and wine in the Eucharist.

Liturgy

The Resurrection of Christ and its profound meaning in our lives is brought home to us in the liturgy of Easter. The Easter services begin with the Easter Vigil, which is held on Holy Saturday night, preferably late in the night, so that the first Easter Mass may begin about midnight. This service is one of the most beautiful and meaningful in all the liturgy. In it we enact in word, ceremony and song the story of our redemption, our passage from death to life by means of water and the Holy Spirit. Christ, the Light of the World, represented by the new Easter fire, comes among us once more, risen from the dead, a guarantee of our future resurrection, provided we live in him and by him. The ceremony begins with the dramatic blessing of the new fire. This is followed by the lighting of the paschal candle, which represents Christ, and the singing of a glorious hymn praising this holy night and the wonder of our redemption. A series of instructions or readings are then sung. This provides an instruction for all, but particularly for those who are to be baptized during the ceremony. After praying the Litany of the Saints the baptismal water is blessed. Then those prepared to become new members of the Pilgrim People of God are baptised. Everyone present is invited to renew his or her baptismal vows. Then follows the first Mass of Easter, celebrated with fullest solemnity.

The Masses of the Easter season are full of the joy of the Resurrection. We follow the risen Christ as he appears to the apostles and the other disciples. On Ascension Thursday we celebrate our Lord's triumphal Ascension into heaven, and begin a nine day's period of prayer to the Holy Spirit in preparation for the glorious feast of Pentecost.

Practice

▲ Read the account of the Lord's Resurrection and of his appearances to his apostles and disciples in John 20:1—30 and Luke 24:1—49.

† † †

*Pilate went back into the praetorium and summoned Jesus.
"Are you the King of the Jews?" he asked him. Jesus answered, "Are you saying this on your own, or have others
been telling you about me?"*

*"I am no Jew!" Pilate retorted. "It is your own people
and the chief priests who have handed you over to me. What
have you done?" Jesus answered: "My kingdom does not
belong to this world. If my kingdom were of this world,
my subjects would be fighting to save me from being handed
over to the Jews. As it is, my kingdom is not here."*

*At this Pilate said to him, "So, then, you are a king?"
Jesus replied: "It is you who say I am a king. The reason I
was born, the reason why I came into the world, is to testify
to the truth. Anyone committed to the truth hears my
voice"*—JOHN 18:33–37.

THE PROPHETS of the Old Testament had described the
Messiah as a ruler who would establish a kingdom. Jesus Christ
fulfilled these prophecies, but in a way different from that which
his disciples expected. "My kingdom," he said, does not belong
to this world"—JOHN 18:36. His kingdom is a spiritual one,
founded on God's great mercy and love. Christ is the king who
now rules over the spiritual kingdom of God on earth, the
Church, and who sits at the right hand of the Father, reigning
triumphantly in heaven. One day he will come to earth again as
king to judge all men. Then, gathering his subjects, he will reign
gloriously in heaven over a kingdom that will have no end.

1. By what right is Christ king?

As God, Christ is king of heaven and earth, because all
things belong to him as God.

In the beginning was the Word;
the Word was in God's presence,
and the Word was God.

He was present to God in the beginning.

Through him all things came into being,
and apart from him nothing came to be. – JOHN 1:1–3.

As man, Christ is king. The Father has given all men to him as his subjects.

> *. . .he showed in raising Christ from the dead and seating him at his right hand in heaven, high above every principality, power, virtue, and domination, and every name that can be given in this age or in the age to come.*
>
> *He has put all things under Christ's feet and has made him, thus exalted, head of the church. . .* – EPH. 1:20–22.

Christ is king of all men because he has redeemed them. As members of a fallen race we had been under the domination of Satan. Christ has paid the price for us, has purchased us with his blood. Therefore we are his.

2. How does Christ exercise his kingship?

a. Christ is king of the angels and saints in his eternal kingdom in heaven.

b. Christ rules as king in his kingdom on earth, his Church, through the pope and bishops.

c. Christ is content to allow his rule of the temporal order to be exercised by lawfully constituted civil authority. Here, although he is king over all things, he chooses not to exercise his rule directly.

3. How did Jesus acknowledge his kingship during his life on earth?

Even as an infant Jesus received the homage of the Wise Men, who came from the East and sought him as the "newly born king of the Jews"–cf. MATT. 2:2.

On Palm Sunday, at his triumphal entry into Jerusalem, he was hailed "king of Israel"–JOHN 12:13.

At his trial before Pilate he publicly acknowledged that he was king—JOHN 18:37.

Shortly before his ascension into heaven Jesus ascribed to himself kingly powers: "Full authority has been given to me both in heaven and on earth"—MATT. 28:18.

4. How did Jesus exercise his office of king during his life on earth?

Jesus not only taught as "one having authority"; he also enacted laws for his kingdom.

He frequently urged his followers to keep his commandments:

Teach them to carry out everything I have commanded you—MATT. 28:20.

The command I give you is this, that you love one another—JOHN 15:17.

In the Sermon on the Mount he quoted the Old Law, which was of divine origin, and on his own authority changed it, saying repeatedly:

You have heard the commandment imposed on your forefathers. . . . What I say to you is. . .—MATT. 5:21–22.

5. What did Jesus teach about his kingdom?

Jesus used many parables in an effort to teach the people what his kingdom really was, a spiritual kingdom, one that extended beyond the Jewish people into the whole world. In speaking of the kingdom of heaven and the kingdom of God, Jesus speaks of his Church, with himself as the head and men throughout the world as the members, and of its completion in heaven.

cf. The parable of the sower—MATT. 13:3–9, 18–23.

The parable of the wheat and the cockle—MATT. 13:24–30, 37–43.

The parable of the mustard seed—MATT. 13:31–32.

The parable of the leaven—MATT. 13:33.

The parable of the fishing net—MATT. 13:47—50.

The parable of the laborers in the vineyard—MATT. 20:1—16.

The parable of the vine-dressers—MATT. 21:33—41.

The parable of the marriage of the king's son—MATT. 22:1—14.

6. Did Jesus delegate his powers to anyone?

Yes. Jesus delegated his powers to his apostles and their successors. As he was about to ascend into heaven he told his apostles:

> . . .*Full authority has been given to me both in heaven and on earth; go, therefore, and make disciples of all the nations.*
>
> *Baptize them in the name 'of the Father, and of the Son, and of the Holy Spirit.'*
>
> *Teach them to carry out everything I have commanded you.*
>
> *And know that I am with you always, until the end of the world!*—MATT. 28:18—20.

7. What did Jesus mean by these words, addressed to the apostles?

With these words Jesus was giving the apostles the commission to teach, sanctify and rule in his kingdom, the Church. He was giving them and their successors a share in his threefold office of prophet, priest and king.

For three years Jesus had lived with these men, teaching them about the kingdom. At the Last Supper he had ordained them priests. After his resurrection he had placed Peter over all the members of his Church and over the other apostles as well, making Peter the visible head of his Church.

After his resurrection Jesus gave the apostles the power to forgive sins. Now, at the moment of his ascension into heaven, he was giving them the commission to teach, sanctify and rule the members of his Church.

8. Did the apostles begin their work immediately after the Ascension of Jesus?

No. The apostles did not begin their work immediately. Jesus had instructed them to remain in Jerusalem in prayer for nine days. He had promised them that on the ninth day the Holy Spirit would come to strengthen them and give them understanding of all he had taught.

9. What do we call the day on which the Holy Spirit descended upon the apostles?

We call that day Pentecost Sunday. The Church, which was born from the pierced side of Christ as he died on the cross, was made manifest to the world on that day.

10. What was the effect of the coming of the Holy Spirit upon the apostles?

After the Holy Spirit had come upon them the apostles were no longer timid or uncertain. They then understood the teachings which Jesus had patiently taught them for three years. They went forth fearlessly, preaching and administering the sacraments in the name of Jesus Christ.

11. How did the apostles fulfill their mission to spread the Church throughout the world?

The apostles remained for a time in their own country, using Jerusalem as a base. Later they went forth to the various parts of the world. Saints Peter and Paul eventually made their way to Rome, of which city St. Peter became bishop.

Liturgy

The feast of Christ the King is celebrated on the last Sunday of the liturgical year. The glorious kingship of Christ is expressed in a beautiful song of thanksgiving and praise, the beginning of the Eucharistic Prayer of the Mass on the feast of Christ the King:

Father, all powerful and ever living God,

We do well always and everywhere to give you thanks.

*You anointed Jesus Christ, your only son with the oil of
gladness, as the universal priest and universal king.*

*As priest he offered his life on the altar of the cross
and redeemed the human race
by this one perfect sacrifice of peace.*

*As king he claims dominion over all creation,
that he might present to you, his almighty Father,
an eternal and universal kingdom:
a kingdom of truth and life,
a kingdom of holiness and grace,
a kingdom of justice, love and peace.*

Practice

▲ Having studied the lessons on the life of our Lord, and
having read some selections from the Gospels, we should now
try to see the life of Christ as a whole.

Read straight through one of the first three Gospels
(Matthew, Mark, or Luke). Afterwards, read straight through
the Gospel according to St. John.

section **13**   The Mystical Body

*You, then, are the body of Christ. Every one of you is a member of it—*I COR. 12:27

It is he who gave apostles, prophets, evangelists, pastors and teachers in roles of service for the faithful to build up the body of Christ, till we become one in faith and in the knowledge of God's Son, and form that perfect man who is Christ come to full stature.

*Let us, then, be children no longer, tossed here and there, carried about by every wind of doctrine that originates in human trickery and skill in proposing error. Rather, let us profess the truth in love and grow to the full maturity of Christ the head. Through him the whole body grows, and with the proper functioning of the members joined firmly together by each supporting ligament, builds itself up in love—*EPH. 4:11—16.

JESUS CHRIST is our high priest, teacher and king. It was to sanctify, teach and rule all people that he became man and lived and died among us. He lived 2,000 years ago, and died in a remote corner of the world, surrounded by only a handful of his friends. How then does he remain among us even though he has ascended into heaven? How does he extend himself into time and space? How does he continue to sanctify, teach and rule men at all times and everywhere in the world?

Christ might have chosen any number of ways to continue his work in the word. He might have chosen to draw each person to himself separately by some sort of illumination from heaven.

84

He might have chosen merely to leave a record of his life and teachings, so that all who read it and accepted those teachings might learn to love and imitate him from afar. As a matter of fact, however, Jesus Christ chose to distribute his graces and to continue his work in the world by taking to himself a new Body, his Church. As Head of the Body, he continues to give life and direction to his members. The Church, therefore, is not merely an organization established by Christ; it is Christ, the fullness of Christ, the Mystical Body of Christ.

1. How does Jesus Christ share the divine life with people?

Jesus Christ shares the divine life with people by joining them to himself in a living union.

Christ said:

I am the vine, you are the branches. He who lives in me and I in him, will produce abundantly, for apart from me you can do nothing–JOHN 15:5.

2. How does Jesus Christ unite people to himself in this life-giving union?

As he died on the cross Christ took to himself another Body. This second Body of Christ is called his Mystical Body, and is the Catholic Church. By being baptized into that Body we become united to Christ, who is its Head, and thus become adopted sons of God and sharers of the divine nature.

3. How did Jesus Christ speak of his Church?

Jesus spoke of his Church,

a. *As his bride,* referring to himself as the bridegroom.

. . . How can wedding guests go in mourning so long as the groom is with them? When the day comes that the groom is taken away, then they will fast–MATT. 9:15.

b. *As his flock,* of which he is the shepherd.

I am the good shepherd. I know my sheep and my sheep know me in the same way that the Father knows me and I know the Father; for these sheep I will give my

*life. I have other sheep that do not belong to this fold.
I must lead them, too, and they shall hear my voice.
There shall be one flock then, one shepherd*–JOHN
10:14–16.

c. *As his kingdom,* calling it the kingdom of heaven (kingdom of God), and the kingdom of his Father, a spiritual kingdom in which he teaches, rules and gives life through the people he empowers to act in his name. Many of the parables of Christ taught of his Church under this aspect.

> *The reign of God is also like a dragnet thrown into the
> lake, which collected all sorts of things*–MATT. 13:47.

d. *As a vine and its branches,* a living organic union between himself and the members of his Church.

> *I am the vine, you are the branches. . .*–JOHN 15:5.

4. How did St. Paul speak of the Church?

The union between himself and his members which Jesus described as his bride, his flock, his kingdom and as the union of vine and branches was described by St. Paul as the union of a living body. "Christ," says St. Paul, "is the head of the body of the Church . . . though many we are one body in Christ." That the Church is the Body of Christ is the theme which is dominant in the teachings of St. Paul.

> *If we would define and describe this true Church of Jesus
> Christ–which is the one, holy, catholic, apostolic, Roman
> Church–we shall find no expression more noble, more
> sublime or more divine than the phrase which calls it "The
> Mystical Body of Jesus Christ." This title is derived from
> and is, as it were, the fair flower of the repeated teaching of
> sacred Scripture and the holy fathers*–Encyclical on the
> Mystical Body 13.

5. Is it true to say that the Church is Christ?

Yes. The Church is "the Mystical Christ." Jesus Christ as he exists today is the God-Man, inseparably linked to his new Body, the Church.

6. How is the Church a body?

A body has many members, which are joined together in such a way as to help one another. So it is with our own body; when one part of the body suffers, all the other parts share its pain, and the healthy parts come to the assistance of the parts which are ailing. Such is the case too, in the Church. The individual members of the Church do not live for themselves alone; they also help their fellow members. All work together for their common good and for the perfect building up of the whole body.

Our bodies, moreover, are not formed by any haphazard grouping of members. They are made up of organs, i.e., members which have different functions, but which work together in such a way that the body lives and acts as a whole. So, too, it is with the Church. In the Church there are many members, millions of men, women and children. As members of the Church, they occupy special positions and exercise special functions; the pope, as the visible head, teaching, sanctifying and ruling in the name of Christ; the bishops—exercising the same functions in union with the Holy Father; the clergy—assisting the bishops in the work of teaching and sanctifying; laymen—each performing some special function; teachers—teaching; parents—forming the youngest members of Christ; doctors, lawyers, farmers, workers—all cooperating, each in his own way, according to his calling in the work of worshipping God, extending the Body of Christ throughout the world and increasing its inner holiness.—cf. Enc. on the Mystical Body.

> *It is thus the Apostle describes the Church when he writes: "As in one body we have many members, but all members have not the same office: so we being many are one body in Christ, and everyone members of one another*—Enc. on the Mystical Body 16.

7. Why is the Church called the Mystical Body of Christ?

The Church is called the *Mystical* Body of Christ:

a. To distinguish it from the physical body of Christ, his human body, which is present in heaven and in the Eucharist under the appearances of bread and wine.

b. To express the uniqueness of this second Body of Christ. The Church is not a physical body (one in which the members are joined physically to one another, as is the case with our own bodies). Neither is it *merely* a moral body (an organization, such as a club, a labor union, or a corporation). It is a unique body, having all the elements of a moral body plus a living soul. This soul, the one unifying life-giving principle which unites all the members to one another and to Christ, the Head, is the Third Person of the Blessed Trinity, the Holy Spirit.

The word *Mystical* must not be taken to mean vague, shadowy or unreal. Rather, it means mysterious, something which is real, but beyond the powers of our intellect fully to understand. The Church is, indeed, a sublime mystery, visible in her external organization but capable of being known only by faith in her inner life.

8. What does the Holy Spirit do as soul of the Mystical Body?

As soul of the Mystical Body the Holy Spirit joins the members of the Church to one another and to Christ, their Head. He is entire in Christ, the Head, entire in the Body, and entire in each of the members. Through his grace he is the cause of every supernatural act in all parts of the Body. He is personally present and active in all the members. He also acts in the members through the ministry of the higher members. He provides for the constant growth of the Church.—cf. Enc. on the Mystical Body 61–63.

9. Is the Mystical Body of Christ visible?

Yes. Like Christ, the Head, who has both an invisible divine nature and a visible human nature, the Church, his Body, has both an invisible inner life (our union with Christ and one another through the Holy Spirit) and a visible, external structure, the hierarchical organization of the Church.

10. How is the union between Christ and his members manifested externally?

The union between Christ and his members is manifested externally by the fact that all the members of Christ profess the same faith, share the same sacred rites, participate in the same sacrifice, observe the same laws and, above all, recognize as visible head of the Mystical Body the pope, the vicar of Christ.

> *As the divine Redeemer sent a Paraclete, the Spirit of Truth, who in his name should govern the Church in an invisible way; similarly he commissioned Peter and his successors, to be his personal representative on earth and to assume the visible government of the Christian community* – Enc. on the Mystical Body 69.

11. Is there another bond of union between Christ and the members of his Mystical Body?

Yes. Besides the visible union and the invisible bond of union, the Holy Spirit, there is yet another bond of union, "those three virtues which link us so closely to each other and to God: Christian faith, hope and charity"—Enc. on the Mystical Body 70.

12. Sometimes the church is called "The Pilgrim People of God." What does this mean?

The term "Pilgrim People of God" was used by the Second Vatican Council to describe the Mystical Body, the Church. The term "pilgrim" indicates the members are travelers from this present life to union with God in heaven. We can never fully reach our goal in this life. Thus we are pilgrims.

The term "people" is less clear but very important. "A people" is a group that shares three things, namely, a) common ancestry, b) common experiences, and c) common goals. Some nations have these characteristics and others do not; e.g. Ireland does while the United States does not.

The common ancestry of the Church is twofold. By Baptism we are children of God. This creates a brotherhood within the Church. Secondly, we are redeemed by Jesus Christ.

The common experiences we share are the liturgical actions of the Church. First, on a given Sunday throughout the world the same Scripture lessons are experienced by being read and explained in the homily. Even though separated by distance and language we do share the same religious experience. Secondly, we share the same seven sacraments, the sources of divine grace. In these sacraments God does come to each of us even though at different times.

The common goals we experience within the Church are to live the Christian message and share it with all of mankind. We also hope to bring mankind with us to eternal happiness in heaven.

The expression "People of God" also stresses the value of each individual member. Each person has opportunities and obligations within the Church. Each has the responsibility to live and share the gift of faith with the rest of mankind. It is not the work of the priests nor bishops, nor pope. It is the common work of all members.

13. What work does Christ do in the Church?

Christ continues the work of redemption which he began in his physical body; now, however, he accomplishes this work through the members of his Mystical Body.

The work of redemption has three phases:

I. While he was on earth in his physical body Christ won grace once and for all for all men.

II. After his death on the cross, he began the second phase of redemption, the distribution and application of those graces through the Mystical Body. Christ teaches and rules through the pope and the bishops. Christ makes men holy through the sacraments. Christ worships the Father through the sacrifice of the Mass, which is continually offered by the whole Mystical Body. Christ still suffers, no longer in his physical body, but in his Mystical Body. Though the sufferings of Christ gained grace for men, this grace must be applied to individual souls. The prayers, the sufferings and the works of the members of the Church bring this about.

. . . In my own flesh I fill up what is lacking in the sufferings of Christ for the sake of his body, the church—COL. 1:24.

90

III. After the end of the world, Christ and those who have accepted his graces of redemption will begin the third phase, when they form one body in heaven, to praise and glorify God for all eternity.

14. Are there any distinguishing marks by which the Mystical Body of Christ can be identified?

Yes. In order to make it possible for men of all ages to recognize his Church, Christ has given it four identifying marks. The Church is one; the Church is apostolic; the Church is holy; the Church is universal (catholic).

Practice

▲ All the members of the Church have a share in the great work of building up and perfecting the Mystical Body of Christ. It would be a great mistake to think that only the clergy have the responsibility for the growth of the Church and the dissemination of her teachings. One of the important developments in modern times is the growth of the lay apostolate in the Church. Pope Pius XII in an address to the Second World Congress for the Lay Apostolate said:

> *It would be a misunderstanding of the Church's real nature and her social character to distinguish in her a purely active element, Church authorities, and a purely passive element, the laity. All the members of the Church, as we ourselves said in the encyclical "Mystici Corporis Christi" are called upon to cooperate in building up and perfecting the Mystical Body of Christ. . . .*
>
> *History shows that from the Church's earliest days laymen have taken part in the activity which the priest carries out in the service of the Church, and today more than ever they must cooperate with greater and greater fervor "for building up the body of Christ" in all forms of the apostolate, especially by making the Christian spirit penetrate all family, social, economic, and political life.*

In most places there are not enough priests to accomplish the vast work which the Church has to do in the world. The influence of one priest must be multiplied by the cooperation of laymen who work with him in the apostolate of the Church.

However, the layman must never think that his cooperation is necessary only because of a shortage of priests. The layman has a work to do which is indispensably his, a work which the priest cannot do. The lay members of the Mystical Body must share in the Church's work of carrying Christ's message to the world. Their words carry particular weight because of the fact that they are living under the same circumstances as those whom they teach. Laymen can be experts in many fields, too, in which the priest ordinarily is not, fields such as the social sciences, psychology, medicine, law, the physical sciences. Here the Church needs laymen who are deeply Christian and who are imbued with the spirit of the apostolate, men and women who by their lives and their work will Christianize the field in which they work, will be apostles to others who work in that field, will do the work of the Church in that place where Christ has placed them.

The Church needs artists, writers, philosophers to apply the teachings of Christ in the great fields of art, literature and architecture. One of the Church's most effective means of teaching, inspiring and ennobling men is by means of art and literature. This vital part of the Church's work will not and cannot be done by priests. It will be done by apostolic lay members of Christ or it will not be done at all.

† † †

The body is one and has many members, but all the members, many though they are, are one body; and so it is with Christ. It was in one Spirit that all of us, whether Jew or Greek, slave or free, were baptized into one body.

All of us have been given to drink of the one Spirit. Now the body is not one member, it is many. If the foot should say, "Because I am not a hand I do not belong to the body," would it then no longer belong to the body? If the ear should say, "Because I am not an eye I do not belong to the body," would it then no longer belong to the body?

If the body were all eye, what would happen to our hearing? If it were all ear, what would happen to our smelling? As it is, God has set each member of the body in the place he wanted it to be. If all the members were alike, where would the body be? There are, indeed, many different members, but one body. The eye cannot say to the hand, "I do not need you," any more than the head can say to the feet, "I do not need you." Even those members of the body which seem less important are in fact indispensable. We honor the members we consider less honorable by clothing them with greater care, thus bestowing on the less presentable a propriety which the more presentable already have. God has so constructed the body as to give greater honor to the lowly members, that there may be no dissension in the body, but that all the members may be concerned for one another. If one member suffers, all the members suffer with it; if one member is honored, all the members share its joy–1 COR. 12:12–26.

THROUGH JESUS CHRIST we have been made members of the family of God. We are joined to Christ and to one another in a union which is far closer than any union on earth. Our Lord himself compared it to the sublime union of the Blessed Trinity, "...that all may be one, even as you, Father, are in me, and I in you; I pray that they may be (one) in us. . ."—JOHN 17:21.

Because we belong to the family of God we are never alone. We are one with Christ and one with one another in the union of the Mystical Body of Christ here on earth. So close is this union that whatever we do or fail to do to one another we do or fail to do to Christ himself.

Because of our union with Christ we are united, too, with all those who share his life in the larger family of God, the Communion of Saints. We on earth, members of the Church Militant, still fighting the good fight as soldiers of Christ, still journeying on our way to our Father's house, are helped by the prayers and encouragement of the victorious and blessed members of the family, the Church Triumphant in heaven. We, who are still able to increase the divine life within us, still able to win God's favors by our cooperation with the grace of Christ, can help the suffering members of the family, those who are being purified in purgatory. They, in turn, although unable to help themselves, can and do pray for us. Thus, through the Communion of Saints we are one with those "'. . . who rest in Christ, who have gone before us with the sign of faith and repose in the sleep of peace;' for whether we live or whether we die still we are not separated from the one and only Christ"—Enc. on the Sacred Liturgy.

1. How do we manifest the love and unity which is ours in the communion of saints?

We manifest the love and unity which is ours in the communion of saints:

a. By praying to the saints in heaven as our patrons and intercessors with God, and by honoring them and imitating them in our daily lives.

b. By praying for our brothers who are undergoing purification in purgatory. They cannot help themselves, cannot shorten their period of purification. But we can help them reach

94

heaven, our common home, more quickly by our prayers and sacrifices, if we offer them to God in their behalf.

c. By praying for, helping and cooperating with our fellow members of the Mystical Body on earth.

2. How do we manifest the love and unity which is ours in the Mystical Body of Christ?

We manifest that love and unity:

a. By offering together the great act of worship of the family of God, the Mass, and by receiving holy communion, the bread of life which both symbolizes and effects our unity.

b. By praying for each other.

c. By helping each other in need.

d. By supporting with our prayers and alms our fellow members of Christ who are laboring in the missions.

e. By working together in the lay apostolate to "restore all things in Christ."

f. By associating and cooperating with one another in the work of the diocese and the parish to which we belong, and in social, economic and civic life.

3. What is a diocese?

A diocese is a territory which is cared for and ruled by a bishop who has been appointed by the Holy Father, the supreme bishop of the Church. The bishop, who is Christ among us, is our spiritual father. It is he who teaches, rules and sanctifies in the name of Christ. The bishop performs these functions both directly and through his representatives and assistants, the pastors of parishes.

4. What is a parish?

A parish is a territory within a diocese, which is administered by the pastor, who has been appointed by the bishop. The parish is the center of our worship and sanctification, and is the community in which we usually manifest our union with one another in the Church.

5. What is the role of the parish?

The role of the parish is the same as that of the Church itself:

a. To worship God. This is accomplished above all through the Mass and through the sacraments.

b. To sanctify its members and through them the whole community. This work of sanctification is accomplished by Christ acting through the sacraments and through the Mass and by the prayers and example of priests and people.

c. To teach its members and the whole community. This work of teaching the word of God is accomplished by the liturgy, by instructions, classes for Catholics, convert and inquiry classes, by the parish school, by the organizations of Catholic Action and by the general efforts of priests and people to witness Christ in their neighborhood.

d. To guide and rule its members. This work is accomplished through the pastor, the shepherd of that portion of Christ's flock which makes up his parish.

6. What is the role of the pastor in a parish?

The role of the pastor in a parish is the role of Christ. The pastor is the representative of the bishop, who is the chief shepherd and spiritual ruler of the diocese.

7. What is the role of the people in a parish?

The role of the people in a parish is that of the members of Christ's kingdom. Theirs is the role of cooperating with the pastor in the total life of the parish, of taking an active part in the worship of the parish, of belonging to and working together in the various parish organizations, of supporting the parish financially, and of carrying the teaching and sanctifying action of the Church into the community in which they live and work.

8. Who is the center of the parish?

The center of the parish and the source of its life is Christ. He is physically present in the Eucharist. He is present in the individuals who possess the divine life. He is present, too, among the community of Christians who meet with him in their midst. Through their meeting with one another in a spirit of fraternal charity the people of the parish give evidence of Christ's presence among them, the sign by which the world can recognize them as members of Christ's kingdom.

Where two or three are gathered together in my name, there am I in their midst—MATT. 18:20.

9. What is the function of a parish in the community?

Since the parish is Christ in the community, its function is twofold: to feed and care for the sheep of the fold and to go out in search of the other sheep, both those who have strayed from the fold, and those who do not yet belong to it.

I have other sheep that do not belong to this fold. I must lead them, too, and they shall hear my voice. There shall be one flock then, one shepherd—JOHN 10:16.

In its task of caring for its members one of the functions of the parish is to help build a better community, one in which people can more easily lead Christian lives.

10. What means does a parish possess for its missionary activity in the community?

The organization of its lay members in movements of the lay apostolate is the means by which a parish can most effectively perform its missionary work in the community. Apostolic organizations, working with the pastor and priests of the parish, can extend and multiply the influence of the parish throughout the community in the work of restoring it in Christ.

Practice

▲ In the Mystical Body we are united not only with Christ, but with all the other members as well. Consequently, there is no escaping the fact that what we do to any member of his Mystical Body we do to Christ. This is the basis for the words of Jesus, spoken to St. Paul at his conversion, "Saul, Saul, why do you persecute me?"—ACTS 9:4. St. Paul did not protest that it was not Christ but the members of Christ's Church he was persecuting. He understood then and there, with the revelation that Christ gave him, that whatever he did to a member of Christ's Body he did to Christ. This, too, is the basis for the words which Jesus will say at the last judgment. "For I was hungry and you gave me food, . . . I assure you, as often as you did it for one of my least brothers, you did it for me"—MATT. 25:35–40.

The things which separate us from one another, wealth, social position, color of skin, difference in nationality, etc., are all minor compared to the bond which unites us as members of Christ and of one another.

Try to keep in mind this week the important fact that whatever we do to any person we do to Christ.

Make an effort to see Christ in your neighbor, and check up on your success or failure in doing so.

† † †

section **15** **The Church is One**

We believe in one holy, catholic and apostolic Church (Nicene Creed).

I do not pray for them alone. I pray also for those who will believe in me through their word, that all may be one as you, Father, are in me, and I in you; I pray that they may be [one] in us, that the world may believe that you sent me. I have given them the glory you gave me that they may be one, as we are one—I living in them, you living in me—that their unity may be complete. So shall the world know that you sent me, and that you loved them as you loved me—JOHN 17:20–23.

98

THIS PRAYER OF CHRIST is realized today in the marvelous oneness which exists within his Church. It is a oneness which is present amid a remarkable diversity. The members of Christ live in all the various countries of the world. They belong to every race on earth. They speak different langauges. They have different cultures, different tastes, different political opinions. But they are one in the great unity of the Body of Christ.

There are, however, millions of men and women who love Christ and worship him as their Savior and their God, who are separated from the unity of the Body of Christ. The prayer of Christ for unity among his members is a prayer also for re-union with his Body.

1. What do we mean when we say that the Church is one?

When we say the Church is one we mean that:

All the members of the Mystical Body believe the same doctrines.

All accept the same sources of life, the seven sacraments.

All worship together in the sacrifice-meal of the Mystical Body, the Mass.

All submit to the same divine authority, that of Christ the Head, who rules the Body through the visible head, our Holy Father the Pope, and the bishops who are in communion with him.

2. Can there be more than one true Church of Christ?

No. There cannot be more than one true Church of Christ because the Church *is* Christ. Christ cannot be divided.

There is but one body and one Spirit, just as there is but one hope given all of you by your call. There is one Lord, one faith, one baptism; one God and Father of all, who is over all, and works through all, and is in all—EPH. 4:4—6.

It follows that among all the nations of earth there is but one People of God, which takes its citizens from every race, making them citizens of a kingdom which is of a heavenly and not of an earthly nature . . .

*All men are called to be part of this catholic unity of
the People of God, a unity which is a harbinger of the universal peace it promotes. And there belong to it or are related to it in various ways, the Catholic faithful as well as all
who believe in Christ, and indeed the whole of mankind.
For all men are called to salvation by the grace of God—*
Constitution on the Church 13.

*. . . all those justified by faith through baptism are incor-
porated into Christ. They therefore have a right to be honored by the title Christian, and are properly regarded as
brothers in the Lord by the sons of the Catholic Church.*

*Moreover some, even very many, of the most significant
elements or endowments which together go to build up and
give life to the Church herself can exist outside the visible
boundaries of the Catholic Church: the written word of
God; the life of grace; faith, hope and charity, along with
the interior gifts of the Holy Spirit and visible elements.
All of these, which come from Christ and lead back to Him,
belong by right to the one Church of Christ.*—Decree on
Ecumenism 3.

**3. There are, in fact, many Churches. Does it make any differ-
ence to which one belongs?**

Yes. Jesus Christ took to himself one Mystical Body. That
Body is the Catholic Church. In the course of history, disputes,
misunderstandings, the pride and greed of men, weaknesses and
abuses within the Church itself have resulted in the rending and
tearing of the Body of Christ. Millions have been separated from
the unity of the Body. Many good people today are deprived,
through no fault of their own, of the life-giving sacraments and
of participation in Christ's sacrifice. Christ wants all of them
to be re-united in his Mystical Body, the Catholic Church.

*I have other sheep
   that do not belong to this fold.
I must lead them, too,
   and they shall hear my voice.
There shall be one flock then,
   one shepherd.*—JOHN 10:16.

100

4. Can those who belong to other Churches be saved?

Yes. God does not deny the means of salvation to anyone. He wants all men to belong to the unity of the Body of Christ. Nonetheless, many through no fault of their own remain outside the Church. God offers these people the grace necessary to save their souls.

Even though these people are not aware that the Church is the one true Church of Christ, it is through the Church that they receive their divine life and their salvation.

5. What is the ecumenical movement?

The ecumenical movement is an attempt on the part of many leaders in the various Christian Churches to work toward the union envisioned and prayed for by Jesus at the Last Supper. Since the Second Vatican Council efforts have concentrated on knowing and understanding the common heritage of the various Christian communities. Some Churches are very similar in ritual and doctrine while others have basic and fundamental differences. These difficulties will have to be resolved before true union can be achieved.

The Council reminded us that all Christians have an obligation to pray for and work for this union. We do not envision a new Church of only the fewest common articles of faith. Rather, pray over and study the total Christian message so all mankind, enlightened by the Holy Spirit will through Jesus find their own true Father in heaven.

Ecumenism means we love our separated brethren because they do possess and share with us many elements of the Christian Revelation.

6. Are all Catholics bound by the same Church laws and customs?

No. Some of the Church laws and customs in the various rites differ. There are two great bodies of law in the Church, one for the Western rite and one for the Eastern rites.

7. What is a rite?

A rite is a system of ritual and prayer used in the worship of God and the administration of the sacraments.

The Latin rite, the one used by Rome and all the West, is the largest. The next largest rite is the Byzantine, which has many national subdivisions. There are also Armenian, Syrian, Chaldean, Malabar, Maronite, Coptic and Egyptian rites, which are used in various countries.

8. How did these various rites originate?

Originally each bishop said Mass and administered the sacraments in his own way. Gradually the customs of certain important cities influenced the surrounding countryside. Rome was the most influential in Italy, Constantinople in Greece, Antioch in Asia Minor, Jerusalem in the Holy Land, and Alexandria in North Africa. In the course of centuries the liturgies of these cities became the basic part of a "rite," although sub-rites developed and still exist. Even in the Latin rite there are variations peculiar to the Dominican and Calced Carmelite orders, and to such cities as Milan, Braga, Lyons and Toledo.

9. What are some of the differences between the Eastern and Western Rites?

a. The ceremonies used at Mass and in the administration of the sacraments are different.

b. In some of the Eastern rites a married man may become a priest (no man may marry after ordination; bishops and monks are unmarried or widowers). In the Western rite the clergy is unmarried.

c. Some of the Eastern rites always have Communion under both species, and use leavened instead of unleavened bread. Members of the Western rite usually receive holy communion only under the form of bread. On special occasions, however, Communion is distributed under both forms.

d. In the Eastern rite the people do not genuflect, but bow profoundly. They also make the sign of the cross from right to left instead of from left to right, as is the practice in the Western rite.

e. Eastern rites have some Church laws different from those of the Western Church.

f. In some of the Eastern rites the people are baptized by immersion, and are confirmed by the priest immediately after Baptism.

There are many other variations. The Church is wise and preserves these customs. The Eastern rites are as old or older than the Western rite. Hence they are not the exception in the Church, but part of the normal way of worshipping God.

10. Did all these rites remain within the Church?

No. In the course of time various groups broke with Rome as did the Orthodox Eastern Churches (Greek, Russian, Georgian, etc.). Throughout the centuries groups of these peoples have returned to union with Rome. When they did so they were allowed to keep their own particular rite. The Church is very solicitous about preserving these rites. Ordinarily one must obtain permission from Rome to change from one rite to another, but a woman may transfer to the rite of her husband without any special permission.

11. What other peoples have separated themselves from the unity of the Church?

Next to the Eastern Schism, the greatest split occurred in the sixteenth century when Martin Luther broke with Rome and began the Protestant Reformation.

12. Why did the Protestants leave the Roman Catholic Church?

The conditions which brought about the Protestant Reformation were very complex. No adequate treatment of the subject could possibly be given here. The following points, however, can be noted:

a. There were real and serious evils in the Church in the sixteenth century. Many of the clergy were not faithful to their vows. There was an over-emphasis on externals and a neglect of the inner religious spirit. Responsible elements in the Church had long been calling for a real reformation to correct these abuses.

b. The spirit of nationalism was growing at that time. There was a strong desire in many countries to rebel against any authority higher than that of the individual state.

c. Martin Luther, whose revolt spearheaded other revolts which resulted in the establishment of many different Protestant Churches, did not at first intend to rebel against the Roman Church itself, but merely to cry out against abuses.

13. What effect did the Protestant Reformation have on the Church?

The Protestant Reformation divided Europe, taking millions away from the unity of the Body of Christ, just as the Eastern Schism had done earlier.

On the other hand, the Protestant Reformation forced the Roman Church to reform herself from the inside. Great saints were raised up within the Church. The Roman Church emerged weaker in numbers but stronger internally.

The division among Christians which exists today is deeply distressing to all who love Christ. Men of good will both within the Catholic Church and among the separated Eastern and the Protestant Churches, pray for the reunion of all the believers and followers of Christ. We can only hope and pray that through charity and mutual understanding, the day will come when all men who follow Christ will once more be re-united.

Practice

▲ It is an interesting and rewarding experience to assist at Mass in a Catholic church of the Eastern rite. Anyone who does so cannot help but be impressed; the ceremonies are so different from those of the Western rite, yet the essentials are the same.

A Latin rite Catholic may fulfill his Sunday obligation by assisting at Mass in a Catholic Eastern rite church. In some of the rites Holy Communion is distributed under the appearances of both bread and wine. A Latin rite Catholic may, of course, receive Holy Communion in one of these rites.

Pray that all men may be joined to the one Body of Christ.

Pray for the gift of faith for someone in particular, a relative or a friend.

✝ ✝ ✝

section **16**   **The Church is Apostolic**

We believe in one holy catholic and apostolic church (Nicene Creed).

This means that you are strangers and aliens no longer. No, you are fellow citizens of the saints and members of the household of God. You form a building which rises on the foundation of the apostles and prophets, with Christ Jesus himself as the capstone—EPH. 2:19—20.

AT THE VERY beginning of his public life Jesus personally selected twelve men who were to be his apostles. During the three years he spent in preaching, teaching and working miracles these twelve were always at his side. Christ spared no effort in instructing and training the apostles, for they were the men on whom he was to rely to extend his kingdom throughout the world. It was on these apostles that Christ founded his Church. He said to Peter, whom he chose to be the head of the apostles, "I for my part declare to you, you are 'Rock,' and on this rock will I build my church. . ."—MATT. 16:18.

The Church of Christ, even in its infancy, was the Church of the apostles. The apostles are among us today in the person of their legitimate successors, the bishops of the Catholic Church. Peter, the first pope, is among us in the person of his successor, our Holy Father the Pope. Christ is among us, teaching,

105

sanctifying and ruling us through the hierarchy of the Catholic Church.

1. What do we mean when we say that the Church is apostolic?

When we say that the Church is apostolic we mean that Christ founded his Church upon the apostles and that the Church in every age is ruled by the successors of the apostles, and teaches the doctrine of the apostles.

2. Who were the apostles?

The apostles were the twelve men whom Jesus chose and called to the work of teaching, ruling and sanctifying in his name. These were the men to whom he gave the mission of extending his Mystical Body throughout the world. They were the first bishops of the Church.

The apostles were simple men; most of them were fishermen; one was a tax gatherer. One of them, Judas Iscariot, betrayed Jesus to his enemies and hanged himself in despair. The other apostles, under the guidance of the Holy Spirit, chose Matthias to replace him. After his ascension into heaven Jesus himself called Saul of Tarsus, whose name he changed to Paul, to be the great Apostle to the Gentiles.

Christ sent the apostles

> **To Teach**—*Go into the whole world and proclaim the good news to all creation*—MARK 16:15.

> **To Rule**—*He who hears you, hears me. He who rejects you, rejects me. And he who rejects me, rejects him who sent me*—LUKE 10:16.

> **To Sanctify**—*"Peace be with you," he said again. "As the Father has sent me, so I send you." Then he breathed on them and said: "Receive the Holy Spirit. If you forgive men's sins, they are forgiven them; if you hold them bound, they are held bound"*—JOHN 20:21–23.

3. What is a bishop?

A bishop is a successor of the apostles. Through the

106

sacrament of Holy Orders and jurisdiction granted by the pope, he has the power not only of administering the sacraments, but also of teaching and ruling the portion of Christ's flock committed to his care.

4. Why is the pope called the head of the bishops?

The pope is called the head of the bishops because he is the successor of St. Peter, who was the head of the apostles. He is, therefore, the visible head of the Church, the one who acts for Christ, the Invisible Head.

5. Where in Scripture do we read that Christ made Peter the visible head of his Church?

Christ, first of all, promised that he would make Peter the visible head of the Church. Later he actually conferred this office upon him.

a. At the time he promised the primacy to Peter, Christ said to him:

> *I for my part declare to you, you are 'Rock,' and on this rock I will build my church, and the jaws of death shall not prevail against it. I will entrust to you the keys of the kingdom of heaven. Whatever you declare bound on earth shall be bound in heaven; whatever you declare loosed on earth shall be loosed in heaven*–MATT. 16:18–19.

It is to be noted that Christ changed Peter's name from Simon to Peter, which means "rock."

b. At the Last Supper, in warning Peter of his coming temptation and denial, Christ said to him:

> *But I have prayed for you that your faith may never fail. You in turn must strengthen your brothers*– LUKE 22:32.

c. In conferring on Peter the primacy among the apostles, which he had earlier promised to him, Jesus told him, "Feed my lambs." Then he said to Peter, "Feed my sheep." The meaning of these words in the language our Lord was speaking gives Peter

107

a clear commission to "feed," i.e., "teach and rule" not only the people (the lambs) but also the leaders of the flock, the bishops, the other apostles (the sheep).

> When they had eaten their meal, Jesus said to Simon Peter, "Simon, son of John, do you love me more than these?" "Yes, Lord," he said, "you know that I love you." At which Jesus said, "Feed my lambs."
>
> A second time he put his question, "Simon, son of John, do you love me?" "Yes, Lord," Peter said, "you know that I love you." Jesus replied, "Tend my sheep."
>
> A third time Jesus asked him, "Simon, son of John, do you love me?" Peter was hurt because he had asked a third time, "Do you love me?" So he said to him: "Lord, you know everything. You know well that I love you." Jesus said to him, "Feed my sheep"– JOHN 21:15–17.

6. Why is the pope the successor of St. Peter?

St. Peter was the first bishop of Rome. The man who succeeds to the See of Rome and becomes bishop of Rome, therefore becomes the successor of St. Peter, and pope.

7. What special guarantee did Christ give the apostles to help them teach in his name?

In order to help them teach in his name Christ guaranteed the apostles infallibility, i.e., he promised that they could not err in teaching his doctrine.

8. How is infallibility found in the Church?

a. The Church as a whole is infallible, that is, the entire Church will never accept a doctrine which is contrary to faith.

b. The bishops as a whole are infallible when they are gathered in an ecumenical council or when they separately all teach the same doctrine.

c. The pope speaking "ex cathedra" is infallible.

9. Where do we read in Scripture that Christ gave the apostles the promise of infallibility?

As he prepared to ascend into heaven, Christ gave to all the apostles the commission to teach, rule and sanctify in his name, saying:

And know that I am with you always, until the end of the world—MATT. 28:20.

The words, "I am with you always" mean, in the language of Scripture, "success in your endeavor." Christ says he will be "with them" in their endeavor, which includes teaching his doctrine. This is a guarantee of success. To teach error in so important a matter would not be success, but failure.

The words, "always, until the end of the world," prove that Jesus gave this guarantee not only to the apostles but also to their successors.

10. What is meant by the infallibility of the pope?

The infallibility of the pope means that by a special protection which Jesus Christ promised to St. Peter and his successors God will not permit the pope to teach error when he is speaking as pope to the whole world on matters of faith or morals.*

In making Peter the supreme pastor of his flock Christ conferred upon him infallibility in matters of faith and morals. If Peter could teach erroneous doctrines to the Church, he would

---

*Infallibility must not be confused with inspiration. The writers of Scripture were inspired to write what they wrote by God himself. Infallibility is rather a negative thing—consisting of a protection which prevents the pope from defining as an article of faith something which was not taught by the apostles. The public revelation of God ceased with the death of the last apostle. Nothing new will be revealed to mankind as a whole. Papal infallibility merely assures that the revelation given to the world by Christ will come down to all generations undistorted and entire. Although nothing new has been revealed to the whole world since the death of the last apostle, there is, of course, an "evolution of dogma." This means that, through study by theologians, more and more can be brought to light which is contained in that revelation. Neither does infallibility mean that the pope cannot sin nor make a mistake in judgment.

actually be poisoning the flock rather than feeding it. Since Peter is the foundation and rock upon which the Church of Christ rests and has the keys by which he can allow men to enter or be excluded from the kingdom of heaven, it follows necessarily that he must be infallible.

11. Must we accept the teachings of the pope even when he does not explicitly use his infallible authority?

Yes. We must accept the teaching of the pope at all times. When the pope speaks he is giving the ordinary teaching of the Church. This teaching is found in papal decrees and encyclicals. We must not only show outward compliance, but also give internal assent, at least out of obedience to the teaching Church.

> *Nor must it be thought that what is expounded in encyclical letters does not of itself demand consent, since in writing such letters the popes do not exercise the supreme power of their teaching authority. For these matters are taught with the ordinary teaching authority, of which it is true to say: "He who heareth you, heareth me"; and generally what is expounded and inculcated in encyclical letters already for other reasons appertains to Catholic doctrine. But if the supreme pontiffs in their official documents purposely pass judgment on a matter up to that time under dispute, it is obvious that that matter, according to the mind and will of the same pontiffs, cannot be any longer considered a question open to discussion among theologians*–Enc. Humani Generis 20.

Liturgy

On the great feast of Pentecost we celebrate the manifestation of the birth of the Church, the coming of the Holy Spirit. In the liturgy of Pentecost Sunday the Church prays for a new outpouring of the Holy Spirit, an increase of his gifts.

Practice

▲ The oldest Christian profession of faith, one which comes

110

down to us from the time of the apostles, is the Apostles' Creed:

I believe in God, the Father Almighty, Creator of heaven and earth. And in Jesus Christ, his only Son, our Lord: who was conceived by the Holy Spirit, born of the Virgin Mary, suffered under Pontius Pilate, was crucified, died and was buried; he descended into hell; the third day he rose again from the dead; he ascended into heaven, sitteth at the right hand of God the Father Almighty. From thence he shall come to judge the living and the dead. I believe in the Holy Spirit, the Holy Catholic Church, the Communion of Saints, the forgiveness of sins, the resurrection of the body, and life everlasting. Amen.

Pray the Apostles' Creed frequently as a profession of faith.

† † †

section **17**   Revelation

An angel of the Lord then addressed himself to Philip: "Head south toward the road which goes from Jerusalem to Gaza, the desert route." Philip began the journey. It happened that an Ethiopian eunuch, a court official in charge of the entire treasury of Candance (a name meaning queen) of the Ethiopians, had come on a pilgrimage to Jerusalem and was returning home. He was sitting in his carriage reading the prophet Isaiah. The spirit said to Philip, "Go and catch up with that carriage." Philip ran ahead and heard the man reading the prophet Isaiah. He said to him, "Do you really grasp what you are reading?" "How can I," the man replied, "unless someone explains it to me?" With that, he invited Philip to get in and sit down beside him. This was the passage of Scripture he was reading. "Like a sheep he was led to the slaughter, like a lamb before its shearer he was silent

111

and opened not his mouth. In his humiliation he was de-prived of justice. Who will ever speak of his posterity for he is deprived of his life on earth?"

The eunuch said to Philip, "Tell me, if you will, of whom the prophet says this—himself or someone else?" Philip launched out with this Scripture passage as his starting point, telling him the good news of Jesus. As they moved along the road they came to some water and the eunuch said, "Look, there is some water right there. What is to keep me from be-ing baptized?" He ordered the carriage stopped, and Philip went down into the water with the eunuch and baptized him. When they came out of the water, the Spirit of the Lord snatched Philip away and the eunuch saw him no more. Nevertheless, the man went on his way rejoicing—ACTS 8:26—39.

THE QUESTION, "How can I unless someone explains it to me" is most important. While everyone is encouraged to read the Bible, understanding it is not always easy. Many sections are difficult for the modern mind to comprehend. Explanations and guidance are required for comprehension.

Where do young people learn about cars? They obtain some knowledge from reading various car magazines, but most of their knowledge comes from talking about and working with engines under the direction of a mechanic or a friend. People learn about cooking in a similar way. The same is true of God. We learn many things about him from the Bible. But we also need some-one to explain the difficult passages, someone to talk to us about God.

Jesus Christ spent his life on earth teaching the truths which lead men to eternal life. Although only a relatively few heard his voice, his message was meant for all people. Jesus relied upon the apostles, the first bishops of the Church, to bring his teach-ings to the whole world. It was they and their successors whom he empowered to teach his word. Even the early successors of the apostles had no written account of the teachings of Jesus Christ. The various parts of the New Testament were written at different times and were not assembled into one book until the end of the second century. It was not until the end of the fourth century that the Church officially declared which books belonged to the New Testament. From the beginning, therefore, there were two sources of revelation, the sacred books of the Jews—the Old Testament, the written word of God—and the oral teachings of the apostles and their successors, called tradition. Later, as the New Testament came to be written, the written source of revelation was, of course, greatly enriched.

There is, therefore, one revelation but it comes in two forms—the written word, the Bible, and the spoken word, tradition. It is the same Holy Spirit who speaks to us through each type of revelation. The written tradition must be interpreted from the living teachings of the apostles and their successors, the pope and the bishops of the Catholic Church.

1. Why do we have revelation?

Human reason, by itself, cannot learn all we need to know about God. So God himself has chosen to give us "revelation." This is God's way of revealing himself to us. He did so gradually. He inspired holy writers and teachers through the centuries. They reflected on the events around them and wrote down the concepts God wanted. However, they were free to compose in their own style, using their own words.

2. Must we accept revelation?

Yes. We must accept God's revelation because it is God revealing himself to us. God is truthful, and can not deceive or be deceived.

3. Where can a person find the contents of revelation?

One part of revelation is called Sacred Scripture, or the Bible. It is a collection of sacred books written by man under the inspiration of God himself. Thus God is the true author. The Bible is divided into two main sections. The first part is called the Old Testament and contains the inspired writings written before the time of Jesus. These forty-five books contain God's revelation to the Jews.

The second and shorter portion of the Bible is the New Testament. It contains the record of the life of Jesus and the writings of some of the early followers of Jesus.

When Jesus died there was no written New Testament. People could learn about Jesus only by listening to his followers teaching his message. Eventually the followers began to write down what they remembered about Jesus. Keep in mind the twenty-seven books of the New Testament have at least eight different authors. The first books were not written immediately after the death of Jesus. At least one was not written until almost sixty years had passed.

St. John reminds us, "Jesus performed many other signs as well—signs not recorded here—in the presence of his disciples. But these have been recorded to help you believe that Jesus is the Messiah, the Son of God, so that through this faith you may have life in his name"—JOHN 20:30.

The other part of revelation is called "tradition." It is the body of truths about God handed down orally within the Church. The truths of tradition can be found in the doctrines of the Church, the decrees of the popes and councils, and in the compositions of the early teachers of the Church, the fathers and doctors of the Church.

4. Who are the fathers and doctors of the Church?

The fathers of the Church are certain writers of the early centuries of Christianity who were characterized by orthodoxy of doctrine and holiness of life.

St. Hilary, St. Athanasius and St. Augustine are examples of the fathers, St. Gregory the Great, who died in 604 A.D. is generally considered to be the last of the fathers of the Western Church, St. John Damascene, who died about the middle of the eighth century, the last of the Eastern Church.

The doctors of the Church are theologians and teachers of later centuries who possess the same qualities, orthodoxy and holiness. St. Thomas Aquinas, who lived in the 13th century, is considered by many the greatest of the doctors.

5. Since the Bible was written over a period of many years by different authors in different countries, who collected them into one book?

There were many books presented to the public all claiming to be divinely inspired. But were they? Who could decide? Only the Church could answer such a problem. A local council in Carthage in 397 compiled a list, accepting 72 books and rejecting others. They sent the list to Pope Siricius who in turn approved it. Thus we do have an authentic list or canon of divinely inspired books.

6. Should a person read the Bible?

Yes, definitely. The Church has always used the Bible in its sacred liturgy or public worship. It encourages all members to read a portion daily in their private devotions. Unfortunately, this has not been as widespread a custom as the Church has desired. The Bible is not easy reading.

7. How does a person prepare to read the Bible?

Before beginning to read from the Bible pray to the Holy Spirit for enlightenment so as to understand the message God is revealing in the passage you are reading. The reason some people have difficulty in understanding the Bible is it is composed in many different literary forms.

8. What are Literary Forms?

The term "literary forms" refers to the different types or styles of literature which can be distinguished from each other. There are many types of literary styles used in the Bible. Thus, the Bible is not a book of only simple prose statements of fact. Some sections of the Bible are written in poetic form while other parts are prophecy. To properly understand each section the reader must be aware of the type of literature being used as well as the rules of interpreting that type of literature.

9. How is the Bible interpreted?

115

Because the Bible has many different literary forms we need assistance in determining the true message. Since it was the Church who compiled the Bible only the Church can give reliable explanations and rules to follow. There are relatively few verses cited for definitive explanation. For the rest of the Bible we rely on the general teaching of the Church to acquire the true meaning of the text.

A practical rule to follow is this: After reading a particular passage, ask yourself this question. "What is the message God is trying to convey to me?"

10. What is the difference between a so-called Protestant Bible and a Catholic Bible?

Actually, very little. Some of the older editions of the so-called Protestant Bible omit some of the books from both the Old Testament and the New Testament. Most recent editions now contain all 72 books.

Practical Points

1. The basic teachings of the Catholic Church are to be found in revelation which consists of two sources, Scripture and tradition. This text uses both. Your instructor will point them out as you progress through the course.

2. It is a good practice to read a portion of the Bible daily. St. Jerome said, "To be ignorant of the scriptures is to be ignorant of Jesus."

3. There are many commentaries available in various Catholic book stores. Your instructor can recommend one to assist you as you read the sacred text.

† † †

We believe in one holy catholic and apostolic Church (Nicene Creed).

Full authority has been given to me both in heaven and on earth; go, therefore, and make disciples of all the nations. Baptize them in the name "of the Father, and of the Son, and of the Holy Spirit." Teach them to carry out everything I have commanded you. And know that I am with you always, until the end of the world—MATT. 28:18–20.

IN THE Old Testament the people of God were the people of only one nation, Israel. Even though God wills the salvation of all men, in the Old Law he made his covenant only with the Jews. With the coming of the Redeemer, however, the kingdom was extended to include the whole world. The covenant Christ made on Calvary was with all mankind.

The Mystical Body of Christ is not confined in its membership to only one race, only one nation, only one class of men. Jesus Christ died for all men. All men are meant to be incorporated into his Body, the Church. The Church, therefore, is catholic (universal). Its universality is one of the essential marks by which the Body of Christ may be recognized.

1. What do we mean when we say that the Church is catholic?

We mean that the Church is for all men, having received from Christ the commission to "make disciples of all nations." The Church was catholic, therefore, even in the earliest days when she numbered only the apostles and a handful of others. True to her mission, the Church is to be found in all parts of the world and in every kind of civilization, and includes among her members all races and classes of men.

117

The Church has a mandate to gather within herself all mankind. The Church must transform all civilizations so as to make them truly Christian.

2. What is the mission of the Church?

The mission of the Church is clear from many Gospel texts:

Go, therefore, and make disciples of all the nations–MATT. 28:19

Go into the whole world and proclaim the good news to all creation–MARK 16:15

You will receive power when the Holy Spirit comes down on you; then you are to be my witnesses in Jerusalem, throughout Judea and Samaria, yes, even to the ends of the earth–ACTS. 1:8.

This good news of the kingdom will be proclaimed throughout the world as a witness to all the nations. Only after that will the end come–MATT. 24:14.

The mission of the Church is as broad as the work of Christ himself. All humanity is the object of the Church's work.

3. Why does the Church send missionaries to other lands, when there are many who are not Catholic where the Church is already established?

a. The Church must be established in every country in the world. Christ told his apostles, "Go into the whole world and proclaim the good news to all creation"–MARK 16:15.

b. The Church is missionary because those who possess the divine life must wish to share it with others as God has so freely shared it with them. The members of the Church must be eager to spread the "good news" of salvation to all men throughout the world.

4. How is the catholicity of the Church manifested in the world today?

a. The Church sends missionaries—priests, brothers, sisters, and lay people to pagan lands.

b. In countries where the Church is already established it continues to grow in numbers and to increase the holiness of her members.

c. In answer to the call of the popes and bishops lay people are trained to apply the teachings of the Church to every phase of human life.

Part of the Church's task is to form the conscience of the individual Christian in order that he might bring the principles of Christ into the realms of education, marriage, recreation, business, etc. The layman lives in two worlds, as it were; one the spiritual (and this is the Church's direct and first care), the other the temporal (and this is the responsibility of laymen themselves). In this second field the Church merely guides and gives principles; she animates this world, but does not organize it or control it.

Catholic laymen have a part in the mission of the Church. They are not passive members of the Church. By the very fact of their membership in the Mystical Body of Christ they have a share in the apostolate of the Church. Theirs is a contribution which only a layman can make.

Practice

▲ Pray this week that the kingdom of God may spread throughout the world.

† † †

*We believe in one holy catholic and apostolic Church
(Nicene Creed).*

*. . . as Christ loved the church. He gave himself up for her
to make her holy, purifying her in the bath of water by the
power of the word, to present to himself a glorious
church, holy and immaculate, without stain or wrinkle
or anything of that sort*—EPH. 5:25—27.

CHRIST is the Anointed of the Lord, the Holy One of God.
In his person he is holiness itself. During his life on earth his
constant concern was to do the will of his Father and to impart
holiness to men. But Christ was not content merely to exhort
men to strive for holiness. He forgave sins; he strengthened souls;
he filled men with his graces; he made men holy.

So it is, too, with the Mystical Christ. The Church is holy
in itself and possesses all the means for the sanctification of all
people.

The history of the Church has been the history of the sanctification of the world. Not only has it preserved the holiness of
Christ; not only has it given life and holiness to its members; but
to whatever extent it has been able to influence a culture or a
civilization, to that extent the Church has elevated it, sanctified
it, Christianized it. Like Christ it is often misunderstood,
hated and falsely accused. But wherever there has been failure
in its work of sanctifying the world, that failure has been due
not to its teachings and means of sanctification, but to a refusal
on the part of the world and of its own members to heed those
teachings, to avail themselves of those means.

One of the chief glories of the Church and one of the strongest evidences of its holiness is the glorious army of saints to

which it has given birth. In every age of its history the Church has produced men and women of heroic sanctity. It is still producing them and will go on producing them, not only canonized saints, who come to the attention of the whole world, but also holy persons whose sanctity is known only to those whose privilege it is to live and work in their company. These holy persons are the truest children of the Church, a living proof that the Body of Christ possesses and communicates the holiness of its Head.

1. What do we mean when we say that the Church is holy?

We mean that the Church, whose Head is Christ and whose Soul is the Holy Spirit, is holy and sacred in its very being.

The Church is called holy, because she is consecrated and dedicated to God. . . . The Church is holy because she is the Body of Christ, by whom she is sanctified, and in whose blood she is washed—Catechism of the Council of Trent.

We mean, moreover, that the Church, as the Mystical Body, continues Christ's priestly work of sanctifying his members and the world through his teachings, the seven sacraments, the holy sacrifice of the Mass and the sacramentals.

2. Besides the Mass, the sacraments and the sacramentals, what other means does the Church offer for the sanctification of men?

a. The teachings of the Church are a powerful means of sanctification. The Church gives us the recipe for holiness in its doctrine. Anyone who lives according to the teachings of the Church is bound to lead a holy life.

b. The examples of holiness which the Church holds out to us provide an incentive for imitation. In every age there have been great saints whom the Church presents to us as models.

c. In addition to liturgical services, Catholic parishes conduct devotions which are an added means of sanctification.

d. The laws of the Church, also, are a means of sanctification, because they oblige us to perform necessary acts of worship, penance and mortification, which we might otherwise neglect.

This is why the Church obliges us to assist at Mass on certain days, to fast and abstain at certain times, and to receive the sacraments of Penance and the Eucharist at least once a year.

> Those who fear the LORD seek to please him,
>   those who love him are filled with his law.
> Those who fear the LORD prepare their hearts
>   and humble themselves before him—SIR. 2:16–17.

e. The religious orders and apostolic movements within the Church provide a way of life which leads to holiness.

The Church has always held up as the ideal the evangelical counsels of poverty, chastity and obedience. Men and women who belong to religious orders take vows which bind them in a special way to the practice of these virtues. In the Church, too, there are many apostolic movements for lay people, movements which have as one of their ends the sanctification of their members.

3. How has the holiness of the Church imprinted itself upon the world?

The Church transformed pagan civilization. Its teaching and influence brought about the eventual disappearance of slavery, a new respect for women, marriage and virginity, and a spirit of mercy and compassion for the poor, the sick and the aged.

Today, when pagan thinking has invaded every sphere of life, the Church refuses to yield to demands to modify the teachings of God on marriage. Thus it protects the family and society in an age in which powerful forces are attempting to destroy them.

4. Is the Church free from faults?

The Church is free from faults in its Head, who is Christ and in its Soul, who is the Holy Spirit. But in its members the Church is not free from faults. Its members are people, who even though made holy by grace and fortified by the sacraments, still have human faults and weaknesses.

122

5. How is the Church perfect in its Head and Soul?

Because the Church is Christ it cannot fail to teach the doctrines of Christ, undiluted and undistorted, with infallible correctness in every age, even though the men who teach these doctrines are imperfect human beings.

Because the Church is Christ it cannot fail to bring holiness to people through the sacraments and the sacrifice of the Mass, even though the people who administer these holy things are frail human beings.

6. Should we not expect perfection in the members of the Church also?

It would be unrealistic to expect that all members of the Church measure up to what the Church desires to make of them.

Christ, in taking a human body, did not dispense it from the weaknesses which are natural to a human body, the need for sleep, food, etc. He made himself subject to suffering and death. Nor did Christ, in taking to himself his Mystical Body, dispense it from the weaknesses which are natural to a body whose members are human.

> And if at times there appears in the Church something that points to the weakness of our human nature, put it down not to the juridical constitution, but rather to that regrettable inclination to evil found in everyone, which its divine founder permits even at times in the most exalted members of his Mystical Body, for the purpose of testing the virtue of flock and shepherds, and that all may increase the merit of their Christian faith. For, as We said above, Christ did not wish to exclude sinners from his Church; hence if some members of the Church are spiritually ill, that is no reason why we should lessen our love for the Church, but rather a reason why we should increase our devotion to her members. Oh, the loving Mother is spotless in the sacraments, by which she gives birth to her children and nourishes them, she is spotless in the faith, which she has preserved inviolate always, in her sacred laws imposed on all, in the evangelical counsels which she recommends, in those heavenly gifts and

extraordinary graces through which, with inexhaustible fe-
cundity, she generates hosts of martyrs, virgins and con-
fessors.

But it cannot be laid to her charge if some members fall
weak or wounded. In their name she prays to God daily:
"Forgive us our trespasses"; and with the brave heart of a
mother turns at once to nurse them back to spiritual health.
When therefore we call the Body of Jesus Christ "mystical,"
we hear a solemn warning in the very significance of the
word. It is a warning that echoes these words of St. Leo:
"Recognize, O Christian, your dignity, and being made a
sharer of the divine nature, go not back to your former
worthlessness along the way of unseemly conduct. Keep in
mind of what Head and of what Body you are a member"
—Enc. on the Mystical Body, 66.

Liturgy

The liturgical season of Lent is the time of the year when the
Church lays particular stress on personal interior renewal. Lent
is a period of forty days set aside by the Church as a preparation
for Easter. If we would rise with Christ to a new life of holiness
on Easter we must die to sin, must practice mortification and
self-denial. The Church obliges us to fast on only two days of
Lent. However, we are strongly encouraged to do so every week-
day of the Lenten season. The Church also urges us to abstain
from amusements and entertainments, and to deepen our prayer-
life. All the liturgical services during Lent are full of encouragement and inspiration for those who are trying to keep the spirit
of the season. The chants and readings in the Mass and the office
extol the merits of fasting and penance. Later, as Lent deepens
into Passiontide, the suffering Savior himself speaks to us, in-
viting us to suffer with him. Passiontide reaches its climax in
Holy Week, when we re-live the awful suffering and death of
Christ.

† † †

Near the cross of Jesus there stood his mother, his mother's sister, Mary the wife of Clopas, and Mary Magdalene.
    Seeing his mother there with the disciple whom he loved, Jesus said to his mother, "Woman, there is your son."
    In turn he said to the disciple, "There is your mother."
From that hour onward, the disciple took her into his care—
JOHN 19:25–27.

WITH THESE WORDS, "There is your son—there is your mother," Jesus was not merely providing for the care of his mother. He was explicitly confirming Mary's position as spiritual mother of the whole human race. Her right to that title was won at the moment she conceived the Son of God in her virginal womb. It had been through a woman that sin had entered the world, when Eve tempted Adam to sin. Christ, the new Adam, who brought redemption to the world, chose to come into the world through a woman. Mary, therefore, is the new Eve, the spiritual mother of mankind.

It was Mary whom the Father chose to be the mother of his Son. But Mary's work did not end even with this most exalted of roles. God chose, also, to use her cooperation in the work of redeeming us. As she stood at the foot of the cross Mary was not merely a mother suffering the agony of seeing her beloved Son die. She, as the new Eve, had to offer him, as he was offering himself, for the sins of men. God required of her that she freely and whole-heartedly join in the sacrifice of her Son. And, as always, she complied perfectly with the will of God. Thus, Mary not only gave Christ to the world, she also gave him back to his Father, receiving in exchange the whole sinful race which had been the cause of his death. By this heroic act of surrender, Mary received an added right to the title Mother of Man, Mother of the Mystical Body of Christ.

Mary was present for the main events in the life of Jesus. She was deeply involved in all of the joyful, sorrowful, and glorious actions in the redemption of the human race. Mary, more than anyone else, listened to and lived the way of life Jesus came to teach us, so we would safely travel this life as pilgrims on the way to heaven.

1. What is the place of Mary in the Mystical Body of Christ?

Mary, as the mother of Jesus, is the mother of the Church, i.e., of the Mystical Body of Christ.

2. Why does our Lady merit the title, "Mother of the Church"?

This title, as well as most of Mary's other titles, stems from three basic facts:

a. It was she from whom the Second Divine Person took his human nature. She is the mother of Christ, our brother, and therefore the mother of all men.

b. By her complete identification with and acceptance of the offering Christ made of himself on the cross Mary cooperated in our redemption, thereby acquiring an added right to the title of mother of all men.

c. All the graces which Christ won for us by his death on the cross and which he as Head applies to the members of his Mystical Body are distributed through her maternal intercession.

3. What other title of our Lady stems from these three facts?

Mary is also called "Queen of Heaven and Earth."

Certainly, in the full and strict meaning of the term, only Jesus Christ, the God-Man, is king; but Mary, too, as mother of the divine Christ, as his associate in the redemption, in his struggle with his enemies and his final victory over them, has a share, though in a limited analogous way, in his royal dignity—Enc. on the Queenship of Mary.

4. Why do we call Mary, the Mother of God?

Mary is the Mother of God because it was from her that the Second Divine Person took his human nature. Mary gave to Jesus what every mother gives her child. But the Person who is her son is not a human person but a Divine Person. The Person whose mother she is, is God; therefore she is, in very fact, the Mother of God.

5. What do we mean by the Immaculate Conception?

By the Immaculate Conception we mean that, by a privilege which was granted to no other human being, our Lady was preserved from original sin from the very first instant of her conception in the womb of her mother.

We declare, pronounce and define that the Most Blessed Virgin Mary, at the first instant of her conception was preserved immaculate from all stain of original sin, by the singular grace and privilege of the omnipotent God, in virtue of the merits of Jesus Christ, the Saviour of mankind, and that this doctrine was revealed by God, and therefore, must be believed firmly and constantly by all the faithful
—Bull, Ineffabilis Dei, Pius IX, Dec. 8, 1854.

6. What is meant by the Assumption of our Lady?

By the Assumption of our Lady is meant that at the end of her earthly life Mary was taken, body and soul, into heaven. God did not allow the body from which his Son took his body to suffer corruption, the fate of all those who have been affected by original sin.

We pronounce, declare and define it to be a divinely revealed dogma that the immaculate Mother of God, the ever virgin Mary, having completed the course of her earthly life, was assumed body and soul into heavenly glory—
Apostolic Constitution, Munificentissimus Deus, Pius XII, Nov. 1, 1950.

Devotion

The devotion to our Lady which is especially dear to her and to her children is the one which is called the rosary. It is predominantly a mental prayer, a meditation on various mysteries in the life of our Lord and our Lady. The Hail Marys which we recite as we meditate on the mysteries in saying the rosary are meant to be a sort of chant in the background. In other words, while we say the various decades of the rosary we should attend to the mystery we are contemplating rather than to the words of the Hail Mary.

The entire rosary is composed of fifteen decades, a decade here means a series of ten beads, corresponding to fifteen mysteries. The five decade rosaries which one commonly sees are really one-third of the rosary itself.

The mysteries on which we meditate in the rosary are divided into three sets and present an outline of the life of Jesus, stressing the key points in the drama of our redemption. Frequent reflection on these principal events will assist us as our faith grows and develops.

   a. The Joyful Mysteries:

     1. The Angel Gabriel announces to Mary that she is to be the Mother of God.
     2. Our Blessed Lady visits her cousin Elizabeth, the mother of St. John the Baptist.
     3. Our Lord is born in Bethlehem.
     4. Our Lord is presented in the temple.
     5. The boy Jesus is found in the temple after he had been lost for three days.

   b. The Sorrowful Mysteries:

     1. Our Lord suffers his agony in the garden of Gethsemani.
     2. Jesus is scourged by the Roman soldiers.
     3. Jesus is crowned with thorns.
     4. Jesus carries his cross to Calvary.
     5. Jesus is crucified.

   c. The Glorious Mysteries:

     1. Jesus rises from the dead.

2. Jesus ascends into heaven.
3. The Holy Spirit descends upon the infant Church.
4. Our Lady is assumed into heaven.
5. Our Lady is crowned Queen of Heaven.

The rosary begins with the recitation of the Apostles' Creed. This prayer is followed by an Our Father, three Hail Marys and the Glory Be to the Father, said on the beads preceding the decades. Each decade is preceded by an Our Father and concludes with the Glory Be to the Father.

section **21**   The Sacred Liturgy

The liturgy is thus the outstanding means by which the faithful can express in their lives, and manifest to others, the mystery of Christ and the real nature of the true Church–Constitution on the Sacred Liturgy 2.

IN DESCRIBING the liturgy the Second Vatican Council relates how Jesus sent the Apostles, filled with the Holy Spirit, to preach the gospel to every creature. They were to proclaim that the Son of God, by his death and resurrection, had freed us from the power of Satan and from death, and brought us into the kingdom of his Father. But the apostles were to be more than teachers. They were to exercise the work of salvation for us through the sacred ceremonies of sacrifice and sacraments, i.e., the liturgy.

The liturgy is an exercise of the priestly office of Jesus. It is through the liturgy that the sanctification of man is manifested by signs perceptible to the senses, and is effected in a way which is proper to each of these signs.

Every liturgical celebration is an action of Jesus, our priest, and of the Church, his Body. No other action of the Church can match the efficacy of the liturgy nor equal it in any way. It is in the liturgy that full public worship is performed by the Mystical Body of Jesus—cf. Constitution on the Sacred Liturgy 6, 7.

Finally, the Council concludes, ". . . the liturgy is the summit toward which the activity of the Church is directed. At the same time it is the fountain from which all her power flows. For the goal of apostolic works is that all who are made sons of God by

130

faith and baptism should come together to praise God in the midst of his Church, to take part in her sacrifice, and to eat the Lord's supper—Constitution on the Sacred Liturgy 10.

The first function of the Pilgrim People of God is to worship God. The second is to teach and sanctify the members. The third is to teach and sanctify the world. In this threefold work of the Church the liturgy plays a vital role. It is through the liturgy that Christ and his members give unceasing worship to God. It is through the liturgy that the members of Christ receive the divine life of sanctifying grace which flows from Christ, the Head. The liturgy of the Church does more than sanctify; it also teaches most effectively because it appeals to the whole person, to the heart as well as the mind.

Liturgy is more than prayer. The liturgy inspires, enlightens, and strengthens the laity in order to apply Christian solutions to the problems of the social order.

1. What is the sacred liturgy?

The sacred liturgy is the official public worship of God by the Mystical Body of Christ. Through this worship we proclaim the reconciliation of man and God. We are sanctified, or made holy, through these sacred actions and symbols.

2. Is the liturgy primarily ritual?

Ritual is essential to the liturgy, but it is by no means the whole of it. We must worship God intelligently with our minds and emotionally with our hearts. Before we can do either of these, the faithful must be instructed in the meaning of the ceremonies and symbols used in the Mass and the sacraments so that they will be well disposed to actively participate with the priest and the rest of the community, e.g., why we use water in Baptism.

While ritual is necessary it could become merely ceremonial. Jesus found fault with his generation because of overemphasis on the ritual by the Jews.

3. How important is a person's active participation in the liturgy?

131

A person does receive some benefit by mere attendance at liturgical services. But when actively participating each member is personally proclaiming approval and acceptance of the sacred doctrine and mysteries being celebrated. Consequently each person should enthusiastically join the congregation in responding to the priest celebrant's call to worship. Everyone should listen attentively to the readings from sacred Scripture and to the homily. The prayers offered by the priest are in behalf of the welfare of all of the people of God but especially for those participating in this particular celebration. The people of God join the priest and unite themselves to God by their fervent responses.

4. Does a person really have an obligation to participate in the liturgy in order to worship God?

Beginning with the Sinai covenant about two thousand years before the birth of Jesus the Jewish people were given minute directions on how and when to worship God. The sacred author of the two books of Kings record God's displeasure with those who did not follow the prescriptions. In the Acts of the Apostles we read of the People of God who in the New Testament from the early days of Christianity gathered gogether on the first day of the week for the breaking of the bread —ACTS 2:42.

5. What is included in the sacred liturgy?

The sacred liturgy includes:

a. The Eucharistic Sacrifice-Meal, the Mass,

b. The seven sacraments,

c. The liturgy of the hours,

d. The sacramentals.

6. What is the liturgy of the hours?

The liturgy of the hours is the daily prayer of the Church. It is composed mainly of the psalms, inspired poems of the Old Testament. This prayer of the Church is prayed every day by all clerics in major orders and by monks and other religious in choir. It follows the cycles of the liturgical year. The two principle sections are the morning hour prayer and evening hour prayer. There are three other sections: the hours of readings, mid-day prayer and night prayer.

The liturgy of the hours with its wealth of psalms, prayers and hymns and readings from Scripture and the Fathers is a great treasure. The laity, although not officially deputed to pray it, may pray part or all of the daily prayer of the Church with great profit to themselves. The breviary is the book containing the text of the liturgy of the hours.

7. What is the liturgical year?

The liturgical year is the means by which the Church relives the life of Christ, by celebrating throughout the year the mysteries of his life, death and resurrection.

8. How does the Church teach and sanctify us during the liturgical year?

Throughout the liturgical year the Church not only presents to us the mysteries of Jesus Christ, it strives to help us take part in them and thereby share more fully in the life of Christ, our Head.

In the four weeks of *Advent* the Church recalls the unfortunate condition of mankind from shortly after creation until the coming of Jesus into the world. Advent is a time of longing for the light of Christ which will enlighten all of us. It is also a time of joy for us because we know we live after the incarnation. We no longer need to walk in the darkness of sin.

Christmas brings us to the stable at Bethlehem and teaches us that the Son of God became flesh for us and for our salvation. We must be born again and undergo a complete reformation by being more intimately united to the Word of God made man.

At the solemnity of the *Epiphany*, we celebrate the call of the Gentiles to the Christian faith. The liturgy exhorts us to give thanks for the blessings of the faith and to seek a deeper faith through prayer and meditation.

133

During the forty days of *Lent*, beginning on Ash Wednesday, the Church issues a call to return to our baptismal innocence. The scriptural lessons of this season reeducate the faithful to purify their intentions and actions. We are called to amend our lives, detest our sins and expiate them by *prayer* and *penance*. Then, on Easter, we can joyfully renew our baptismal promises.

Holy Week begins with a representation of the triumphant entry of Jesus into Jerusalem on Passion (Palm) Sunday. Holy Thursday calls attention to the great gifts of the Holy Eucharist and the priesthood. On Good Friday the sufferings of Jesus are put before us. The Church invites us to follow in the blood-stained footsteps of our Lord, to carry the cross willingly with him, to reproduce in our hearts the spirit of atonement and to die together with him so we can rise with him on Easter.

The *Easter* season commemorates the triumph of our Savior over sin and death. The Church reminds us that we should rise with him to a new life of greater fervor and holiness, aspiring only to the things of heaven.

At *Pentecost* the Church urges us to be more docile to the action of the Holy Spirit, so that we may become holy, as Christ and his Father are holy.

During the course of the liturgical year, besides the mysteries of Jesus Christ, the feasts of some of the saints are celebrated. These feasts are of a lower and subordinate order. Through them the Church strives to put before us examples of sanctity from every age in order to move us to cultivate in ourselves the virtues of Christ.

section **22** The Mass, the
Christian Sacrifice-Meal

*Christ the Lord, Eternal Priest according to the order of
Melchisedech, loving his own who were in the world, at the
last supper, on the night he was betrayed, wishing to leave
his beloved spouse, the Church, a visible sacrifice, such as
the nature of men requires, that would represent the bloody
sacrifice offered once on the cross, and perpetuate its
memory to the end of time, and whose salutary virtue
might be applied in remitting those sins which we daily
commit . . . offered his body and blood under the species
of bread and wine to God the Father, and under the same
species allowed the apostles, whom he at that time constituted the priests of the New Testament, to partake thereof;
commanding them and their successors in the priesthood to
make the same offering*—Enc. on the Sacred Liturgy 67.

AS LOVING CHILDREN we long to offer gifts to God, our
Father. But what gift can we find which would be worthy to offer to the Almighty? The food we eat, the clothes we wear, our
most precious possessions, even our very lives are his already.
People before the time of Christ longed to offer gifts to God; but
all they could offer were the fruits of the land and the beasts of
the field. How could these gifts atone for sin? The priests, too,
who offered these gifts in the name of the people were members
of the same fallen race. There was no gift worthy to be offered to
God. Yet God did accept the offerings made by his people in the
Old Testament. He was pleased to accept these offerings because
they foreshadowed the perfect gift which would one day be offered to him by the perfect priest, the gift of Christ himself which
his Son, as priest, would offer to him on the cross.

Christ offered himself to his Father once on the cross. He

135

continues to offer himself, day after day, in that re-offering of his sacrifice of Calvary in which we now have a part, the eucharistic sacrifice of the Mass.*

1. What is sacrifice?

Sacrifice is the public offering by a priest of a gift to God. The gift, or victim, is something good which we possess. When we present it for sacrifice we are giving up all our claims to it. In some sacrificial ceremonies, the eating of the gift is a sign of participation and unity among those who make the offering.

2. Why do we offer gifts to God?

We offer gifts to God in an attempt to give ourselves to him. We have a need to thank God for previous favors. We also have a duty to praise God for being God. We sometimes have need to apologize for having offended him through sin and plead for forgiveness. Finally we petition him to continue to provide for our basic needs.

The gift we offer represents us. We offer it as a sign that we acknowledge God's supreme ownership of us and of all things.

3. Have men always offered gifts to God?

Yes. From the very beginning the Bible mentions that people offered gifts to God. The principal persons throughout Old Testament offered sacrifices to God. The Jews offered many sacrifices as God had instructed them to do.

4. What was the only perfect offering which was made to God the Father?

The only perfect offering made to God was the offering which Jesus Christ made when he offered himself to the Father in perfect love and obedience.

---

*The Holy Eucharist is a marvelous gift from God. It will be considered in four chapters. First, as a sacrifice (22), second, the ceremony in which it is confected (23), third, the sacramental form (28), and fourth, as a sacrificial meal (29).

5. When did Jesus Christ offer himself to the Father?

Jesus Christ offered himself to the Father as he died on the cross. He began by offering himself in a sacrificial meal at the Last Supper. He often expressed it, "I have come to do the will of the Father!"

6. What was the significance of the Last Supper?

The Last Supper was the living memorial of the death and resurrection of Christ. At the Last Supper Jesus told the apostles that they were to celebrate this sacrificial meal in memory of him. This we do in the Mass. The Mass is the re-offering of that sacrificial meal which makes Christ's death and resurrection present among us.

> *At the Last Supper, on the night when He was betrayed, our Savior instituted the Eucharistic sacrifice of His body and blood. He did this in order to perpetuate the Sacrifice of the cross throughout the centuries until He should come again, and so to entrust to His beloved spouse, the Church, a memorial of His death and resurrection: a Sacrament of love, a sign of unity, a bond of charity, a Paschal Banquet in which Christ is eaten, the mind is filled with grace, and a pledge of future glory is given to us—*Constitution on the Sacred Liturgy 47.

7. In what ways are the Last Supper, the crucifixion and the Mass the same?

At the Last Supper Jesus changed bread into his body and wine into his blood. These were separated as a sign that the death of Jesus was to be "for the forgiveness of sin."

On the cross once again the body and blood of Jesus were separated and Jesus died for the forgiveness of the sins of mankind.

In the Mass, Jesus, through a priest, once again changes bread into his body and wine into his blood, separates them, and offers them for the forgiveness of sins.

In all three ceremonies the body and blood of Jesus are separated, indicating death. In all three Jesus is the principal agent or priest. And all three are brought about for the explicit purpose of the forgiveness of sins.

8. How are the Last Supper and the Mass the fulfillment of the ancient Jewish Passover?

The Passover was the meal which celebrated the covenant which God had made with the Israelites through Moses on Mt. Sinai. The Last Supper took place in the Passover observance. Our re-offering, the Mass, celebrates the new, perfect and everlasting covenant which God made with mankind through Christ, that covenant which was sealed in the blood of Christ as he died on the cross.

The Passover commemorated the saving actions God had worked for his people in the Old Testament. The Last Supper introduces the New Testament rite of redemption, the Mass. It was most appropriate that while observing the Passover commemoration Jesus should introduce the new covenant sacrifice.

9. What did the death of Christ as a sacrifice accomplish?

   a. It gave infinite worship to God.

   b. It redeemed us by atoning for our sins, thereby restoring divine life to the human race.

   c. It gave perfect thanks to God for all his favors to man.

10. Why is the Mass called the Eucharistic celebration?

The word "eucharist" means "thanksgiving." The Mass is the great act of praise and thanksgiving which Christ and the whole Church offer in loving thankfulness to God for the saving death and resurrection of Christ.

11. Is attendance and participation at the Mass an obligation or an opportunity?

While we properly speak of the divine obligation of taking part in the Mass a believer in the Christian revelation sees the Mass as the perfect opportunity to meet God and to respond to God's love for us.

138

Practice

▲ Even while we are attending instructions we should join in the prayers of the congregation at Mass. We should learn and pray the prayers which the people offer and we should sing the hymns which the people use at Mass.

† † †

section **23** The Structure of the Mass

EVERY IMPORTANT event requires a suitable preparation. The Mass, the most sublime act of worship is no exception. At the Last Supper, our Lord surrounded the moment of sacrifice with ceremonies, the supper itself, the washing of feet, a sermon and a hymn. The Church does likewise. In the earliest days the Mass followed the same pattern as the Last Supper. For centuries it was preceded by a meal. Later conditions brought about changes. The Mass today in the Latin rite is divided into two main parts, the Liturgy of the Word and the Liturgy of the Eucharist. The Liturgy of the Word is composed of an entrance rite, a service of Scripture reading, a homily on the Word of God from Scripture and the Prayer of the Faithful. The Liturgy of the Word prepares us for the Liturgy of the Eucharist. The Liturgy of the Eucharist is composed of three parts, the preparation of gifts, the sacrificial act itself, and the sacrificial meal, the Eucharistic banquet.

Each of the two principal parts has two themes.

The Liturgy of the Word	We speak to God
	God speaks to us
The Liturgy of the Eucharist	We give to God
	God gives to us

An understanding of the ceremonies of the Mass will aid in our appreciation of the Mass itself and will enable us to participate more fully.

1. What is the origin of the Liturgy of the Word?

In the earliest days of the Church, the Mass began just as the Last Supper did with a meal. It was celebrated in the evening in the homes of the people. Later the Mass was separated from the meal and came to be celebrated in the morning. In place of the preparatory meal there was substituted an adaption of the Jewish synagogue service, which the earliest Christians had continued to hold, at first with the Jews in the synagogue and later by themselves. This service of prayer and instruction is the basis of our present Liturgy of the Word. In the course of the centuries other parts have been added.

2. What is the structure of the Liturgy of the Word?

a. We speak to God

1. *The Entrance Rite.* There are various optional ways to begin the Liturgy. The more common form is to sing a hymn while the celebrant enters. Occasionally the congregation is blessed with holy water. We now speak to God our first word, namely we call to mind our sins, express sorrow for them, and plead forgiveness.

2. *The Gloria.* Here we express our second word, one of praise. It is addressed to the three persons in the Trinity.

3. *The Opening Prayer.* Here we express our third and fourth words, those of thanksgiving for past favors and of petition for future favors.

b. God speaks to us.

1. *The First Reading* is usually a reading from one of the books of the Old Testament. We listen to part of the early revelation of God to his chosen people.

2. *The Responsorial Psalm* is a reflective prayer carrying on a theme from the lesson. It is a meditative response to the words of God. It is prayed alternately by the lector and congregation.

3. *The Second Reading* (used only on Sundays and some feast days) is usually from the New Testament which contains God's later revelation.

4. *The Gospel Acclamation* or alleluia is the short introduction to the Gospel reading of the day.

5. *The Gospel* reports the actions and very words of our Redeemer, Jesus.

6. *The Homily* is an instruction by the priest based on the Scripture readings of this Mass. God, speaking through the priest, applies the message of Scripture to contemporary times.

7. *The Creed.* We respond to the words of God by an act of faith. This ancient formula of what we believe is a list of the saving actions of God. When praying it we are united to Christians of all ages who have also used it to express the basic tenets of our faith.

8. *The Prayer of the Faithful* is a series of petitions for the needs of the Church, civil government and all humanity.

The various parts of the Liturgy of the Word are not just so many readings. Frequently the readings and responses develop a theme or plan for that day. Each part is tied together with the others to teach a special lesson for the assembled Christian community to apply to their daily living.

3. What is the structure of the Liturgy of the Eucharist?

The Liturgy of the Eucharist includes the following:

a. We give to God.

1. *The Preparation of the Gifts* begins with a few members of the congregation, representing the entire

141

assembly, bringing gifts of bread and wine and water to the celebrating priest. Other gifts such as the collection, alms for the poor, and symbolic offerings might be included. In addition to the principal gifts of bread, wine and water, we should offer ourselves. At this time we should reoffer ourselves to God the Father. We should pledge to strengthen our faith and hope through charitable works. The collection taken up at this time is a part of the procession. We should regard what we offer in the collection as part of our gift to the Christian community.

2. *The Eucharistic Prayer.* This, the most important part of the Mass is introduced by a song of thanksgiving, called the Preface. During the Eucharistic Prayer, Jesus offers the sacrifice of his body and blood to his Father. Once again he renews the offering he made of his life on the cross. The Consecration occurs in the center of the Eucharistic prayer. At that time Jesus, through the priest, changes bread and wine into his body and blood. Then the priest invites the assembled congregation to proclaim their faith in the new eucharistic presence of Jesus on the altar.

Before and after the moment of sacrifice the Church prays for various people—the pope, the bishops, the faithful, the living, the dead, sinners, ourselves, and for the things of earth we use.

The Eucharistic Prayer has a beautiful ending. Christ, our high priest, mediator between God and Man, drawing all things to himself, presents them to his Father. "Through him, with him, in him, in the unity of the Holy Spirit, all glory and honor is yours, almighty Father, forever and ever." The people answer, "Amen," which signifies their thankful commitment in faith to the act which Christ has just performed. The "Amen" could mean "I believe."

There are four different ordinary Eucharistic

Prayers, as well as two for reconciliation and three for children.

b. God gives to us.

1. *The Lord's Prayer.* The communion service begins with the prayer Jesus taught us. We ask for the bread which is our Lord, and we forgive those who have offended us, as we wish God to forgive us.

2. *The Rite of Peace.* Before approaching the altar to receive Jesus in Holy Communion we should be at peace with our families and our neighbors. We follow the local parish custom and extend a sign of peace to those nearby, symbolizing our peace with all of mankind.

3. *Holy Communion.* The priest now gives to us the true bread of life. Through this sacred meal we are intimately united to Jesus and to all others who participate in this holy banquet.

4. *The Conclusion.* After a short thanksgiving the priest gives us his blessing and we are sent to live the message of the word and the Eucharist.

4. What is the importance of Communion in the Mass?

Communion is the part of the Mass in which our union with one another and with Christ is most deeply symbolized and increased. The Mass, the Eucharistic Celebration, is a sacrifice-meal. Every member of the congregation should take part in Communion at Mass. Not to do so would be to fail to participate fully in the Mass.

5. What is meant by the different roles which are fulfilled in the celebration of Mass?

By the different roles we mean that various actions and prayers are proper to different members of the congregation to perform and say during Mass.

a. The *celebrant,* or concelebrants, preside at the assembly.

He sums up the petitions of the people in the opening prayer. He preaches the homily after the reading of the Gospel. He prepares the bread and wine. He alone prays the great sacrifical prayer of the Mass, the Eucharistic Prayer, and the words of consecration.

b. The *deacon,* if there is one, assists the celebrant and reads the Gospel.

c. The *commentator* assists the congregation by announcing the parts of the Mass and giving brief explanations of their meaning.

d. The *readers* proclaim the Word of God to the whole congregation in the Scripture readings.

e. The *choir* assists the whole congregation in singing their parts of the Mass and provides music which helps the people to pray and meditate.

f. The *people* sing and pray together the people's parts of the Mass.

g. The *servers* assist the priest at the altar.

6. What is a concelebrated Mass?

A concelebrated Mass is one at which several priests gather at the same altar to offer together, to con-celebrate, the Eucharist. Usually only one priest celebrates the Mass, but on occasions two or more priests may celebrate together.

7. Why does the priest wear special vestments at Mass?

The garments worn are different from any contemporary culture. They serve to call to our minds the fact that the ceremony we are witnessing is not ordinary. This meal is different. It is our meeting with God.

8. Why are the priest's vestments of different colors?

Vestments of different colors are used to indicate the spirit of the Mass or the season of the liturgical year, e.g., during Advent and Lent violet vestments are worn, during the Christmas and Easter season white vestments, on Pentecost red vestments.

144

On the ordinary Sundays of the year green vestments are worn. On the feasts of other saints, our Lord and our Lady, white vestments are worn.

Practice

▲ We should take our full part in the Eucharistic Celebration by enacting fully the role which is ours in the Mass.

Mother Church earnestly desires that all the faithful should be led to that full conscious, and active participation in liturgical celebrations which is demanded by the very nature of the liturgy. Such participation by the Christian people as "a chosen race, a royal priesthood, a holy nation, a redeemed people"—1 PET. 2:9; cf. 2:4–5, *is their right and duty by reason of their baptism.*

In the restoration and promotion of the sacred liturgy, this full and active participation by all the people is the aim to be considered before all else; for it is the primary and indispensable source from which the faithful are to derive the true Christian spirit—Constitution of the Sacred Liturgy 14.

1. Readers, commentators and leaders of song fulfill their role by performing these functions reverently and carefully.

Servers, lectors, commentators, and members of the choir also exercise a genuine liturgical function. They ought, therefore, to discharge their office with the sincere piety and decorum demanded by so exalted a ministry and rightly expected of them by God's people.

Consequently they must all be deeply imbued with the spirit of the liturgy, each in his own measure, and they must be trained to perform their functions, in a correct and orderly manner—Constitution of the Sacred Liturgy 29.

2. The congregation performs its role by listening to the readings and homily with a mind and heart open to the Holy Spirit and by saying and singing their parts of the Mass together in a spirit of prayer.

To promote active participation, the people should be encouraged to take part by means of acclamations, responses,

145

psalmody, antiphons, and songs, as well as by actions, ges-
tures and bodily attitudes. And at the proper times all
should observe a reverent silence–Constitution on the Sacred
Liturgy 30.

▲ The most basic and important participation in the Eucharistic Celebration is taking part in the Eucharistic meal, Holy Communion. We should take part in Communion at Mass as often as
we can. We should do so with the realization that we, as members of God's great family, are partaking of God's family meal.
Through this meal we are united to each other and to God.

The Church, therefore, earnestly desires that Christ's faith-
ful, when present at this mystery of faith, should not be
there as strangers or silent spectators; on the contrary,
through a good understanding of the rites and prayers they
should take part in the sacred action conscious of what they
are doing, with devotion and full collaboration. They should
be instructed by God's word and be nourished at the table of
the Lord's body; they should give thanks to God; by offering
the Immaculate Victim, not only through the hands of the
priest, but also with him, they should learn also to offer
themselves; through Christ the Mediator, they should be
drawn day by day into ever more perfect union with God and
with each other, so that finally God may be all in all.–Constitution on the Sacred Liturgy 48.

▲ We should realize that we pray when we sing, not only
when we speak words. We should recall the words of St. Augustine, "He who sings well prays doubly well."

The musical tradition of the universal Church is a treasure
of inestimable value, greater even than that of any other
art. The main reason for this pre-eminence is that, as sacred
song united to the words, it forms a necessary or integral
part of the solemn liturgy.

Therefore sacred music is to be considered the more holy
in proportion as it is more closely connected with the litur-
gical action, whether it adds delight to prayer, fosters unity
of minds, or confers greater solemnity upon the sacred rites.
But, the Church approves of all forms of true art having the

needed qualities, and admits them into divine worship—
Constitution on the Sacred Liturgy 112.

▲ There are many different forms of music which are suitable for use in liturgical celebrations. Composers have used different forms of music to express religious ideas. While a person may have a preference for one type of music we should try to learn to appreciate different forms. Compositions used in the sacred liturgy should be true music. Texts should present true religious concepts. Tunes should not be chosen for sentimental or nostalgic reasons, but because they help us think of God and our relationship to him.

† † †

section **24** Prayer

One day he was praying in a certain place. When he had finished, one of his disciples asked him, "Lord, teach us to pray, as John taught his disciples." He said to them, "When you pray, say:
  Father, hallowed be your name,
    your kingdom come.
  Give us each day our daily bread.
  Forgive us our sins
    for we too forgive all who do us wrong;
  and subject us not to the trial"—LUKE 11:1–4.

THROUGH the liturgy, the Church prays to God. As members of the Mystical Body of Christ we pray with and through the Church by taking part in the liturgy.

We must also pray privately. Our response to God for all the gifts he has given us must be to converse lovingly with him

147

through prayer and meditation. Only if we cultivate the spirit of prayer in our lives through private prayer will we be able to pray with the Church as we should in liturgical prayer and deepen our life in Christ.

There are many different ways of praying privately. We can pray by using words which someone else has composed; we can pray by speaking to God in our own words. But however and whenever we pray, we should pray as Christ taught us.

Prayer, then, is conversation with God. It gives us an opportunity to communicate to God our joys, disappointments, our desires, as well as our appreciation and gratitude.

We can and should pray for or petition God for whatever is good. We can converse with God about everything that is a part of our lives.

1. How should we pray?

a. "Father, . . ."

We should pray with *simplicity* and *trust*, as a child speaks to its father. We should pray with the realization that God knows and loves us individually and personally, but always mindful of the fact that we are members of the family of God, united to our brothers.

> *As for clothes, why be concerned? Learn a lesson from the way the wild flowers grow. They do not work; they do not spin. Yet I assure you, not even Solomon in all his splendor was arrayed like one of these. If God can clothe in such splendor the grass of the field, which blooms today and is thrown on the fire tomorrow, will he not provide much more for you, O weak in faith!–* MATT. 6:28–30.

b. "Hallowed be your name . . ."

We should, first of all, *adore God* in our prayer. We should think of his goodness and his mercy and express our adoration and love in acts of faith, hope, love, and adoration.

> *More than this we need not add;*
> *let the last word be, he is all in all!*

148

> *Let us praise him the more, since we*
> * cannot fathom him,*
> * for greater is he than all his works;*
> *Awful indeed is the LORD's majesty,*
> * and wonderful is his power*–SIR. 43:28–30.

c. "Your kingdom come."

We should pray *as members of the Body of Christ*, conscious of our duty of witnessing Christ to the world and of extending his kingdom.

> *In the same way, your light must shine before men so that they may see goodness in your acts and give praise to your heavenly Father*–MATT. 5:16.

d. "Give us each day our daily bread."

We should *ask God for the things we need*, first of all for spiritual gifts for ourselves and for others.

> *Seek first his kingship over you, his way of holiness. . .*
> –MATT. 6:33.

We should also ask God for the needs of everyday life and even for special favors, praying for these latter things on the condition that it is the will of God that we have them.

> *Ask, and you will receive. Seek, and you will find. Knock, and it will be opened to you.*
> *For the one who asks, receives. The one who seeks, finds. The one who knocks, enters. Would one of you hand his son a stone when he asks for a loaf, or a poisonous snake when he asks for a fish?*
> *If you, with all your sins, know how to give your children what is good, how much more will your heavenly Father give good things to anyone who asks him!*–MATT. 7:7–11.

e. "Forgive us our sins for we too forgive all who do us wrong. . ."

We should pray for *forgiveness of our sins*, resolving to avoid sin in the future, and mindful of our Lord's words:

> *Then in anger the master handed him over to the*

torturers until he paid back all that he owed. My heavenly Father will treat you in exactly the same way unless each of you forgives his brothers from his heart—MATT. 18:34—35.

f. "... Subject us not to trial."

We should pray for *help in time of temptation* and for strength to avoid the occasions of sin, humbly admitting that without such help from God we would not be able to remain faithful to him.

2. What should be the qualities of our prayer?

a. We should pray with *reverence and sincerity*, remembering that it is God to whom we are speaking.

When you are praying, do not behave like the hypocrites who love to stand and pray in synagogues or on street corners in order to be noticed. I give you my word, they are already repaid. Whenever you pray, go to your room, close your door, and pray to your Father in private. Then your Father, who sees what no man sees, will repay you—MATT. 6:5—6.

b. We should pray with childlike *humility* and with *confidence* that our Father will hear and answer us.

In your prayer do not rattle on like the pagans. They think they will win a hearing by the sheer multiplication of words. Do not imitate them. Your Father knows what you need before you ask him—MATT. 6:7—8.

c. We should pray with *faith* and *perseverance*, refusing to give up in discouragement because God does not seem to answer our prayer immediately.

In reply Jesus told them: "Put your trust in God. I solemnly assure you, whoever says to this mountain, 'Be lifted up and thrown into the sea,' and has no inner doubts but believes that what he says will happen, shall have it done for him. I give you my word, if you are ready to believe that you will receive whatever you ask for in prayer, it shall be done for you"—MARK 11:22—24.

d. We should pray with *submission* to the will of our Father, who alone knows whether what we ask is really good for us. We should pray as our Lord prayed: "My Father . . . let it be as you would have it, not as I"—MATT. 26:39.

3. Does God always answer our prayers?

Yes. Our Lord said, ". . . whatever you ask the Father, he will give you in my name"—JOHN 16:23.

Our prayers are always answered, but not always in the way we expect.

4. When should we pray?

We should pray every day:

In the morning, as we begin our day we should greet God first of all and offer ourselves and our day to him.

In the evening before retiring we should thank God for the blessings of the day and ask his pardon for the faults we have committed.

Before and after meals we should ask God's blessing on the food he has provided for us and thank him for it.

In time of temptation we should ask God for help. Frequently during the day we should elevate our hearts and minds to God with short prayers such as, "My Jesus, mercy," "All for thee, most Sacred Heart of Jesus," "My God I love you."

5. To whom should we pray?

a. We should pray to God, through Christ, our mediator. Thus the Church prays most frequently in her liturgy: to God the Father, through Christ, in union with the Holy Spirit.

b. We should pray to each of the Divine Persons individually: e.g., we pray to the Holy Spirit for light and inspiration.

c. We should pray to our Lord Jesus Christ as man: e.g., we pray to the Sacred Heart as the symbol of Christ's humanity; we pray to Christ in the Eucharist.

d. We should pray to the Blessed Virgin Mary, the Mother of God and our mother.

e. We should pray to the saints, to St. Joseph, Patron of the universal Church, to the saints whose names we bear, to other saints to whom we have a special devotion, and to our guardian angel.

6. With whom should we pray?

We should pray with Christ and our fellow members in Christ by participating in the public worship of the Church, the liturgy.* We should pray with others by taking part in devotions such as the way of the cross, May and October devotions, common recitation of the rosary, holy hours, etc. We should pray as families, e.g., the family rosary, grace before and after meals. We should pray by ourselves.

7. Why should we pray to the saints?

The doctrine of the Communion of Saints teaches us that there is a union between the faithful on earth, the souls in heaven and the souls in purgatory. The saints in heaven can know our needs and intercede for us with God. The souls in purgatory are unable to earn any help for themselves, but can be aided by our prayers. The faithful on earth, too, can aid one another by their prayers.

8. Why should we pray to the Blessed Virgin Mary?

We should pray to the Blessed Virgin Mary because she is the Mother of God and our mother. Our Lady intercedes with God for us at all times. God is certainly pleased when we pray to her and honor her in a special way. In honoring her we are only imitating what God himself has done, since he has blessed her above all his other creatures.

---

*The term "public prayer" is used officially for liturgical prayer (the Mass, the sacraments, the divine office). Services which are non-liturgical, such as the way of the cross and the recitation of the rosary, even when they involve a large group of people, are called "private devotions."

Liturgy

During the course of the liturgical year the feasts of the various saints are celebrated day by day. The great feasts of our Lady brighten the year, the Immaculate Conception in the midst of Advent on December 8th, the Assumption on August 15th, as well as her lesser feasts throughout the year. Special feasts of our Lord, too, are celebrated at regular times, such as the feast of Christ the King in November and the Sacred Heart in June. All the saints are honored together on November 1st, and all the souls in purgatory remembered especially on All Souls Day, November 2nd.

Practice

▲ We should begin to acquire the habit of daily prayer, if we have not already done so. The minimum should be: a) a short offering of ourselves and our day to God made in the morning, (cf. The Morning Offering pg. 24); b) a brief examination of conscience and an act of contrition (sorrow) at night (cf. pg. 18).

It is highly desirable also to pray the Rosary and to say meal prayers.

Grace before meals:

Bless us O Lord and these your gifts which we are about to receive from your bounty through Christ our Lord. Amen.

Thanksgiving after meals:

We give you thanks for all thy benefits, Almighty God, Who lives and reigns forever. May the souls of the faithful departed, through the mercy of God, rest in peace. Amen.

*. . . He had to pass through Samaria, and his journey brought
him to a Samaritan town named Shechem near the plot of
land which Jacob had given to his son Joseph. This was the
site of Jacob's well. Jesus, tired from his journey, sat down
at the well.*

*The hour was about noon. When a Samaritan woman
came to draw water, Jesus said to her, "Give me a drink."
(His disciples had gone off to the town to buy provisions.)
The Samaritan woman said to him, "You are a Jew. How
can you ask me, a Samaritan and a woman, for a drink?"
(Recall that Jews have nothing to do with Samaritans.) Jesus
replied: "If only you recognized God's gift, and who it is
that is asking you for a drink, you would have asked him instead, and he would have given you living water." "Sir," she
challenged him, "you do not have a bucket and this well is
deep. Where do you expect to get this flowing water? Surely you do not pretend to be greater than our ancestor Jacob,
who gave us this well and drank from it with his sons and his
flocks?" Jesus replied: "Everyone who drinks this water
will be thirsty again. But whoever drinks the water I give
him will never be thirsty; no, the water I give shall become
a fountain within him, leaping up to provide eternal life."*
—JOHN 4:5—14.

OUR LORD JESUS CHRIST is the source of the "living
water," the divine life. He gives us this life and increases it within us by means of the seven channels of grace which are called
the sacraments. Through the sacraments Jesus Christ unites us to
himself, ever deepening our union with him, ever increasing our
holiness. Through the sacraments Christ is with us throughout
our lives to provide us with all the help and strength we need to
grow in the divine life. At the very beginning of our life our Lord

154

is there to join us to his Mystical Body and give us the divine life. At the end, he is there to forgive our sins, strengthen us for our last battle with the enemy and prepare us for heaven. All throughout our lives he is there to strengthen us, to forgive us, to nourish us, and to fit us for the vocation in which we serve him in the Church.

1. What is a sacrament?

A sacrament is a sacred sign instituted by Christ to give grace.

2. How many sacraments are there?

There are seven sacraments:

Baptism, Confirmation, Penance, Holy Eucharist, Anointing of the Sick, Holy Orders and Marriage.

3. In what way are the sacraments sacred signs?

Signs are things or actions which convey an idea. A smile or a frown is a sign of one's feelings. A flag is a sign of a nation. Words are signs which convey an idea. In the sacraments the words together with the action constitute the sacred sign.

The sacraments are signs which not only communicate an idea but also produce what they signify. The sacraments not only make us aware of the divine life; they actually produce this life within us.

Water, since it is so necessary for life, can be used as a sign of life; hence water is an appropriate sign of the divine life. But in the sacrament of Baptism it not only signifies that life; it actually produces it. Oil is used to strengthen the body. In Confirmation it is used to signify the strength we receive from this sacrament and to give us that strength. Oil is also used as a medicine. In the sacrament of the Anointing of the Sick it is used both to signify and to impart health of soul and body.

The Sacrament	The Sign	
Baptism	Pouring of water	I baptize you in the name of the Father, and of the Son, and of the Holy Spirit.

155

The Sacrament	The Sign	
Confirmation	Anointing with oil	Be sealed with the gift of the Holy Spirit.
Penance	The confession of the sinner and the absolution of the priest.	I absolve you from your sins in the name of the Father, and of the Son, and of the Holy Spirit. Amen.
Holy Eucharist	Bread and wine	This is my body; This is my blood.
Anointing of the Sick	Anointing with oil	Through this holy anointing may the Lord in his love and mercy help you with the grace of the Holy Spirit. May the Lord who frees you from sin save you and raise you up.
Holy Orders	The imposing of the bishop's hands	We ask you, all-powerful Father, give these servants of yours the dignity of the presbyterate. Renew the Spirit of holiness within them. By your divine gift may they attain the second order in the hierarchy and exemplify right conduct in their lives.
Marriage	The exchange of marriage vows	

4. What do we mean when we say that the sacraments were instituted by Christ?

We mean that Jesus himself gave us the sacraments and that they are instruments by which he is now present with us and through which he shares his divine life with us.

5. Can we say the sacraments are acts of Jesus Christ?

Yes. Even though it is a human being who administers the sacraments, we can truthfully say that it is Christ who baptizes, Christ who confirms, Christ who forgives sin, etc. Christ acts in

156

and through the one who administers the sacrament. This person must have power from Christ to do so, and must intend to do what Christ intends. But because the sacraments are Christ's actions the holiness of the one administering them does not essentially affect them.

All the sacraments are administered by a priest or bishop, except Marriage which is administered by the couple. Baptisms may be administered by a deacon, and, in an emergency, by a lay person.

7. Do the sacraments always give grace?

If a sacrament is properly received it will always give grace, provided we do not place an obstacle in the way. An example of such an obstacle would be mortal sin in one who receives Confirmation, Holy Orders or Marriage. In such a case the grace which should have been given, but was impeded by the obstacle of mortal sin, will be given when the sinner repents.

8. What kind of grace do the sacraments give?

All the sacraments give the divine life of sanctifying grace. In addition, each sacrament gives its own particular actual graces and a right to future actual graces.

9. How long do the effects of the sacraments last?

While the ritual of the sacrament lasts but a few minutes, the effects are much longer. For example, once we are baptized, God promises all of the graces we need, when we need them, until we die.

10. What part do the sacraments play in the life of the Church?

Each of the sacraments plays an indispensable part in the life of the Church. Baptism, Confirmation, Marriage and Holy Orders confer an office in the Mystical Body. Baptism makes us members of the Body and gives us a share in the priesthood of Christ. Confirmation makes us mature and responsible Christians and increases our participation in Christ's priesthood. Holy Orders confers the actual powers of the priesthood and provides for the continuation of the Church. Marriage makes a man and woman one and provides for the growth of the Body of Christ by conferring the vocation of parenthood and guaranteeing the graces which enable parents to guide the youngest members of Christ.

Anointing of the Sick restores the sick member of Christ's Body to health, so that the person can re-join the other members in celebrating the Eucharist. If it is the sick person's time to die, this sacrament serves as preparation for entrance into the ranks of the Church Triumphant in heaven. Two other sacraments are at our disposal at all times to provide for our everyday spiritual needs; the sacrament of Penance to give us pardon for sin and strength to resist temptation, and the sacrament of the Eucharist to nourish our souls and give us an increase of the power to love God and our neighbor.

11. What other effects do the sacraments have?

Three of the sacraments, Baptism, Confirmation and Holy Orders, give to the soul a mark which can never be lost. This mark or character is a badge of our membership in Christ, a participation in his eternal priesthood, by which we are dedicated to sacred worship. These sacraments may be received only once.

Practical Points

1. In order to receive Confirmation, Holy Eucharist, Anointing of the Sick, Holy Orders and Marriage lawfully, we must be in possession of the divine life, or be in the state of sanctifying grace. If we are in the state of serious sin we should receive the sacrament of Penance first. One who knowingly receives any of these sacraments in mortal sin would thereby commit a very serious sin of sacrilege.

2. The more faith and love we have when we receive the sacraments the more grace they will confer on us. It is true that the sacraments worthily received always give grace, even if they are received without due preparation. But it is also true that the

better prepared we are to receive them the more fruitful will be our reception.

3. Whenever possible the entire family should participate in the preparation for reception of the sacraments, especially Baptism, first Penance, first Holy Communion, and Confirmation. When each member of the family shares in the preparation for these sacraments family love and stability are strengthened.

† † †

section 26 Baptism

Are you not aware that we who were baptized into Christ Jesus were baptized into his death? Through baptism into his death we were buried with him, so that, just as Christ was raised from the dead by the glory of the Father, we too might live a new life. If we have been united with him through likeness to his death, so shall we be through a like resurrection. This we know; our old self was crucified with him so that the sinful body might be destroyed and we might be slaves to sin no longer—ROM. 6:3–6.

IN THE early days of the Church, people were baptized by immersion. When they entered the pool, stripped of their clothes, and were submerged in its waters, they understood that they were dying to their former sinful selves and were being buried in the waters to rise as Christ did to a new life. When they left the water they put on white garments to show that they were alive with the new life of Christ.

This practice symbolized most strikingly what our Lord does for us in Baptism. Through the waters of Baptism he washes away sin and gives us a new life in God. By Baptism Christ unites us to himself and gives us the grace he merited by his life, death and resurrection.

1. What is Baptism?

Baptism is the sacrament of rebirth through which Jesus Christ gives us the divine life of sanctifying grace and joins us to his mystical body.

2. What did Christ say about the necessity for Baptism?

Speaking to Nicodemus, who came to him by night to inquire about his teaching, Our Lord told of the necessity for Baptism in these words:

> *"I solemnly assure you, no one can see the reign of God unless he is begotten from above." "How can a man be born again once he is old?" retorted Nicodemus. "Can he return to his mother's womb and be born over again?" Jesus replied, "I solemnly assure you, no one can enter into God's kingdom without being begotten of water and Spirit. Flesh begets flesh. Spirit begets spirit"*—JOHN 3:3–6.

3. When did Jesus Christ institute Baptism?

Jesus Christ instituted Baptism after the resurrection when he sent his apostles into the world to bring to all people the "good news" of the redemption, telling them:

> *"Full authority has been given to me both in heaven and on earth; go, therefore, and make disciples of all the nations. Baptize them in the name 'of the Father, and the Son, and of the Holy Spirit.' Teach them to carry out everything I have commanded you. And know that I am with you always, until the end of the world!"*—MATT. 28:18–20.

4. What does Jesus Christ accomplish in us through Baptism?

a. Jesus removes our sins.

> *. . . sin will no longer have power over you; you are now under grace, not under the law*—ROM. 6:14.

The grace received at Baptism remedies the "graceless" condition of the soul called original sin.

For those old enough to have sinned Jesus also takes away their personal sins and the punishment due to them when the recipient is properly disposed.

b. Jesus gives us a new life, the divine life, and makes us adopted children of God. He welcomes us into a life of intimacy with the Persons of the Blessed Trinity, Father, Son and Holy Spirit.

> *See what love the Father has bestowed on us in letting us be called children of God! Yet that is what we are*–1 JOHN 3:1.

Along with the divine life Christ also gives us powers which enable us to act as children of God and grow in the divine life. Among these powers are faith, hope and charity.

c. Christ unites us to himself and to the members of his Mystical Body.

> *There is but one body and one Spirit, just as there is but one hope given all of you by your call. There is one Lord, one faith, one baptism; one God and Father of all, who is over all, and works through all, and is in all*–EPH. 4:4–6.

After Baptism we can no longer pray or suffer alone. When we pray we pray to a common Father in heaven, and our prayers are heard because of our union with Christ. Our sufferings have value for the entire Church. St. Paul says, "Even now I find joy in the suffering I endure for you. In my own flesh I fill up what is lacking in the sufferings of Christ for the sake of his body, the Church"–COL. 1:24.

d. The Holy Spirit joins Himself to us in a close relationship.

> *Are you not aware that you are the temple of God and that the Spirit of God dwells in you? If anyone destroys God's temple, God will destroy him. For the temple of God is holy, and you are that Temple*–1 COR. 3:16–17.

161

e. Christ gives us a share in his priesthood through the baptismal character. It is by means of this sharing in Christ's priesthood that we participate in the Mass, unite our prayers and sacrifice with those of Christ, and obtain the right to receive the other sacraments.

5. Is Baptism the only way of receiving the divine life of sanctifying grace for the first time?

Baptism is the normal way of receiving sanctifying grace. But the mercy and love of Jesus is so great that he gives the divine life in an extraordinary manner whenever a person, through no fault of his own, cannot receive Baptism.

a. One who has sorrow for his sins out of love of God and sincerely desires Baptism, receives the divine life of sanctifying grace by virtue of his desire.

b. One who does not know of the necessity of Baptism but who has such sorrow and desires to do the will of God receives the sanctifying grace by virtue of his implicit desire for Baptism.

c. An unbaptized person who gives his life for his belief in God is baptized, as it were, in his own blood, thereby receiving the divine life of sanctifying grace.

6. What actual graces does Jesus give in Baptism?

The actual graces given at baptism assist the new Christian to develop the new life in Christ.

But more than that, a Christian is expected to rise above a mere observance of the moral law. He or she is expected to imitate Jesus and become holy. In every way possible the total personality must resemble Jesus. St. Paul describes this new personality as follows:

> *See to it, then, that you put an end to lying: let everyone speak the truth to his neighbor, for we are members of one another. If you are angry, let it be without sin. The sun must not go down on your wrath; do not give the devil a chance to work on you. The man who has been stealing*

must steal no longer; rather let him work with his hands at honest labor so that he will have something to share with those in need. Never let evil talk pass your lips; say only the good things men need to hear, things that will really help them. Do nothing to sadden the Holy Spirit with whom you were sealed against the day of redemption. Get rid of all bitterness, all passion and anger, harsh words, slander, and malice of every kind. In place of these, be kind to one another, compassionate, and mutually forgiving, just as God has forgiven you in Christ—EPH. 4:25—32.

Thus the actual graces of Baptism are:

a. The grace to call God our Father and to rely on that relationship.

b. The graces needed throughout our earthly lives to acquire the various virtues which enable us to fulfill our commitment to live the Christian life.

c. The grace to resist temptation which invites us to sin.

These graces are always available whenever needed by the baptized.

7. What is the sign used in Baptism?

The sign used in Baptism is washing with water and the saying of the words:

I baptize you in the name of the Father, and of the Son, and of the Holy Spirit.

Water is a most appropriate symbol of the effects of Baptism.

a. Water is used for cleansing. The flowing waters of Baptism symbolize the cleansing of the soul of sin.

b. Water is also life-giving. Irrigation makes a desert bloom. In the book of Genesis water is described as one of the elements from which the life of the world came.

In the beginning, when God created the heavens and the earth, the earth was a formless wasteland, and darkness covered the abyss, while a mighty wind swept over the waters—GEN. 1:1—2.

163

8. Who administers the sacrament of Baptism?

Baptism normally is administered by a priest or deacon. In case of necessity, however, anyone can baptize, even an unbeliever, provided he performs the actions, says the proper words and has the intention of doing what Christ intends.

9. What are the baptismal promises?

The priest asks the person about to be baptized to reject Satan, and to renounce the works of sin.

On the positive side, the candidate is asked three basic questions about the faith so as to profess his acceptance and belief.

Every year, during the Easter solemnities, we are invited to renew our baptismal promises.

10. What happens to unbaptized infants?

Neither the Bible nor tradition gives a solution to this question. We have to leave this to the mercy and justice of God.

The salvation of one who does not have the use of reason depends upon the efforts of others. Therefore, parents have a serious obligation to see that their children are baptized soon after birth, within a month.

11. Why does it sometimes happen that a person who had been baptized a Protestant is baptized again when he becomes a Catholic?

Whenever a Christian desires to become a member of the Catholic Church and enter into full communion with it he would not be baptized again if proof of valid Baptism in another Christian church can be produced. If there is doubt about the validity or of the existence of such a baptism a priest would privately, conditionally baptize that person. If such a person has been truly baptized he makes a Profession of Faith in the Catholic Church and is thus received into the Church.

12. When can an adult be baptized?

An adult may be baptized when he/she has finished a course of basic instructions. The ideal day would be Holy Saturday evening at the Easter Vigil Mass. The season of Lent is one of training for new members of the Pilgrim People of God. It is also a time when the full fledged members go through a period of "re-training" by penance and study of the selected scriptural readings so they can "renew" their baptismal vows and commitments with the rest of the People of God on Easter, the greatest feast day of the Church year.

13. What is the purpose of sponsors at Baptism?

Parents have the first responsibility to train the newly baptized child in the practice of the faith, to bring him up to keep God's Commandments as Jesus taught. In the ritual the priest asks the sponsors, "Are you ready to help the parents of this child in their duty as Christian parents?"

Practical Points

1. Everyone should be given a saint's name at Baptism. The saint, then, is the special protector and model for the person to imitate.

2. One godparent or sponsor is required, but two are allowed. Godparents must be baptized, practicing Catholics who are at least fourteen years of age. One non-Catholic "Christian witness" may be admitted along with the regular sponsor.

3. A dying infant may be baptized by anyone who pours natural water over the child's head and says, "I baptize you in the name of the Father, and of the Son, and of the Holy Spirit." A dying adult should express some desire to be baptized and should believe at least that there is one God in three Persons, who rewards the good and punishes the evil, and that Christ is the Son of God.

4. Baptized adults, who by profession of faith are entering into full communion with the Church will have to receive the sacrament of Penance before they can receive Holy Communion.

Practice

▲ If you are preparing for Baptism it is time to select a patron saint, either the one whose name you already bear or one of your own choosing. Perhaps you can find out something about the life of your patron saint.

† † †

section **27** **Confirmation**

When the day of Pentecost came it found them gathered in one place. Suddenly from up in the sky there came a noise like a strong, driving wind which was heard all through the house where they were seated. Tongues as of fire appeared, which parted and came to rest on each of them. All were filled with the Holy Spirit. They began to express themselves in foreign tongues and make bold proclamations as the Spirit prompted them. Staying in Jerusalem at the time were devout Jews of every nation under heaven. These heard the sound, and assembled in a large crowd. They were much confused because each one heard these men speaking his own language. The whole occurrence astonished them. They asked in utter amazement, "Are not all of these men who are speaking Galileans? How is it that each of us hears them in his native tongue? We are Parthians, Medes and Elamites. We live in Mesopotamia, Judea and Cappadocia, Pontus, the province of Asia, Phrygia and Pamphylia, Egypt and the regions of Libya around Cyrene. There are even visitors from Rome—all Jews, or those who have come over to Judaism; Cretans and Arabs too. Yet each of us hears them speaking in his own tongue about the marvels God has accomplished"–ACTS 2:1–11.

THE MARK of maturity is responsibility. All the actions of a new-born child center about himself. Not for years does he begin to do things for others. Gradually, however, he assumes more and more responsibility as he becomes more mature. A similar growth from childhood to maturity takes place in the supernatural life. Here, however, the growth is not gradual; it comes about instantaneously through the sacrament of Confirmation.

The Church was born from the pierced side of Christ on Good Friday; but it was not until the Holy Spirit descended upon her on Pentecost that she manifested herself to the world and assumed the responsibility of bearing witness to Jesus. Somewhat the same thing happens in the life of a Christian. Those born into a new life at Baptism reach supernatural maturity and assume full responsibilities to bear witness to Christ when the Holy Spirit comes in a special way in Confirmation. A person is a full member of the Church once he has received the sacraments of Baptism, Confirmation and Holy Eucharist.

1. What is the sacrament of Confirmation?

Confirmation is the sacrament through which Jesus confers on us the Holy Spirit, making us full-fledged and responsible members of the Mystical Body. We also receive the graces of the Holy Spirit especially those which enable us to profess, explain and spread the faith.

2. When was the sacrament of Confirmation given to the Church?

The Scriptures do not give us the scene of the actual institution. But Christ's institution of the sacrament of Confirmation is revealed in Scripture by the fact that he promised to send, and actually did send the Holy Spirit to strengthen the apostles, and by the fact that the apostles did administer this sacrament soon after the Resurrection.

> *Philip, for example, went down to the town of Samaria and there proclaimed the Messiah. . . . When the apostles in Jerusalem heard that Samaria had accepted the word of God they sent Peter and John to them. The two went down*

to these people and prayed that they might receive the Holy Spirit. It had not as yet come down upon any of them since they had only been baptized in the name of the Lord Jesus. The pair upon arriving imposed hands on them and they received the Holy Spirit—ACTS 8:5, 14–17.

3. What does Jesus Christ accomplish in us through the sacrament of Confirmation?

Jesus gives us:

a. an increase of the divine life.

b. a new and deeper relationship with the Holy Spirit.

c. the sacramental mark or character of Confirmation.

d. an increase of the strength to profess, defend and spread the faith.

4. What is the sign of the sacrament of Confirmation?

The sign of the sacrament of Confirmation is the imposition of hands and anointing with chrism. The bishop says, "Be sealed with the gift of the Holy Spirit."

The imposition of hands signifies the conferring of full and perfect adulthood. This is an ancient ceremony, which signifies the giving of a special power.

Chrism, the oil used in Confirmation, is a mixture of olive oil or a vegetable oil and a perfume called balm, consecrated by the bishop at the Holy Week Chrism Mass.

5. What is the effect of the distinctive character given in Confirmation?

The character is a spiritual power, a sharing in the priesthood of Christ. The baptismal character admits us to the Church and enables us to receive the sacraments and participate in the Mass. The character given in Confirmation consecrates a Christian for the defense of the faith and the winning of others to Christ.

6. What is the role of the Holy Spirit in Confirmation?

Our new relationship with the Holy Spirit is similar to that of the apostles after the first Pentecost. On that day they were enlightened so as to better understand the mysteries of God. They were also strengthened to be able to bear witness to Jesus.

At our Confirmation this same Holy Spirit comes with the special sacramental graces to enlighten our minds and strengthen our wills so we will be able to live up to our Christian commitments.

7. What are the powers which enable us to profess, defend and spread the faith?

These powers are the gifts of the Holy Spirit and the actual graces of the sacrament of Confirmation. These actual graces enable us to meet the challenges to our faith and to take advantage of the possibilities of spreading the faith in our every-day life.

> *When they bring you before synagogues, rulers and authorities, do not worry about how to defend yourselves or what to say. The Holy Spirit will teach you at that moment all that should be said*—LUKE 12:11—12.

8. How do the gifts of the Holy Spirit help us?

The gifts render us docile to the inspirations of the Holy Spirit. In Baptism we receive these gifts in embryo. At Confirmation they become more fully developed. The seven gifts are wisdom, understanding, right judgment, courage, knowledge, love and the spirit of reverence in God's service.

9. Why must a confirmed person be concerned with world problems and Social Justice?

In the Gospels Jesus teaches his followers that they must not only show concern for everyone, but each Christian must actively, as well as possible, work to resolve the problems of Social Justice. In the parable of the Last Judgment Jesus promises eternal life to those who feed the hungry, give drink to the thirsty, etc. This is a duty, not an optional activity. Those choosing to ignore and neglecting to perform these basic duties in behalf of others were cast into eternal punishment—cf. MATT. 25:31—46.

Responding to the question, "Who is my neighbor?" Jesus told the parable of the Good Samaritan. Here Jesus taught us the duty to assist anyone in need—cf. LUKE 10:25—27.

In another parable, Jesus relates the story of a rich man and a beggar named Lazarus. The rich man did not abuse or directly harm Lazarus. However, he was guilty of neglecting to provide care for the basic needs of a suffering person. The rich man too entered into eternal punishment for failure at least to attempt to alleviate human misery and suffering—cf. LUKE 16:19—31.

From these teachings of Jesus it is easy to see the duty of Christians to be concerned with the problems facing any and all of the members of the human family. A confirmed Christian can not limit his area of concern and assistance just to relatives and those of his immediate circle of acquaintances. At first glance it might seem to be impossible for individuals to do much about the social problems of far distant peoples. This is not true. Moreover, many of the problems, especially of poverty and starvation, are very real to people some of them living in our own country. The popes of recent years have issued a series of Encyclical Letters giving us Christian guidelines on how to attempt to resolve the basic injustices which are daily occurrences to many suffering people. The problems of Social Justice are many and varied. They include world hunger, peace, distribution of wealth, exchange of goods between nations, education, job opportunities, urbanization, etc., just to name a few. Obviously, these problems are broad and complex and it is impossible to explain them adequately here. Your instructor can guide you to a deeper study of the teaching of the Church on Social Justice.

Jesus came to save all people. He loves all people. As long as any one person is a victim of any form of injustice each Christian must cooperate to find ways to alleviate the problem.

10. How does a Christian profess and spread his faith?

A Christian professes and spreads his faith by:

a. praying for all people.

First of all, I urge that petitions, prayers, intercessions and thanksgivings be offered for all men—1 TIM. 2:1.

b. professing belief in Christ

Whoever acknowledges me before men I will acknowledge before my Father in heaven. Whoever disowns me before men I will disown before my Father in heaven—MATT. 10:32–33.

c. giving good example,

You are the light of the world. A city set on a hill cannot be hidden. Men do not light a lamp and then put it under a bushel basket. They set it on a stand where it gives light to all in the house. In the same way, your light must shine before men so that they may see goodness in your acts and give praise to your heavenly Father—MATT. 5:14–16.

d. doing the works of mercy,

Then the just will ask him: "Lord, when did we see you hungry and feed you or see you thirsty and give you drink? When did we welcome you away from home or clothe you in your nakedness? When did we visit you when you were ill or in prison?" The king will answer them: "I assure you, as often as you did it for one of my least brothers, you did it for me"—MATT. 25:37–40.

e. aiding the foreign missions by prayers, alms, the encouragement of vocations to the missions, and by actually taking part in the work of the missions,

f. participating in the apostolate of suffering,

Our hope for you is firm because we know that just as you share in the sufferings, so you will share in the consolation—2 COR. 1:7.

g. taking part in the work of the Church, which is to sanctify the members, and through them to teach and sanctify the world. Once confirmed we have an obligation to strive to live

more perfectly the commandments, the virtues and characteristics of a good Christian as described throughout the pages of
Sacred Scripture.

> *But how shall they call on him in whom they have not
> believed? And how can they believe unless they have
> heard of him? And how can they hear unless there is
> someone to preach? And how can men preach unless
> they are sent? Scripture says, "How beautiful are the
> feet of those who announce good news!"* –ROM.
> 10:14–15.

11.. How do the special actual graces of Confirmation affect our lives?

The actual graces of this sacrament are:

a. the grace of enlightenment so we can understand the
teaching of Jesus as given to us through his Church.

b. the grace of strength to do what the Holy Spirit tells us
to do. For example, to worship God on the Lord's day, to respect life, to do penance for our sins, etc.

c. the grace to defend or explain the faith whenever anyone inquires about any part of it.

d. the grace to spread the faith or grace of good example
so we will always live and act in such a way that our religious
convictions are evident.

e. the grace to promote Social Justice throughout the
world.

These actual graces do not all come to us at one time only
on the day of Confirmation. They are given as needed throughout our lifetime. We should occasionally make a "renewal" of
our Confirmation so to strenthen our appreciation of our relationship with the Holy Spirit.

12. When may a person be confirmed?

An adult may be confirmed on the day he is received into
full communion with the Church. If he wishes, he can wait

172

until the bishop comes to his parish for the regular Confirmation class.

In the Latin rite children are confirmed by the bishop at about the age of 10, but this can vary by diocesan practice.

Practical Points

1. In ordinary cases it is the bishop who administers the sacrament of Confirmation. A pastor may do so if the bishop is not available when one of his parishioners who has never been confirmed is dying. The priest who receives a person into full Communion with the Church or baptizes him may confirm the person at that time.

2. When confirming the bishop may appoint some priests to assist him to confirm some of the members of the class along with the bishop.

3. A sponsor is required at Confirmation. The sponsor must be at least fourteen years of age, a practicing Catholic who has been confirmed. Your baptismal sponsor can also be your Confirmation sponsor.

4. An additional patron saint my be selected at the time of Confirmation or the baptismal patron alone may be used.

5. Every member of the Church is called to be apostolic. We have been called by Jesus through Baptism and now, strengthened by the Holy Spirit in Confirmation, share the responsibility of carrying the message of the Gospel to all peoples. In reality this means to our families, friends and co-workers. We must manifest the principles of Christian living by our activities. Employers must create a Christian atmosphere for the workers. Students must work diligently and honestly, hospital personnel manifest a Christian attitude toward all they meet in their daily work. The confirmed Christian who has teaching ability should become active in teaching Christian doctrine in religious education classes. These are just a few of the thousands of ways to be a contemporary apostle.

Prayer of the Holy Spirit

*Come, Holy Spirit, fill the hearts of your faithful and
enkindle in them the fire of your love.*

*Send forth your Spirit and they shall be created
And you shall renew the face of the earth*

*Let us pray. O God, who did instruct the hearts of the
faithful by the light of the Holy Spirit, grant us by the
same Spirit to have a right judgment in all things and
ever to rejoice in his consolation. We ask this through
Jesus Christ, Our Lord. Amen.*

† † †

section **28** The Eucharist

*During the meal Jesus took bread, blessed it, broke it, and
gave it to his disciples. "Take this and eat it," he said,
"this is my body." Then he took a cup, gave thanks,
and gave it to them. "All of you must drink from it," he
said, "for this is my blood, the blood of the covenant,
to be poured out in behalf of many for the forgiveness of
sins.*

*I tell you, I will not drink this fruit of the vine from
now until the day when I drink it new with you in my
Father's reign"–MATT. 26:26–28.*

THE LOVE OF GOD, our Father, knows no bounds. The
greatest expression of the love of God for us is the gift he has
given us, his own Son, Jesus Christ. "Yes, God so loved the
world that he gave his only Son, that whoever believes in him
may not die but may have eternal life"–JOHN 3:16.

The love of Jesus Christ for us, too, is a love without limit.

174

Christ proved that love by offering his life to his Father for our salvation. "There is no greater love than this: to lay down one's life for one's friends"—JOHN 15:13.

But Christ was not content even with offering himself once upon the cross. Such is his love for us that on the night before he died he gave us his greatest gift, himself in the Eucharist. By means of the Eucharist Christ continually re-offers himself to the Father through the ministry of his priests in the sacrifice of the Mass. By means of it, too, he comes to us to be the food of our souls and to unite us in Holy Communion. Finally, this greatest of gifts is Christ's continual and abiding presence among us in this, the most wonderful of all his sacraments.

"... Compare the Eucharist to a fountain; the other sacraments to rivulets. For the Holy Eucharist is truly and necessarily to be called the fountain of all graces containing as it does ... the fountain itself of celestial gifts and graces, and the author of the other sacraments, Christ our Lord ..."—Council of Trent.

1. What is the Holy Eucharist?

The Holy Eucharist is the sacrament and the sacrifice in which Jesus Christ under the appearances of bread and wine is contained, offered and received.

2. What is the sign of the sacrament of the Eucharist?

The sign of the Eucharist is wheat bread and pure grape wine over which the words: "This is my body" and "This is my blood," are said.

3. When did Christ institute the Eucharist?

Christ instituted the Eucharist at the Last Supper.

During the meal he took bread, blessed and broke it, and gave it to them. "Take this," he said, "this is my body." He likewise took a cup, gave thanks and passed it to them, and they all drank from it. He said to them: "This is my blood, the blood of the covenant to be poured out on behalf of many"—MARK 14:22–24.

175

4. How do we know that Christ is truly present in the Eucharist?

a. The words, "This is my body;" "this is my blood," were spoken in fulfillment of a promise Jesus had made that he would give his flesh to eat and his blood to drink. When he made this promise he said, ". . . so the man who feeds on me will have life because of me"—JOHN 6:57.

The people to whom Jesus spoke these words took them literally. Jesus, who could read their minds, did not correct them. Rather he let them go away in disbelief, and would have allowed even the apostles to leave unless they would accept his words literally—cf. JOHN 6:61—70.

b. St. Paul, speaking of the Holy Eucharist says:

". . .This cup is the new covenant in my blood. Do this, whenever you drink it, in remembrance of me." Every time, then, you eat this bread and drink this cup, you proclaim the death of the Lord until he comes!

This means that whoever eats the bread or drinks the cup of the Lord unworthily sins against the body and blood of the Lord. A man should examine himself first; only then should he eat of the bread and drink of the cup. He who eats and drinks without recognizing the body eats and drinks a judgment on himself.

That is why many among you are sick and infirm, and why so many are dying.

If we were to examine ourselves, we would not be falling under judgment in this way—1 COR. 11:25—31.

c. It has been the constant, infallible teaching of the Church that in the Eucharist the body and blood, soul and divinity of Jesus Christ are contained under the appearances of bread and wine.

5. To whom did Jesus give the power of changing bread and wine into his body and blood?

Jesus gave this power to the apostles at the Last Supper. He gives it to his priests in the sacrament of Holy Orders.

176

6. What happens when the priest pronounces the words, "This is my body; this is my blood,' over the bread and wine?

At these words the actual bread and wine cease to exist. In their place is the body and blood, soul and divinity of Jesus Christ.

7. Does anything remain of the bread and wine after the words of consecration have been spoken?

Only the appearances of bread and wine remain; that is, the looks, taste, smell, etc., remain, although the bread and wine themselves have been changed into Christ.

8. Are both the body and blood of Christ present under the appearances of bread alone?

Yes. It is the living Christ who is present in the Eucharist. Under the appearance of bread alone (and under the appearance of wine alone) both the body and blood of Christ are present.

Practice

▲ Our Lord is actually present in every Catholic church. We should not only pay him reverence each time we pass a church; we should stop in and visit him whenever we have the opportunity.

† † †

177

Then the Lord said to Moses, "I will now rain down bread from heaven for you. Each day the people are to go out and gather their daily portion. . . . On seeing it, the Israelites asked one another, "What is this?" for they did not know what it was. But Moses told them, "this is the bread which the Lord has given you to eat." . . . . Morning after morning they gathered it, till each had enough to eat–EX. 16:4–21.

Let me firmly assure you, he who believes has eternal life. I am the bread of life. Your ancestors ate manna in the desert, but they died. This is the bread that comes down from heaven for a man to eat and never die. I myself am the living bread come down from heaven. If anyone eats this bread he shall live forever; the bread I will give is my flesh, for the life of the world. At this the Jews quarreled among themselves, saying, "How can he give us his flesh to eat?" Thereupon Jesus said to them: "Let me solemnly assure you, if you do not eat the flesh of the Son of Man and drink his blood, you have no life in you. He who feeds on my flesh and drinks my blood has life eternal, and I will raise him up on the last day. For my flesh is real food and my blood real drink. The man who feeds on my flesh and drinks my blood remains in me, and I in him. Just as the Father who has life sent me and I have life because of the Father, so the man who feeds on me will have life because of me. This is the bread that came down from heaven. Unlike your ancestors who ate and died nonetheless, the man who feeds on this bread shall live forever." He said this in a synagogue instruction at Capernaum–JOHN 6:47–59.

HOW PRIVILEGED were the men and women who lived in

the Holy Land at the time of Christ They could see his face, hear his voice, and feel the touch of his hand as he blessed them. And yet we today enjoy an even greater intimacy with our Savior. We cannot see him with the eyes of the body. But ours is the far greater privilege of receiving his sacred body into our own, of eating his flesh and drinking his blood. The marvel by which this intimacy is achieved is the precious legacy which Christ gave to his Church the night before he died, his greatest gift, the most Holy Eucharist. By means of the sacrament of the Holy Eucharist we have his continual and abiding presence among us. Jesus once told the apostles, "I will not leave you orphans." True to his promise, he has indeed remained among us, actually and physically present in the Holy Eucharist.

What other nation is there so honored as the Christian people? Or what creature under heaven so beloved as a devout soul, to whom God cometh, that he may feed her with his glorious flesh? O unspeakable grace; O wonderful condescension! O infinite love, singularly bestowed on man— Thomas a Kempis, "The Imitation of Christ."

1. How did Jesus prepare the apostles for the gift of the Eucharist?

About a year before he died on an occasion after preaching to a crowd, Jesus fed a great number of people with only five barley loaves and a couple of dried fish—cf. JOHN 6:1—15.

During the same night the apostles began to sail across the sea. Suddenly Jesus was seen walking on the water. Then he got into the boat—cf. JOHN 6:15—24.

The next day the crowd found Jesus in Capernaum when he gave them the discourse on the bread of life quoted above. Jesus taught he would somehow, through bread, make himself the true food which alone satisfies the hungers of the human family.

2. What is meant by the expression, Holy Communion?

Holy Communion is the expression used when speaking about receiving the Holy Eucharist.

179

The expression is very appropriate. It sums up the most important effect of the Holy Eucharist, the strengthening of the union between Jesus and his members and of the union between the members themselves.

Is not the cup of blessing we bless a sharing in the blood of Christ? And is not the bread we break a sharing in the body of Christ?—1 COR. 10:16–17.

3. Why are bread and wine appropriate material for the Holy Eucharist?

Bread is the staple food in the diet of most people, and wine is the staple drink of a great part of mankind. Therefore, bread and wine are appropriate material for the Eucharist, which is the food of our soul.

Bread and wine, too, are wonderful symbols. The bread is made of many grains of wheat baked into one wafer; the wine is made up of many grapes, crushed into one draught of wine. This is symbolized by the union of all the faithful with each other in Christ.

4. When may we receive Holy Communion?

We may receive Holy Communion every day. The Church encourages everyone to do so. Since Holy Communion is the sacrificial meal, it is most fitting to receive it in the Mass.

5. How often may a person receive Holy Communion?

Ordinarily one would receive Holy Communion only once a day, with the following exceptions: even though we have already received Holy Communion we may do so a second time at masses of Baptisms, first Communions, Confirmations, weddings, funerals and ordinations, etc.

6. How does Jesus help us through Holy Communion?

Through Holy Communion Jesus gives us:

a. an increase in the divine life of sanctifying grace; and consequently a deeper union with God,

b. an increase of faith, hope and charity,

180

c. a closer union with himself, and with every member of the Pilgrim People of God,

d. a pledge of our resurrection and our future glory,

e. the forgiveness of our daily faults and the grace to overcome our inclination to sin,

f. the promise of actual graces to help us love God and others more.

7. How does Communion unite us with our neighbor?

Our Lord gave us Communion in the form of a banquet in which we all eat of the same food. Communion, therefore, both symbolizes and deepens our union with one another in the Mystical Body. It symbolizes our union, because eating and drinking together is a sign of love and friendship. It deepens that union, because it gives us an increase of the divine life and of the power to love one another.

I pray also for those who will believe in me through their word, that all may be one as you, Father, are in me and I in you; I pray that they may be (one) in us, that the world may believe that you sent me. I have given them the glory you gave me that they may be one, as we are one – JOHN 17:20–22.

8. What effect does Communion have upon our bodies?

Holy Communion lessens the difficulty we experience in bringing the impulses of the body under control. Frequent and daily Communion is the greatest means we can use to become chaste, temperate, patient, etc.

9. How is the Eucharist a pledge of our future glory?

Our Lord promised,

He who feeds on my flesh and drinks my blood has life eternal and I will raise him up on the last day – JOHN 6:54.

10. How does Communion remove our daily faults?

Our union with Christ in the Holy Eucharist is a union based on love. Because of this love Christ forgives us our venial sins; the love thus engendered in our hearts merits for us the forgiveness of all or part of the punishment due to sin.

St. Pius X in his decree on frequent Communion said,

The desire of Jesus Christ and of the Church that all Christians should daily approach the holy banquet is based chiefly on this, that Christians united to God through the sacrament should derive from there the strength to conquer concupiscence, and wash away light faults of daily occurrence, and should forestall more serious ones to which human frailty is exposed. . .

11. What is required in order to receive Communion?

To receive Holy Communion worthily a person must

a. have a good intention, i.e., the desire to love God more

b. be free from mortal sin.

12. How can we make our reception of Holy Communion more fruitful?

We can make our reception of Holy Communion more fruitful by a good preparation before and a good thanksgiving after receiving.

Preparation includes not only the desire to be united to Christ and an intelligent and active assistance at Mass, which is the immediate preparation for Holy Communion, but also an attempt to practice love of our neighbor in our daily lives and a desire for an increase of the gift of charity.

Thanksgiving includes not only some moments of private prayer after Communion, a practice which is highly recommended, but also an attempt to use the graces of the sacrament by practicing love of God and of our neighbor.

13. Is it necessary to go to confession before receiving Communion?

No. It is not necessary to go to confession before receiving

Communion unless we have committed a mortal sin. Many people who receive Communion daily or weekly go to confession frequently. If we have committed a mortal sin, however, even though we have made an act of perfect contrition, we must go to confession before Communion.

14. What kind of sin would it be to receive Communion in the state of mortal sin?

To receive Communion knowingly in the state of mortal sin would be a most serious sin of sacrilege.

15. Why do Catholics of the Latin rite usually receive Holy Communion under the appearance of bread alone?

The Catholics of the Latin rite usually receive Holy Communion under the appearance of bread alone because Jesus is present, body and blood, under the appearance of bread and wine. When we receive under the appearances of either alone we do receive both the body and blood of the Lord.

There are some special occasions when we do receive communion under both forms. For example:

a. newly baptized adults in the Mass which follows their baptism,

b. confirmed adults in the Mass of their Confirmation,

c. those who were previously baptized and are received into full communion with the Church,

d. the bride and groom in the nuptial Mass,

e. wedding anniversary Masses,

f. during special spiritual exercises such as retreats, etc.

16. How is the Eucharist Christ's abiding presence among us?

The Eucharist is reserved in the tabernacle of Catholic churches. Jesus is, therefore, actually present in our churches at all times. He is there just as truly as he is in heaven, except that here, under the appearances of bread, he can be seen only with the eyes of faith.

17. Why do we adore the Holy Eucharist?

We adore the Holy Eucharist because Jesus, present in the Eucharist is truly God. That is why we genuflect whenever we pass in front of the tabernacle. It is an act of adoration of God.

Practical Points

1. Every Catholic is invited to receive Communion each time he assists at Mass, although normally we receive it only once a day.

2. The goal of every Catholic should be to participate at Mass and receive Communion daily, or at least frequently during the week.

   > *Two classes of people should communicate often, the perfect because, being well prepared, they would be very wrong not to approach the fountainhead of perfection; and the imperfect, that they might acquire perfection; the strong that they might preserve their strength, the weak that they might become strong; the sick that they might find a cure; the healthy, that they might be preserved from sickness*–Introduction to a Devout Life, St. Francis de Sales.

3. Catholics are bound under penalty of mortal sin to receive Communion at least once a year during the Easter time, that is from the first Sunday of Lent until Trinity Sunday.

4. In addition to Holy Thursday we celebrate a great feast in honor of the blessed Sacrament on the Sunday after Trinity Sunday, the feast of Corpus Christi or the body and blood of the Lord.

Practice

▲ When, for some reason, we are unable to receive Holy Communion we should make a "spiritual communion" at the Communion part of the Mass; that is, we should tell our Lord that we regret our inability to receive him in the Blessed

Sacrament here and now, but desire to be united to him and to our neighbor in a deeper love.

If you are taking instructions and are as yet unable to receive Holy Communion, make such a spiritual communion every time you take part in Mass.

† † †

section **30** Penance

THE FIRST CHAPTERS of the Book of Genesis describe God creating everything. Hence all of creation, especially mankind, was good. But early in human history man committed the first sin. Mankind, not God, was responsible for moral evil in the world.

Throughout Old Testament history God frequently sent special messengers to call mankind back to lead a morally good life. The prophets dramatically preached the need for repentance and reconciliation. John the Baptist, the last of the prophets, proclaimed this theme, "Reform your lives. The reign of God is at hand"—MATT. 3:2.

In the fullness of time God the Father sent his only Son, Jesus, who said, "Reform your lives and believe in the gospel"—MARK 1:15.

Jesus calls every person to live a holy life. In the Sermon on the Mount he admonishes us, "You must be made perfect as your heavenly Father is perfect"—MATT. 5:48. Consequently a Christian will strive to build his life around three basic tenets,

a. to love God above all things with his whole heart,

b. to love his neighbor as himself,

c. to strive to follow God's call to perfection.

185

Jesus spent almost three years in public teaching. While he denounced sin he manifested great personal love for sinners. God desires not the death of the sinner, but that he be converted and saved—cf. EZ. 33:11. The following story illustrates how Jesus treated sinners.

The scribes and the Pharisees led a woman forward who had been caught in adultery. They made her stand there in front of everyone. "Teacher," they said to him, "this woman has been caught in the act of adultery. In the law, Moses ordered such a woman to be stoned. What do you have to say about the case?" (They were posing this question to trap him so that they could have something to accuse him of.) Jesus bent down and started tracing on the ground with his finger. When they persisted in their questioning, he straightened up and said to them, "Let the man among you who has no sin be the first to cast a stone at her." A second time he bent down and wrote on the ground. Then the audience drifted away one by one, beginning with the elders. This left him alone with the woman, who continued to stand there before him. Jesus finally straightened up and said to her, "Woman, where did they all disappear to? Has no one condemned you?" "No one, sir," she answered. Jesus said, "Nor do I condemn you. You may go. But from now on avoid this sin."—JOHN 8:3–11.

The story of the woman taken in adultery is only one of the many incidents in the Gospels which give us a glimpse of the love and tenderness of Jesus in his dealings with sinners. Often in the Gospel narrative we see Jesus looking deep into the heart of a man or woman, seeing the frightful condition of that soul after a lifetime of sin, and then applying his healing with the words, "Your sins are forgiven." Often the sinner approached our Lord in the hope of obtaining a cure of his bodily disease. But before healing the body Jesus healed the soul. Sometimes the sinner did not even ask for forgiveness. No matter; Jesus could see what was in the heart and mind, could see not only the sin but the sorrow for sin as well. And His unfailing response was, "Your sins are forgiven."

Hopefully, we will never be guilty of serious sins. But no

matter how great or small the offense against our heavenly Father and regardless of how often we have sinned, whenever we, truly sorry, approach God begging forgiveness God can and will forgive us all of our sins. As indicated above, Jesus, who is true man and true God, knows and thoroughly understands human nature. He not only calls for a conversion but he gives us the sacrament of Penance to make reconciliation possible. Confession should be a joyful experience. In it we hear God speaking through the priest saying, "I forgive you." In fact, God seems to be unable to resist a humble penitent pleading for mercy.

> *As Jesus said, "I tell you, there will likewise be more joy in heaven over one repentant sinner than over ninety-nine righteous people who have no need to repent"*–LUKE 15:7.

1. What is the sacrament of Penance?

Penance is the sacrament by which Jesus, through the absolution of the priest, forgives sins committed after Baptism.

2. When did Jesus institute the sacrament of Penance?

On Easter night when Jesus appeared to the apostles he said to them:

> *"Peace be with you," he said again, "As the Father has sent me, so I send you." Then he breathed on them and said: "Receive the Holy Spirit. If you forgive men's sins they are forgiven them; if you hold them bound, they are held bound"*–JOHN 20:21–23.

3. What is the sign of the sacrament of Penance?

The sinner's manifestation of sorrow by word or gesture, the sins confessed, the sinner's willingness to make satisfaction and the words of the priest. "I absolve you from your sins in the name of the Father, and of the Son, and of the Holy Spirit," constitute the sign of the sacrament of Penance.

4. How does Jesus help us in this sacrament?

First of all, we know God himself speaks through the priest

absolving us of our sins. In the sacrament of Penance God forgives mortal sin and restores the divine life of sanctifying grace in ever greater abundance.

God also forgives all venial sins which we confess with contrition, and gives us an increase of the divine life of grace.

God gives us a pledge of the actual graces needed to atone for past sins and to avoid sin in the future and the graces needed to live the Christian life.

God also removes the temporal punishment due for sins, all or part of it, depending on the depth of our sorrow for sin and the strength of our purpose of amendment.

5. What do the actual graces of this sacrament do for the sinner?

The special actual graces proper to this sacrament are:

a. the grace to appreciate the mercy of God, our forgiving Father.

b. the grace to do penance or atone for our sins.

c. the grace to avoid sin in the future.

An illustration will explain this third grace. Suppose a person has committed only one sin, that of stealing. He confesses and is absolved. God now promises special help whenever that person is tempted to steal again. Similar assistance would have been promised and available if he had been guilty of and confessed other sins.

6. Why did Jesus make confession a part of the sacrament of Penance?

Christ made confession a part of the sacrament of Penance because of his understanding of the needs of the human heart. He realized that the confession of sin helps the sinner. The priest in the confessional is father and counsellor to the sinner. In order to help the sinner amend his ways and grow in the love of God the priest needs to know the sins the person has committed and the person's attitudes and feelings.

7. How does confession help the sinner?

a. The urge to confess is natural to man. A sorrow or shame is lessened when shared with another.

b. Confession makes us conscious of our sinfulness. It forces us to think of our sins. We cannot bury them and forget about them. We have to face them time and time again. This has the effect of making us conscious of them and of helping us overcome them, and of helping us realize how weak we are and how merciful God is.

c. People need reassurance God has actually forgiven them. The sinner is not as apt to have this reassurance if he merely says in his heart, "I am sorry." When Jesus forgave sins he announced the fact, in order that the sinner would know that he was forgiven. In the parable of the Prodigal Son the younger son was sorry for sins. But he knew he had to go to his father and personally admit his guilt. Notice how the father blessed the repentant son for doing so—cf. LUKE 15:11—31.

d. When using the open confessional or "face to face" approach, the penitent can receive the sacrament in a more relaxed manner. This approach gives time for in-depth reflection and confession. It encourages a more thorough explanation of the current state of the sinner's relationship with God and neighbor. It invites a dialogue which will lead to a better understanding of the penitent's condition making it easier for the priest to advise and guide the penitent toward a more grace-filled life.

e. The sinner, now forgiven, is also reconciled to the Christian community.

8. Why must we confess our sins to a priest?

Sin offends both God and mankind and the sinner needs the forgiveness of both. Sometimes, because of the nature of our sin we should not or cannot approach the person offended. Nor are we obliged to testify publicly and specifically against ourselves. The priest, who is the representative of both God, our merciful Father, and of the Pilgrim People of God can and does speak for both whenever he absolves our sins and reconciles us to God and to the Church.

Jesus no longer walks the earth in his physical body. Nonetheless, he continues his work as healer of souls through the Church. He still pronounces those words which alone can bring peace and comfort. "Your sins are forgiven." Now he does so through Penance, the sacrament of divine mercy. In his great love for sinners our Lord has provided a means whereby his healing action can penetrate to every corner of the earth. On Easter Sunday Jesus gave the power to forgive sins to the Apostles. The Church in turn has passed this power on to the priests when they are ordained. True, the priest cannot read the mind and heart of the sinner as Jesus could. But after a confession of sins and the absolution of the priest the sinner of today can be just as assured as was the woman taken in adultery that the words of Jesus, "Nor do I condemn you" have been addressed to him.

9. If the main purpose of the sacrament of Penance is to forgive mortal sin, should we receive it when we have no mortal sins?

We should receive the sacrament of Penance frequently, even if we have no mortal sins. Pope Pius XII says in his Encyclical on the Mystical Body:

> *To hasten daily progress along the path of virtue, we wish the pious practice of frequent confession to be earnestly advocated. Not without the inspiration of the Holy Spirit was this practice introduced into the Church. By it genuine self-knowledge is increased, Christian humility grows, bad habits are corrected, spiritual neglect and tepidity are countered, the conscience is purified, the will strengthened, a salutary self control is attained, and grace is increased in virtue of the sacrament itself*–88.

10. How does the sacrament of Penance help us grow in the divine life?

The sacrament of Penance not only forgives sin; it also develops virtues which make us more Christ-like.

a. The virtue of penance is based on a sense of the holiness of God. The realization of the goodness of God must be the basis of all our sorrow. This realization should grow each time we say the act of contrition or go to confession.

b. Penance reminds us of the great love God has for us. Love must engender love; we should grow in the love of God and neighbor each time we receive the sacrament.

c. The sacrament of Penance increases our hope. We realize that even though we are sinners we can obtain from God the help we need to reach heaven.

11. What is necessary for a worthy reception of the sacrament of Penance?

a. examination of conscience,

b. sorrow for sin,

c. resolution to avoid sin in the future,

d. confession,

e. acceptance of the penance.

12. What is an examination of conscience?

An examination of conscience is a reasonable effort to recall the sins committed since our last confession. In examining our conscience, we must avoid two dangers: on the one hand, carelessness and lack of effort to recall our sins, on the other, anxiety and excessive soul searching, which would make the sacrament of Penance a burden.

A good examination of conscience will also be concerned with the performance of good works. A person should ask questions such as, "Do I try to help my neighbor in time of need?" "Do I ever speak kindly toward others?" A Christian must not only avoid sin, but must manifest his love of God and neighbor in a positive manner.

13. How do we make an examination of conscience?

First of all, we should pray to the Holy Spirit for light to know our sins and for the grace to be sorry for them. Then we should call to mind the commandments of God and of the Church and the obligations of our state in life. Then we should ask ourselves wherein we have failed to live up to them. If we go to confession frequently we can simply ask ourselves whether we have sinned in thought, word or deed against God, neighbor or self.

14. What is to be done if we find that we have no sins to confess, or if our confessions have become routine?

In the first case, we usually can discover sins and defects in ourselves if we examine our conscience more carefully on the subject of charity or one of the other virtues. The holiest people are always well aware of their shortcomings.

In the second case, we should select one or two faults for which we are truly sorry, instead of reciting a whole catalogue of "the usual venial sins," and make an effort to recall the number of times we have committed such faults.

In both cases it will help to seek the advice of our confessor.

15. What is contrition?

Contrition is sorrow for and detestation of our sins, together with the intention of not sinning in the future. Without this sorrow there can be no forgiveness or reconciliation. God himself cannot forgive a sin if we do not want to give it up.

16. What are the qualities of true contrition?

a. We must mean what we say. There must be a true resolve to reform our lives.

b. Our sorrow must be based on the love, or at least the fear of God. If we are sorry for our sins only because we are in disgrace, because we are disgusted with ourselves or for any other merely human reason, our sorrow is not true contrition.

c. We must hate sin more than any other evil. Our detestaion for sin does not have to be felt to be sincere. Contrition is a matter of the will, not of the feelings.

d. We must be sorry for all our mortal sins. It is not enough to be sorry for one and not another. When we sin mortally we separate ourselves from God. To be reunited with God, we must give up all our mortal sins.

17. Are there different kinds of contrition?

There are two kinds of contrition, perfect and imperfect. They are different by reason of their motives. In each case we are sorry for our sins because they are an offense against God. In imperfect contrition the motive is fear of the justice of God and of the punishment which our sins deserve. In perfect contrition the motive is the goodness of God, which prompts us to love him above all else for his own sake.

Perfect contrition removes all sins, even mortal sins. Imperfect contrition by itself will remove only venial sins. However, in the sacrament of Penance imperfect contrition suffices.

18. What is the procedure in going to confession?

There are two ways to go to confession. One way is to make a private preparation and to approach a priest for the sacrament. Another way is the communal celebration. Here, we meet with a number of our fellow Christians and after the reading of the Scriptures we make a general examination of conscience. Then we individually approach one of the priests to privately confess our sins and personally receive absolution immediately from him.

There are two types of confessionals. One is the traditional confessional whereby we are separated from the priest by a screen which makes identification difficult and preserves anonymity for those who desire it. The second way is to go "face to face." This method provides a more personal approach to the sacrament.

Begin with words like these: "Bless me, Father, for I have sinned. It has been ____weeks since my last confession. I am married, single, widowed, etc." Next, either you or the priest may read a short passage from Scripture. Then, tell your sins. When you have confessed all of them say, "I am sorry for these and all of the sins of my whole life." The priest might give some spiritual advice. Then he assigns a penance to perform. After the sinner has expressed sorrow by praying an act of contrition the priest gives the individual sinner absolution. Then say, "Thank you, Father," and leave the confessional area.

19. What is the purpose of reading Scripture when receiving the sacrament of Penance?

The purpose of the Scripture reading is to help the sinner call to mind the mercy of God and to arouse in the person a sincere desire to reform his/her life.

Some people select a passage for use in confession, but they also use it as a guide for examining their conscience day by day between receptions of this sacrament. For example, the beatitude "Blest are the peacemakers: they shall be called sons of God," —MATT. 5:9. Using this every day you might ask yourself, "Do I bring peace to my family by the way I treat them? Do I cause hard feelings and disappointment? etc."

In a communal celebration the Scripture lesson would be read by a lector for the benefit of the assembled congregation. In a private reception either the priest or the penitent selects a reading.

20. What sins must we confess in confession?

a. We must confess all our mortal sins:

- their number, as nearly as we can remember.
- their kind, e.g., "I stole $100" (it is not enough to say, I broke the 7th commandment).
- any circumstances which might change the nature of the sin, e.g., "My husband has a violent temper and I was afraid."

b. We are encouraged to confess also our venial sins. However, this is not necessary. The reception of any of the other sacraments, an act of imperfect contrition, or any virtuous act will also remove venial sins.

If we forget to mention a mortal sin, the sin is forgiven nevertheless. We need not remain away from communion, nor go back to confession immediately. In our next confession we should say, "In my last confession I forgot to mention _____ _____."

21. What is meant by a "bad confession"?

A "bad confession" is one in which the penitent deliberately conceals a mortal sin. This renders the confession invalid and sinful and all future confessions invalid and sinful until the sin is confessed.

22. What is meant by a "resolution not to sin again"?

By a resolution not to sin again is meant a sincere intention not to sin again. Even God will not forgive a sin unless the sinner intends not to commit it again. Unless a person is resolved not to repeat his offense he can hardly be said to be sorry for it. The resolution to avoid sin in the future, therefore, is necessary for the forgiveness of sin.

In the case of venial sin, unless we are sorry for those we confess, and intend not to commit them again, we would do better not to confess them, since they will not be forgiven. Only those venial sins which we intend to avoid in the future will be pardoned.

In the case of mortal sins, unless we are sorry for all our mortal sins and intend not to commit any kind of mortal sin in the future, none of our sins will be forgiven. In Lesson 36 the difference between mortal and venial sin will be explained.

It is important to remember, however, that all God demands in the way of a resolution for the future is that we intend to do our best. No one may safely say, "I am certain that I shall never commit this sin." All we can say is, "With God's help I shall do my best. I intend never to commit this sin again, and shall keep away from anything which would cause me to fall again."

23. What is the penance given by the priest?

Usually the penance is the saying of a few prayers, or performing some good work. The acceptance of the penance shows our willingness to make amends to God.

24. What is meant by "the punishment due to sin"?

The punishment for unrepented mortal sin is eternal separation from God, or hell.

Then he will say to those on his left: "Out of my sight, you condemned, into the everlasting fire prepared for the devil and his angels"–MATT. 25:41.

Venial sin does not deserve such a severe punishment. Yet one who sins venially should try to make amends for his sins.

25. How can we make amendment for our sins?

Besides the sacramental penance given by the priest another means we have is the *virtue* of penance. This virtue, or good habit, becomes visible when a person undergoes a "metanoia," or conversion. Every Christian is called to live a life of higher moral standards. Jesus calls us to be the light of the world. If the Christian finds he has failed and sinned he needs a conversion or i.e., turning back to God. To do this the sinner should receive the sacrament of Penance. But he should also live this reconciliation by performing acts of virtue such as additional and more fervent prayer, fasting, almsgiving and other charitable activities. In doing this he forces himself to look into his own life and find ways to concentrate his efforts to remain faithful to the baptismal commitments. In a sense, he attempts to make up for the damage his personal sins have caused to his neighbor, and to show God that he is trying to reform his life.

Practical Points

1. We *should* go to confession frequently.

2. We *must* receive the sacrament of Penance when we are guilty of serious sin because we must become reconciled to God before we may approach the sacrament of the Holy Eucharist.

3. It is not necessary to go to confession each time we receive Communion unless we have committed mortal sin.

4. We are bound under pain of mortal sin to go to confession at least once a year, but only if we are guilty of serious sin.

5. If possible, we should have a regular confessor.

Practice

▲ You should not wait until the time of your first confession to begin the practice of examining your conscience. It is highly recommended that everyone make an examination of conscience every day. Just before retiring at night is a good time to do so. An effort to recall the sins committed during the day, followed by an act of contrition for these as well as all past sins will help a person to advance spiritually.

† † †

section **31** The Sacrament of the Sick

Is there anyone sick among you? He should ask for the presbyters of the church. They in turn are to pray over him, anointing him with oil in the Name (of the Lord). This prayer uttered in faith will reclaim the one who is ill, and the Lord will restore him to health. If he has committed any sins, forgiveness will be his. Hence, declare your sins to one another, and pray for one another, that you may find healing–JAMES 5:14–15.

ON ALMOST EVERY PAGE OF THE Gospels we read of Jesus curing or healing someone from almost every type of disease and physical ailment. Jesus had a deep sympathy and compassion for the sick. He was able to restore health to those with whom he came into contact.

The Church, the new Body of Jesus Christ, shares the same concern for those suffering from all forms of ailments, whether physical, mental, or emotional. Thus it is fitting for the Church to have a special sacrament for its members who are suffering from a serious illness.

This sacrament is not just for those who are so sick they have only a few minutes to live. But it is for the seriously ill. Jesus loved those people. The Church likewise loves today's seriously ill people.

Throughout history the Church encouraged many of its members to establish hospitals and various institutions for the care of the sick, the diseased, and the dying. Many members have joined religious communities of priests, brothers, or sisters, whose mission was to minister to the sick.

Any serious illness can be a frightening experience. People with such illnesses need the consolation and satisfaction of Jesus coming with and through the Church to reassure and comfort them. Whenever the Church brings this Sacrament of the Sick the sick person knows that God and the People of God share his concern.

1. What is the Sacrament of the Sick?

The Sacrament of the Sick is the sacrament in which Jesus, through the anointing and prayers of the priest, gives health and strength to the person who is now seriously ill.

2. What does Jesus accomplish through the Sacrament of the Sick?

Through the Sacrament of the Sick, Jesus:

a. increases the divine life in the ill person,

b. sometimes restores health to the person,

c. gives the actual graces needed to accept the illness,

d. forgives sin and removes the temporal punishment due to sin. When confession is impossible, he forgives even mortal sin through this sacrament.

3. **What are the actual graces of this sacrament?**

The actual graces of this sacrament are:

a. the grace to be resigned to the illness;

b. the grace to be able to bear the illness with the proper disposition;

c. the grace to hope for eternal happiness in heaven.

4. **What is the sign of this sacrament?**

The sign of this sacrament is the anointing with a special oil, called the oil of the sick, together with the words of the priest, "Through this holy anointing may the Lord in his love and mercy help you with the grace of the Holy Spirit. May the Lord who frees you from sin save you and raise you up." While praying the priest anoints the sick person on the forehead and the palms.

5. **How is the Sacrament of the Sick administered?**

This sacrament may be administered to individuals or to groups. While the structure of the ritual is the same there is a certain added dimension to the communal celebration of the Sacrament of the Sick. In the communal ceremony a group of sick or elderly people gather with their friends and family to receive the anointing in common. Since the sick and elderly should be a special concern to all of the members of the Church it is fitting to show this concern publicly. The ill are encouraged and strengthened by the presence of the People of God. They find motivation to unite their sufferings to those of Jesus. Those attending can begin to see the Christian value of pain and illness.

The ceremony begins with the priest calling to prayer those assembled. They begin with an admission of guilt of sin and pray for forgiveness. A short service of the Word of God follows. The priest reads passages revealing the healing activity of Jesus. Then he invites those who are witnessing the sacrament to join him in prayer in behalf of the sick.

The priest then silently lays his hand on the sick person. This is an invocation to Jesus to come and cure the illness.

If the oil of the sick was not previously blessed by the bishop the priest now blesses it. The actual anointing follows.

Those attending the anointing conclude the ceremony by praying together the Lord's Prayer.

6. Who may receive this sacrament?

Anyone who is seriously ill due to sickness or old age may receive this sacrament. A prudent judgement is all that is necessary to determine whether the sickness is serious enough to warrant the sacrament. The sick person need not be in danger of death. An old person who is in a weakened condition may be anointed although no serious illness is present. A person undergoing surgery because of a dangerous illness may be anointed. Sick children who have sufficient use of reason to be comforted by this sacrament may be anointed.

7. Is this sacrament given to the dying?

While the primary purpose of this sacrament is to restore health it can be given to the dying. Not every seriously sick person dies. Some illnesses, such as terminal cancer, can last for several months. It would be wrong to deny such a person the consolation of this sacrament and its actual graces. Many of those once regarded as dying are very much alive.

In addition to this sacrament the Church has the last rites for the dying. These include holy Viaticum (Communion), the prayers for the dying and the Apostolic Blessing.

Practical Points

1. Those who have the care of a sick person should call the priest as soon as they discover the illness is serious. The person, fortified by the actual graces of this sacrament can then honestly face life or death, whichever God in his providence has designated.

2. For a sick call provide the following items for the priest: a crucifix, the two blessed candles, a glass of water, and a

200

spoon. These articles should be on a table which is covered with a white linen cloth.

3. When the priest comes to the house on a sick call, the members of the family should remain in the sick room, except while the priest is hearing the confession. If the priest is bringing the Blessed Sacrament, he should be met at the door with a lighted blessed candle and led to the sick room.

4. Catholics should be careful to let the parish priest know whenever there is any serious illness in the family. The priest can judge what ought to be done. In the case of a prolonged illness the priest will bring Communion even when there is no danger of death.

5. If someone is injured seriously, the priest should be called immediately.

6. The priest should be called even though to all appearances death might have taken place. The prayers for the dying are a consolation to the family and friends.

† † †

section **32**   Holy Orders

Every high priest is taken from among men and made their representative before God, to offer gifts and sacrifices for sins. He is able to deal patiently with erring sinners, for he himself is beset by weakness and so must make sin offerings for himself as well as for the people. One does not take this honor on his own initiative, but only when called by God as Aaron was. Even Christ did not glorify himself with the office of high priest; he received it from the One who said to him, "You are my son; today I have begotten you"–HEB. 5:1–5.

JESUS CHRIST, mediator between God and man, is the eternal priest. In the crowning act of his priesthood he offered himself to the Father on the cross for our sake. But Christ was priest not only on the cross; in his very being he is *the* priest, and his priesthood is an eternal one: ". . . but Jesus, because he remains forever, has a priesthood which does not pass away. Therefore he is always able to save those who approach God through him, since he forever lives to make intercession for them"—HEB. 7:24—25.

But Jesus is not content to live his priesthood only in heaven. He desires to live on and exercise that priesthood here on earth until the end of time. Jesus, the merciful priest who forgave sinners, the gentle priest who blessed the people, the zealous priest who sought out the lost sheep, the loving priest who offered himself and fed his disciples with his own flesh, and blood, still lives and continues his priestly work in the world. He does so by means of the sacrament of Holy Orders, through which he shares his priesthood with man. Through this sacrament Jesus gives to human beings the staggering power of changing bread and wine into his body and blood, the power of forgiving sins, the awesome powers of his priesthood.

Some people are shocked at the idea that a priest should claim to possess such powers. "How," they ask, "can an ordinary man forgive sin?" The answer is that a priest is not an ordinary man. He is a man who has been made "another Christ" through the sacrament of Holy Orders. It is Jesus who has performed this wonder. It is Jesus who will have it so. He desires to work through men. He desires to forgive sinners, to teach and preach, to give the divine life, to renew his sacrifice on the cross through human beings, those whom he consecrates and empowers as his priests through this great sacrament.

The reason a priest has these powers is so the members of the Pilgrim People of God who need these special services will have someone designated to care for their needs. A priest is ordained not for himself, but to provide spiritual services for the members of the Church. A priest is a bridge builder. He brings God to the people and the people to God.

The priest is like "another Christ" because he is marked with an indelible character, making him, as it were, a living image of our Saviour. The priest represents Christ who said, "As the Father has sent me, I also send you; he who hears you hears me." Admitted to this most sublime ministry by a call from heaven, he is appointed for men in the things pertaining to God, that he may offer gifts and sacrifices for sins. To him must come anyone who wishes to live the life of the divine Redeemer and who desires to receive strength, comfort and nourishment for his soul; from him the salutary medicine must be sought by anyone who wishes to rise from sin and lead a good life. Hence all priests may apply to themselves with full right the words of the Apostle of Gentiles: "We are God's helpers"—Enc. on the Development of Holiness of Priestly Life 7.

1. What is the sacrament of Holy Orders?

Holy Orders is the sacrament through which Christ gives the power and the grace to perform the sacred duties of bishops, priests and deacons of the Church.

2. When did our Lord institute Holy Orders?

After changing bread and wine into his body and blood, Jesus told his apostles, "Do this in commemoration of me." With these words he conferred the priesthood on the apostles.

3. What is the sign of the sacrament of Holy Orders?

The sign of this sacrament is the laying on of the hands by the bishop.

When the apostles ordained deacons, priests or bishops they did so by the laying on of hands.

. . . for this reason, I remind you to stir into flame the gift of God bestowed when my hands were laid on you— 2 TIM. 1:6.

4. What does Jesus accomplish through the sacrament of Holy Orders?

Through the sacrament of Holy Orders our Lord:

a. increases the divine life of the one who is ordained,

b. gives a new character to the soul,

c. gives the right to all the actual graces needed to fulfill the sacred office.

d. gives special duties and obligations to the ordained,

e. gives the powers of the priesthood to fulfill those obligations.

5. Who administers Holy Orders?

The bishop administers Holy Orders.

6. What are the degrees in Holy Orders?

The orders of deacon, priest, and bishop comprise the sacrament of Holy Orders.

A bishop has the fullness of the priesthood and ecclesiastical jurisdiction over a diocese.

A priest has the power to offer Mass and administer the sacraments.

A deacon may assist a priest or bishop at Mass, preach, distribute Holy Communion and baptize.

7. How is Holy Orders a social sacrament?

Holy Orders is given to a man primarily for the benefit of others. The five sacraments we have studied are for the salvation and personal growth in holiness of the individual. The other two, Marriage and Holy Orders, provide for the life of the community, the Church.

8. What are the actual graces of this sacrament?

The ordained priest throughout the years of priestly ministry receives these actual graces to assist in the priestly work:

a. the grace to preach,

b. the grace to lead the Christian community in worship,

c. the grace to heal the wounds of sin through the sacrament of Penance, *d.* the grace to be a servant to the Pilgrim People of God,

e. the grace to direct the spiritual advancement of a person.

9. What is the work of a bishop?

Bishops, as a group, replace the twelve apostles. They have the fullness of the priesthood. Their main work is to govern their diocese and to lead the Pilgrim People of God by teaching, ruling, and sanctifying them.

10. What is the work of a priest?

The work of a priest is the work of Christ, the teaching and sanctifying (and in the case of bishops, who have the fullness of the priesthood), the ruling of the members of the Mystical Body of Christ. The priest, as Christ among men, also has a missionary work, that of bringing Christ to all persons and all persons to Christ.

The work of the Church in the modern world is so extensive that priests are to be found working in many fields.

Some priests are missionaries, carrying the gospel to other lands, or doing missionary work in their own country.

Some priests are teachers in Catholic schools. Some are chaplains of Catholic students in secular universities. Some priests are engaged in administrative and specialized work.

Some priests are in monastic orders, living the life and doing the work which is special to the order or congregation to which they belong.

Some priests are working in parishes, as pastors or as associates of the pastor.

The primary function of all priests, whatever their field of special work, is to offer Mass and to pray the liturgy of the hours. These functions they perform officially, in the name of the whole Church.

11. What is the work of a priest in a parish?

The work of a priest in a parish is a most varied work. It partakes of something of each of the special fields outlined above.

The parish priest does missionary work. He has the care not only of the healthy members of the parish, but also of those who have fallen away, those who have married outside the Church, and those who are lukewarm and weak in their faith. He also works for those who are not Catholics and tries to bring them into contact with the Catholic Church and its teachings.

The parish priest also teaches, instructing those who wish to come into full communion with the Church, and teaching religion in the parish school and to children in religious education programs.

The parish priest has the care of the sick within the parish. He visits them in their homes and in the hospitals. He brings Holy Communion to the sick and anoints them.

The priest in a parish administers the sacraments to the people; he baptizes, hears confessions, prepares couples for marriage and assists at the wedding, and buries the dead.

The parish priest acts as chaplain for the various parish organizations. Many parish priests are chaplains of groups who are working in the lay apostolate, the Legion of Mary, the Marriage Encounter, Cursillos and many other organizations of men, women and youth.

12. What is the work of a deacon?

There are two kinds of deacons, transitional and permanent. A transitional deacon is a student preparing for ordination to the priesthood. He is ordained a deacon usually near the end of this third year of seminary preparation. Most likely he spends part of his last year of training working full-time in a parish.

The permanent deacon is frequently a married man who has full-time employment, but volunteers part of his free time to serve the People of God. The permanent deacon's role primarily should be one of service in the parish, in a diocesan institution, or some other capacity. Some visit the sick and those in prison, or help the poor, or work with various service organizations. Others do marriage counselling, marriage preparation, etc.

Both types of deaconate have as their responsibility to

206

preach the gospel, serve at the altar, and to assist in various works of charity.

Practice

▲ Parents should consider it a great blessing to have a son who aspires to the priesthood, and they should do all in their power to foster his vocation.

▲ Parents should be pleased to have their sons serve at the altar.

▲ Learn the name of the bishop of the diocese in which you live. Pray for him at Mass where we mention the pope and bishop. Pray too, for priests, particularly the priest who is giving you instructions, and for the priests of your parish.

▲ Since preaching the word of God is such an important function of the priest, it is fitting for you to pray to the Holy Spirit before Mass begins so he will inspire the priest to give a good homily.

† † †

section **33** Marriage

Defer to one another out of reverence for Christ. Wives should be submissive to their husbands as if to the Lord because the husband is head of his wife just as Christ is head of his body the church, as well as its savior. As the church submits to Christ, so wives should submit to their husbands in everything. Husbands, love your wives, as Christ loved the church. He gave himself up for her to make her holy, purifying her in the bath of water by the power of the word, to present to himself a glorious church, holy and immaculate, without stain or wrinkle or anything of that sort. Husbands should love their wives as they do

their own bodies. He who loves his wife loves himself.
Observe that no one ever hates his own flesh; no, he
nourishes it and takes care of it as Christ cares for the
church for we are members of his body. "For this reason
a man shall leave his father and mother, and shall cling
to his wife, and the two shall be made into one." This
is the great foreshadowing; I mean that it refers to Christ
and the church. In any case, each one should love his
wife as he loves himself, the wife for her part showing
respect for her husband–EPH. 5:21–33.

SOME, AFTER READING this quotation from St. Paul, feel he is degrading women. St. Paul could not and does not mean that. Paul sees the union between a Christian and Jesus as so close as to be similar to a grafting to each other. Paul sees this same type of union between husband and wife. They do become one. Now parts of a body can not be in rebellion or disobedient to the total person. Neither should husband and wife fail to love or be subject to each other. Paul sees husband and wife as totally united and working in harmony in the Lord.

Within the Mystical Body of Christ each member has his function to perform. "Furthermore, God has set up in the church first apostles, second prophets, third teachers. . ." 1 COR. 12:28. Certain of the sacraments give us our vocation within the Pilgrim People of God and guarantee us the graces to live up to that vocation. It is the sacrament of Marriage which confers the vocation of parenthood. Christian fathers and mothers, therefore, have a special sacrament which fits them for the very important office which is theirs, that of giving life and Christian education to the newest members of Christ, their children. The sacrament of Marriage sanctifies the natural love of man and woman, raises it from the natural order to the supernatural and makes it the vehicle of God's grace.

The intimate partnership of married life and love has been
established by the Creator and qualified by his love. It is
rooted in the conjugal covenant of irrevocable personal con-
sent. Hence, by that human act whereby spouses mutually

bestow and accept each other, a relationship arises which by divine will and in the eyes of society, too, is a lasting one. For the good of the spouses and their offspring as well as of society, the existence of this sacred bond no longer depends on human decisions alone.

For God Himself is the author of matrimony, endowed as it is with various benefits and purposes. All of these have a very decisive bearing on the continuation of the human race, on the personal development and eternal destiny of the individual members of a family, and on the dignity, stability, peace and prosperity of the family itself and of human society as a whole. By their very nature, the institution of matrimony itself and conjugal love are ordained for the procreation and education of children and find in them their ultimate crown—Pastoral Constitution on the Church No. 48.

1. What is the Sacrament of Marriage?

Marriage is the sacrament in which Christ unites a Christian man and woman in a life-long union, making them two in one flesh. In entering marriage the man and woman and God enter into a covenant whereby they pledge their mutual and total commitment to each other.

2. What is the sign of the sacrament of Marriage?

The sign of the sacrament of Marriage is the expression on the part of the bride and groom of their consent to marriage.

3. When did Jesus Christ raise marriage to the dignity of a sacrament?

Neither the exact time nor the exact words in which Jesus definitely made Marriage a sacrament are recorded in Sacred Scripture. The institution of the sacrament may have taken place at the marriage feast of Cana—JOHN 2:1–10, or on the occasion of Christ's remarks about marriage to the Pharisees—MARK 10:2–12. The Church teaches infallibly that Christ instituted the sacrament of Marriage, as he did all the others.

4. What does Christ accomplish through the sacrament of Marriage?

Through the sacrament of Marriage Christ confers:

a. an increase of divine life;

b. all the actual graces needed throughout married life to bring about an ever deeper union of man and wife in soul and body to help them live up to what they promised in their marriage vows when they said: "I take you for my lawful wife (husband) to have and to hold, from this day forward, for better, for worse, for richer, for poorer, in sickness and in health, until death do us part."

5. What are some of the actual graces of marriage?

Some of the actual graces of matrimony which God pledges to provide throughout the life of the marriage are the following:

a. the grace of *dialogue or communication* which enables the spouses to better understand themselves and express their feelings to each other so they can freely communicate on all levels, verbal and non-verbal.

b. the grace of *unity* which helps a couple solve the problems which are divisive. This grace unites spouses to each other and to Jesus.

c. the grace of *healing.* The marriage covenant can be wounded by acts of selfishness, uncharitableness, etc. This grace is a salve for such injuries.

d. the grace of *parenthood* assists parents in raising and educating their children to discover God's plan for themselves and to participate in it.

e. the grace of *sanctification* assists the spouses in helping each other remove all forms of evil and sin from their own home and to acquire virtuous habits and conduct.

The graces of the sacrament of Marriage are given not just on the day of marriage, but continually to be used in the daily life of a Christian husband and wife. They are meant to work in conjunction with, not independently of the graces of the other sacraments. Married people should use the sacraments of Penance and the Holy Eucharist with their vocation in mind seeking by means of confession to rid themselves of the faults which prevent a more perfect marriage union and family life, and by means of Communion to grow in love for one another in Christ.

6. What did our Lord teach about marriage?

Then some Pharisees came up and as a test began to ask him whether it was permissible for a husband to divorce his wife. In reply he said, "What command did Moses give you?" They answered, "Moses permitted divorce and the writing of a decree of divorce." But Jesus told them: "He wrote that commandment for you because of your stubbornness. At the beginning of creation God made them male and female; for this reason a man shall leave his father and mother and the two shall become one. They are no longer two but one flesh. Therefore let no man separate what God has joined." Back in the house again, the disciples began to question him about this. He told them, "Whoever divorces his wife and marries another commits adultery against her; and the woman who divorces her husband and marries another commits adultery"–MARK 10:2–12.

Jesus taught:

a. that marriage was instituted by God,

b. that husband and wife find their fulfillment in each other,

c. that marriage is to last for life,

d. that marriage must be between one man and one woman.

7. When did God institute marriage?

The Lord God formed man out of the clay of the ground and blew into his nostrils the breath of life and so man became a living being. . . . The Lord God said: "It is not good for the man to be alone. I will make a suitable partner for him". . . . So the Lord God cast a deep sleep on the man and while he was asleep, he took out one of his ribs and closed up its place with flesh. The Lord God then built up into a woman the rib that he had taken from the man. When he brought her to the man, the man said, "This one, at last, is bone of my bones and flesh of my flesh; This one shall

211

be called 'woman', for out of 'her man' this one has been taken." That is why a man leaves his father and mother and clings to his wife, and the two of them become one body—GEN. 2:7, 18, 21—24.

The sacred author of Genesis teaches that from the very beginning of human history God instituted marriage for the first people he created.

8. For what purpose did God institute marriage?

Marriage and conjugal love by their nature bring about the begetting and educating of children. Children are the greatest gift of marriage. They contribute substantially to the welfare of their parents. God who said, "It is not good for man to be alone"—GEN. 2:18, and "Who made man from the beginning male and female"—MT. 19:4, wished to share with mankind special participation of his own creative work. Thus he blessed male and female, saying: "Increase and multiply"—GEN. 1:28.

Thus the purpose of marriage is to bring about both the enrichment and personal fulfillment of the couple and the continuation of the human race by bringing children into the world. It is difficult to separate these two goals because one brings about and strengthens the other. The presence of children causes the continued personal development of the couple as they must adjust and perhaps even sacrifice for the welfare of each other and the children.

9. What did Jesus teach about divorce?

Jesus said, "Therefore let no man separate what God has joined"—MARK 10:9. He clearly teaches, "Whoever divorces his wife and marries another commits adultery against her"—MARK 10:11. Jesus, God, teaches that an attempted marriage following a "divorce" would be invalid and adulterous.

In the Old Testament God had permitted divorce to the Jews because of the hardness of their hearts. The Old Law was imperfect in this as well as in other respects. Christ restored marriage to what God had intended in the beginning, a union of one man and one woman for life.

212

10. What did Jesus do for marriage by elevating it to the dignity of a sacrament?

For as God of old made Himself present to His people through a covenant of love and fidelity, so now the Savior of man and the Spouse of the Church comes into the lives of married Christians through the sacrament of Matrimony. He abides with them thereafter so that, just as He loved the Church and handed Himself over on her behalf, the spouses may love each other with perpetual fidelity, through mutual self-bestowal"–Pastoral Constitution on the Church 28.

In making marriage a sacrament Jesus gave it a new meaning, a new beauty and a new power of sanctifying. Marriage is now not merely the lawful union of man and wife; it is a source of holiness, a means of a closer union of each with God as well as with each other. The union of husband and wife in marriage is a type of the union of Christ and his Church.

Finally, by making marriage a sacrament Jesus gives the couple the assistance of the actual graces which make possible continued personal growth by comforting and supporting each other.

11. In what way is the union of husband and wife a symbol of the union of Christ and his Church?

The union between Christ and his Church is a vital, life-giving union. The union of husband and wife is a life-giving union, imparting grace to their souls.

The union between Christ and his Church is an organic union, the union of head and body. The union of husband and wife is a union of two in one flesh and one spirit.

The union between Christ and his Church is a union of infinite love, love which is constant and unwavering, love which is self-sacrificial. The union of husband and wife is also a union of love, love which is exclusively given to one's spouse, love which is unselfish, love which lasts as long as life.

12. Who administers the sacrament of Marriage?

The bride and groom administer this sacrament to each other. The first gift they give to each other as man and wife is the gift of the divine life.

13. What laws safeguard marriage?

a. Since marriage was instituted by God, there are divine laws, such as the indissolubility and unity of marriage.

b. Since marriage was made a sacrament by Jesus, the head of the Church, there are laws made by the Church which protect it. For example, it is the Church law which fixes the age for a valid marriage, forbids mixed marriages, etc.

c. Since marriage is the basis of human society, the state makes laws governing it. Such laws are those which require a marriage license, blood tests, legal age for marriage, etc.

14. Has the state the power to grant a divorce?

The state has no power to dissolve a valid sacramental Marriage. Consequently the Church does not ordinarily recognize the subsequent marriages of divorced persons. The state may, however, dissolve the civil aspects of a valid Marriage. This is called in civil law a divorce; but in the eyes of God the Marriage still exists.

15. Has the Church the power to grant a divorce?

Not even the Church has the power of dissolving a valid, sacramental Marriage which has been consummated. Therefore, when the Church declares that a Marriage is null and void, she is merely declaring that something existed at the time of the marriage which rendered the marriage invalid from the very beginning, e.g., in the case where one of the parties to the marriage did not give true matrimonial consent.

There are cases in which the Church (not the state) has the power of dissolving the *natural* bond of marriage. One such instance is the well-known "Pauline Privilege"—cf. 1 COR. 7:12–16.

Practical Points

1. Marriage is a sacred covenant between the spouses and God. A couple should prepare themselves for marriage by prayer and shortly before the marriage date they *should* also receive the sacrament of Penance.

2. No one would accept a position from which he could never resign without a great deal of thought and investigation. No one would enter a profession without adequate preparation. Yet thousands enter into marriage with little or no preparation. To remedy this situation most dioceses provide Pre-Cana conferences or other types of marriage preparation. Engaged couples should avail themselves of these services.

3. Married couples can derive great benefit from a Marriage Encounter or a Cana Conference. In some places these programs are held regularly in various parishes throughout the diocese. They provide an excellent means of stirring up the graces which are in the married couple, in order that their union may become ever more perfect.

4. Catholics must be married in one of the following ways in order to have a truly valid, convenant marriage. They must be married by a priest or a deacon in the presence of two witnesses. Or, if the bishop grants a dispensation from canonical form, as in the case of a mixed marriage, the marriage could be witnessed by someone other than a Catholic priest.

5. Catholics not married according to the rules given in 4 above can enter a new marriage. Before doing so ask your parish priest for advice and how to proceed.

6. "Divorced" persons, we must remember, are still married in the eyes of God. To keep company with such a person could lead to serious sin. Many a marriage outside the Church has resulted from such company-keeping. Persons in such situations should consult their parish priest for advice.

7. The Church has set up certain impediments to marriage, conditions which render a marriage either unlawful or both

unlawful and invalid. When there is a sufficient reason to do so, the bishop may grant a dispensation from certain impediments, provided the impediment does not affect the essence of marriage.

8. Couples planning marriage should consult the parish priest of the bride at least two months before the marriage. The publication of the banns in Church is done usually on the three Sundays before the marriage date.

9. Catholics should be married at Mass. Only for a serious reason should a Catholic couple deprive themselves of the great privilege of being married at Mass.

10. At their wedding Mass the new couple may present the gifts of bread and wine and water to the priest. Thus their first action as man and wife is to make an offering to God, their covenant partner. Catholics may receive Holy Communion under the both forms, i.e., the form of bread and the form of wine.

11. The couple may select the scripture texts and certain other optional features for their wedding Mass. Consult your pastor for details.

12. The minister of the non-Catholic party to a mixed marriage may offer a congratulatory type prayer when the wedding is celebrated in a Catholic church. A priest can do the same when a dispensation has been granted for the marriage to take place in a non-Catholic church.

13. Sometimes because of serious and unresolvable problems a couple can not continue to live together. Separation and even civil divorce might have to take place. Consult your parish priest for advice and contact the Chancery office for assistance.

14. Catholics who have obtained civil divorce may and should continue to participate in the sacramental life of the Church. The unique burdens these persons carry are of special con-

cern to the Church. The Family Life Bureau is available to assist such persons.

† † †

section **34**   The Sacramentals

At one point, children were brought to him so that he could place his hands on them in prayer. The disciples began to scold them, but Jesus said, "Let the children come to me. Do not hinder them. The kingdom of God belongs to such as these." And he laid his hands on their heads before he left that place—MATT. 19:13–15.

OUR LORD has given us seven sacraments, by which he sanctifies and strengthens us and fits us for our role in his Mystical Body. In imitation of Christ, her head, the Church has given us the sacramentals, by means of which she sanctifies the ordinary things of life, calls down God's blessings upon us and reminds us in a practical and vivid way of the truths by which we live. The Church blesses many of the objects which we use in daily life. We need never be out of reach of her blessing. We are never abandoned to our own weakness in any emergency. The Church is constantly at our side, asking God to bless us and the things we use.

1. What are sacramentals?

Sacramentals are special blessings or blessed objects which the Church gives us in order to inspire our devotion and to gain for us certain spiritual and temporal favors.

2. How do the sacramentals differ from the sacraments?

217

Christ instituted the sacraments; the Church the sacramentals. The sacraments were instituted to give grace; the sacramentals to impart a blessing or some special protection.

3. What are the effects of the sacramentals?

The effects of the sacramentals are:

a. the remission of venial sin and of the temporal punishments due to sin;

b. the repression of evil spirits;

c. the giving of actual grace through the prayer of the Church;

d. health of body and material blessings.

4. What are some of the principal sacramentals?

The ceremonies, actions and prayers which surround the essential act in the sacraments are sacramentals. The anointings in Baptism, the prayers used in the Last Anointing and the nuptial blessing given in Marriage are a few examples of such sacramentals.

The sign of the cross, holy water, the rosary, the way of the cross and benediction of the Blessed Sacrament are examples of sacramentals which are used frequently.

5. What are the sacramentals which are given on certain days during the year?

Candles are blessed and distributed on Candlemas Day, Feb. 2. The blessing of throats is given on St. Blaise Day, Feb. 3. Blessed ashes are placed on our forehead on Ash Wednesday, to remind us of our death and to urge us to do penance during Lent. Blessed palms are distributed on Palm Sunday, as a reminder of our Lord's triumphal entry into Jerusalem to begin his Passion. The blessing of fields takes place on August 15. Other sacramentals, such as the blessing of a home or of a mother during pregnancy and a blessing after childbirth, can be given at any time.

6. How should we use the sacramentals?

We should use the sacramentals with faith and reverence, as the Church instructs us to do. We must avoid superstition in our use of medals and other blessed objects, remembering that they, as well as the other sacramentals, produce their effect not automatically, but as a result of the prayers of the Church and the devotion they inspire in us.

Devotion

Many laymen wish to associate themselves with various religious orders in order to participate in the prayers and good works of those orders. Originally these people were allowed to wear the religious habit of the order with which they were associated. Now they wear the scapular—two small pieces of cloth connected by strings and worn over the shoulders. There are sixteen scapulars in which Catholics may be invested. The oldest and most common of these is the scapular of our Lady of Mount Carmel, by which the wearer shares in the fruits of the good works and prayers of the Carmelite Order.

In place of the actual scapular one may wear the scapular medal, which has an image of the Sacred Heart on one side and of our Lady on the other. There are many spiritual privileges attached to wearing the scapular. Converts may be enrolled in any or all of the scapulars after they have made their First Communion.

Practice

▲ Pictures, statues and crucifixes can be an aid in prayer and in keeping us mindful of God and the things of God. Every Catholic home should have a crucifix or some religious picture or statue in a prominent place.

Care should be used in selecting these objects, however. They should be in good taste, not merely "religious," the kind which will inspire devotion, rather than mere sentiment. Nowadays good religious art is available. We need not be satisfied with anything less.

section **35** **The Great Powers
of a Christian**

*Beloved,
let us love one another
because love is of God;
everyone who loves is begotten of God
and has knowledge of God.*

*The man without love has known nothing of God,
for God is love.*

*God's love was revealed in our midst in this way:
he sent his only Son to the world
that we might have life through him.*

*Love, then, consists in this:
not that we have loved God
but that he has loved us
and has sent his Son as an offering for our sins.*

*Beloved,
if God has loved us so,
we must have the same love for one another–*
1 JOHN 4:7–11.

*The way we came to understand love
was that he laid down his life for us;
we too must lay down our lives for our brothers.*

*I ask you, how can God's love survive in a man
who has enough of this world's goods
yet closes his heart to his brother
when he sees him in need?*

Little children,
let us love in deed and in truth
and not merely talk about it–1 JOHN 3:16–18.

WE HAVE been made children of God, having been "born again of water and the Holy Spirit." In Baptism we have received a new life from Christ. We must therefore live a new life, a life consistent with the dignity of a Christian.

The Christian life is a life of love.

"You shall love the Lord your God with your whole heart, with your whole soul, and with all your mind."

This is the greatest and first commandment. The second is like it:

"You shall love your neighbor as yourself"–MATT. 22:37–39.

I give you a new commandment:
Love one another.
Such as my love has been for you,
so must your love be for each other.
This is how all will know you for my disciples:
your love for one another"–JOHN 13:34–35.

This is my commandment:
love one another
as I have loved you.
There is no greater love than this:
to lay down one's life for one's friends.
You are my friends
if you do what I command you"–JOHN 15:12–14.

We would not be able to love God or one another as children of God without a special gift from God, the gift of charity. This gift is one of the great powers which God gives us with the gift of the divine life, the power to believe God, the power to hope in him and the power to love him and to love our fellowmen as children of God, the virtues of faith, hope and charity. These gifts, together with the gifts of the Holy Spirit and the other helps which God gives us enable us to live according to the new life which is ours as members of the Mystical Body of Christ,

222

to make a return to God for the gifts he has given us. The return gift we give to God must be no less than God's gift to us—Christ. We return Christ to God by allowing Christ to live in us, by living the Christ life ever more fully.

1. Why do we receive the divine life here on earth?

We receive the divine life here on earth because God wants us to be born again and begin to share his life here and constantly increase it. The greater the degree of the divine life we possess, the more like God we become, the greater glory we give God and the happier we shall be in heaven.

2. How do we receive the divine life?

The ordinary way of receiving the divine life is through Baptism, to which we are led by faith.

The man who believes in it and accepts baptism will be saved— MARK 16:16.

3. How does the divine life grow within us?

When God gives us the divine life he also gives us new powers which enable us to *act* and grow in that life. These new powers are the virtues of faith, hope and charity, the moral virtues of prudence, justice, temperance and fortitude and the gifts of the Holy Spirit.

4. What is faith?

Faith is a power given us by God which enables us to believe God in whatever he has told us. Our minds cannot fully understand the mysteries which God has revealed to us. But faith makes us *certain* of the truth of everything God has said, more certain than we are about things we see or hear, because faith rests on the authority of God himself. Finally, faith is a responsive obedience to God's revelation.

5. Can we earn the gift of faith?

No. We receive faith from God as a free gift. There is nothing we can do to earn it. But God, who ". . . wants all men to be saved and come to know the truth"—1 TIM. 2:4 offers the gift of faith to all men.

6. What is an act of faith?

An act of faith is an *expression* we give to the gift of faith. An act of faith is a great act of humility; it demands that we submit our minds to God and accept his word for something we cannot see for ourselves.

*Trust me when I tell you that whoever does not accept the kingdom of God as a child will not enter into it—*LUKE 18:17.

7. How do we live by faith?

We live by faith by acting according to what we believe rather than according to what the world tells us. To live by faith means also to strive ever for a deeper faith and to desire the will of God rather than our own.

My brothers, what good is it to profess faith without practicing it? Such faith has no power to save one, has it? If a brother or sister has nothing to wear and no food for the day, and you say to them, "Good-bye and good luck! Keep warm and well fed," but do not meet their bodily needs, what good is that? So it is with the faith that does nothing in practice. It is thoroughly lifeless.

*To such a person one might say, "You have faith and I have works—is that it?" Show me your faith without works, and I will show you the faith that underlies my works!—*JAMES 2:14—18.

*Be assured, then, that faith without works is as dead as a body without breath—*JAMES 2:26.

8. What is hope?

Hope is a power given us by God which enables us to have confidence that God will grant us pardon for our sins, the divine life, and heaven itself. Hope also includes a desire for the rewards which God has promised those who love him, a desire to possess God, the source of everlasting happiness.

You who fear the LORD, wait for his mercy,
turn not away lest you fall.

You who fear the LORD, trust him,
and your reward will not be lost.

You who fear the LORD, hope for good things,
for lasting joy and mercy.

Study the generations long past and understand;
has anyone hoped in the LORD and been disappointed?

Has anyone persevered in his fear and been forsaken?
has anyone called upon him and been rebuffed?

Compassionate and merciful is the LORD;
he forgives sins, he saves in time of trouble–SIR. 2:7–11.

9. What is an act of hope?

An act of hope is an *expression* we give to the gift of hope. Like the act of faith it is a great act of humility. Left to ourselves we have no right to hope for forgiveness or to aspire to heaven. But clinging to Christ, our Savior, who has paid the price of our salvation, we rely on the goodness of God, who has promised to save us if we cooperate with the help he gives.

10. What is charity?

Charity is the gift given by God which enables us to love him above all things for his own sake and to love ourselves and all our brothers as children of God.

11. How are faith, hope and charity increased within us?

Faith, hope and charity are increased within us by use; the more we exercise faith the stronger becomes our faith; the more we exercise hope and love the stronger become our hope and love.

12. What are the mortal virtues?

The moral virtues are:

a. prudence, the virtue which inclines us to form right judgments about what we should or should not do,

b. justice, the virtue which inclines us to give to all men whatever is due to them, *c. temperance,* the virtue which inclines us to govern our appetite according to what is right and pleasing to God,

d. fortitude, the virtue which inclines us to do what God desires, even when it is hard and disagreeable.

13. What are the gifts of the Holy Spirit?

The gifts of the Holy Spirit are:

a. counsel, the gift which moves us to act with prudence, especially in difficult cases,

b. piety, the gift which moves us to love God as our Father and to have affection for all persons and things consecrated to him,

c. fear of the Lord, the gift which moves us to fear offending God and being separated from him whom we love,

d. fortitude, the gift which moves us to do great things for God joyfully and without fear of difficulties and obstacles,

e. knowledge, the gift which moves us to see the things of this world in their true perspective, in their relation to God,

f. understanding, the gift which moves us to a deeper insight into the truths that God has revealed to us,

g. wisdom, the gift which moves us to judge all things, human and divine, as God sees them and to have a relish for the things of God.

All the gifts of the Holy Spirit make us docile and receptive to the guidance of God and the graces he sends us, and so enable us to act quickly and easily in the performance of his will.

14. How can we express our love for God?

As children of God we can express our love for our Father:

a. by offering him ourselves and everything we do;

We offer ourselves to God in the Morning Offering (cf. p. 24) and throughout the day by doing all we do as well as we can out of love for God.

. . . whether you eat or drink—whatever you do—you
should do all for the glory of God—1 COR. 10:31.

We offer ourselves to God above all in the Mass. In the Mass we offer ourselves in and with and through Christ. There is no better way of offering ourselves than by daily Mass.

b. by doing his will, by making our own the prayer of Christ,

Let it be as you would have it, not as I—MATT. 26:39.

This means, first of all, that we keep the commandments and do not separate ourselves from God by serious sin. Secondly, we must strive to avoid all sin, even that which is not serious.

We can be sure that we love God's children when we love
God and do what he has commanded. The love of God
consists in this: that we keep his commandments—and his
commandments are not burdensome—1 JOHN 5:2—3.

c. by imitating Christ, whom God has sent not only as our Savior but also as our model.

Learn from me, for I am gentle and humble of heart. . .
—MATT. 11:29.

d. by uniting ourselves to Christ by eating his flesh and drinking his blood in the Eucharist;

The man who feeds on me will have life because of
me—JOHN 6:57.

e. by recalling God's mercy to us; he has forgiven our sins; we can love him all the more by being grateful for his forgiveness;

I tell you, that is why her many sins are forgiven—be-
cause of her great love. Little is forgiven the one whose
love is small—LUKE 7:47.

f. by praying; our prayers should not be merely those in which we ask God for favors; we should also tell him we love him and ask him for an increase of the gift of love;

g. by loving others; we love God only if we love one an-other.

227

I ask you, how can God's love survive in a man who has enough of this world's goods yet closes his heart to his brother when he sees him in need?—1 JOHN 3:17.

15. How do we express love for our fellowmen?

We express love for our fellowmen by treating all men with the reverence which is due them as sons of God. This means much more than "not bothering" people or refraining from insulting or injuring them. We must treat every man as we would Christ himself. We must practice the works of mercy. Christ tells us that at the last judgment he will say to us:

Come. You have my Father's blessing! Inherit the kingdom prepared for you from the creation of the world. For I was hungry and you gave me food, I was thirsty and you gave me drink. I was a stranger and you welcomed me, naked and you clothed me. I was ill and you comforted me, in prison and you came to visit me. Then the just will ask him: "Lord, when did we see you hungry and feed you or see you thirsty and give you drink? When did we welcome you away from home or clothe you in your nakedness? When did we visit you when you were ill or in prison?" The king will answer them: "I assure you, as often as you did it for one of my least brothers, you did it for me"—MATT. 25:34—40.

16. What are the works of mercy?

The works of mercy are:

to feed the hungry,	to admonish the sinner,
to give drink to the thirsty,	to instruct the ignorant,
to clothe the naked,	to counsel the doubtful,
to visit those in prison,	to comfort the sorrowful,
to shelter the homeless,	to bear wrongs patiently,
to visit the sick,	to forgive all injuries,
to bury the dead,	to pray for the living and the dead.

Often we fail to see opportunities to practice the works of mercy because we fail to understand them properly. "The naked" are not only those who have no clothes at all, but those

228

who do not have enough clothes. "The homeless" are not only displaced persons, but families who cannot find a decent place to live because landlords refuse to rent to couples with children or to people of certain races. The words of St. John, "I ask you, how can God's love survive in a man who has enough of this world's goods yet closes his heart to his brother when he sees him in need?"—1 JOHN 3:17—apply to nations as well as to individuals. Yet today there are countries which are too small in area to support their people, while other countries with enormous space restrict immigration. There are countries where abject poverty is so widespread as to be the rule, countries which need financial and technical aid in order to feed and clothe their people. A Christian, mindful of these words of St. John, may not close his eyes to such conditions, nor condone a policy of apathy or opposition to measures which would help his brothers in need in other countries.

17. Why do we have to love all men?

When Jesus was asked the question, "Who is my neighbor?" he replied by telling the story of the good Samaritan, which teaches us that our neighbor is *every man,* not only those who belong to *my* race, *my* country, *my* religion. Even those who hate us and injure us must be included in our love. Jesus tells us in the Sermon on the Mount:

> *My command to you is: love your enemies, pray for your persecutors. This will prove that you are sons of your heavenly Father, for his sun rises on the bad and the good, he rains on the just and the unjust*—MATT. 5:44—45.

Practice

▲ Study the acts of faith, hope and love. Become familiar enough with the content of these prayers to be able to express your faith, hope and love to God in your own words.

An Act of Faith

O my God! I firmly believe that you are one God in three Divine Persons, Father, Son, and Holy Spirit. I believe that your Divine Son became man and died for our sins, and that he will come to judge the living and the dead. I believe these and all the truths which the holy Catholic Church teaches because you have revealed them, who can neither deceive nor be deceived.

An Act of Hope

O my God! relying on your infinite goodness and promises, I hope to obtain pardon of my sins, the help of your grace, and life everlasting, through the merits of Jesus Christ, my Lord and Redeemer.

An Act of Love

O my God! I love you above all things with my whole heart and soul because you are all-good and worthy of all love. I love my neighbor as myself for the love of you. I forgive all who have injured me, and ask pardon of all whom I have injured.

▲ In your examination of conscience check as to whether you are actually sharing with others the knowledge you are acquiring about God and his Church.

▲ Are there any sick friends or acquaintances whom you have not visited lately? Are there any newcomers in the neighborhood whom you might welcome by a visit?

Prayer of St. Francis

Lord, make me an instrument of Your peace.
Where there is hatred, let me sow love;
*   where there is injury, pardon,*
*   where there is doubt, faith,*
*   where there is despair, hope,*
*   where there is darkness, light,*
*   and where there is sadness, joy.*

Oh Divine Master, grant that I may not so much
seek to be consoled as to console; to be understood
as to understand, to be loved as to love; for it is in
giving that we receive, it is in pardoning that we are
pardoned, and it is in dying that we are born to
eternal life.

† † †

section **36** Sin and Its Consequences

I declare and solemnly attest in the Lord that you must no
longer live as the pagans do—their minds empty, their under-
standing darkened. They are estranged from a life in God
because of their ignorance and their resistance; without
remorse they have abandoned themselves to lust and the
indulgence of every sort of lewd conduct.
That is not what you learned when you learned Christ!
I am supposing, of course, that he has been preached and
taught to you in accord with the truth that is in Jesus:
namely, that you must lay aside your former way of life
and the old self which deteriorates through illusion and
desire, and acquire a fresh, spiritual way of thinking. You
must put on that new man created in God's image, whose
justice and holiness are born of truth—EPH. 4:17–24.

GOD THE FATHER looking down upon his Son, Jesus
Christ, said: "This is my beloved Son. My favor rests on
him"—MATT. 3:17. Through Christ we have become adopted
sons of God. As good and loving children of God, it should be
our constant desire to live under the smile of our Father, to
merit his approval, to hear in our hearts the Father saying,
"These, too, are my beloved children, members of the Body of
my Son, in them I am well pleased."

231

In order to be pleasing to our Father we must, like Christ, do always what is pleasing to him. We must at the very least refrain from acting ungratefully and rebelliously against him. We must avoid sin.

When we speak of sin and the evil of sin we usually mean serious, or mortal sin. Mortal sin is the greatest of all evils. It is a rejection of God, a breaking of our friendship with God.

Venial sin is not to be compared with mortal sin. It is not a rejection of God. It is an offense against him, but in a manner which does not destroy our friendship.

But it is only by comparison with mortal sin that venial sin seems slight. In itself venial sin is no trivial matter. It is an offense against God or our neighbor, and therefore a failure to love as a child of God should love.

As children of God we must, as St. Paul exhorts us, "put on the new man, which has been created according to God in justice and holiness of truth." We must avoid not only mortal sin, but deliberate venial sin as well.

1. What is sin?

Against you only have I sinned, and done what is evil in your sight—PS. 51:6.

Sin is doing what God forbids. Sin is saying no to God and to God's plan for us. Sin is willful disobedience to God. This disobedience may be an action, a thought, a desire, or an intention.

But sin also offends our neighbor and ourselves, e.g. God's seventh commandment forbids us to steal. In the act of theft we offend our neighbor by depriving him of some of his property. We also make it possible to ruin our own reputation when our sinful crime becomes public knowledge. Our sins disrupt the common good of the whole community.

2. How can an internal act be sinful?

Actually, the essence of sin lies in the thought, desire or intention. As soon as we deliberately desire or intend to perform a sinful act we have already offended God. We may lack

232

the courage or the opportunity of putting our desire into action, but that does not change the fact that we have withdrawn our obedience from God. All actions for which we are responsible begin with a desire or intention; the action is merely the carrying out of that desire or intention. This fact explains the words of Christ,

> *What I say to you is: anyone who looks lustfully at a woman has already committed adultery with her in his thoughts*—MATT. 5:28.

3. What are the different kinds of sins?

The different kinds of sins are:

a. original sin, the sin of our first parents. We suffer from the *effects* of original sin, but we are not personally guilty of it;

b. personal sin, a sin which we ourselves commit. Personal sin may be mortal or venial.

4. What is mortal sin?

> *Anyone who sees his brother sinning, if the sin is not deadly, should petition God, and thus life will be given to the sinner. This is only for those whose sin is not deadly. There is such a thing as a deadly sin; I do not say that one should pray about that. True, all wrong doing is sin, but not all sin is deadly*—1 JOHN 5:16—17.

Mortal sin is called deadly because it causes us to lose the divine life of sanctifying grace and consequently God no longer lives in us. Mortal sin is a serious offense against God. In order to be mortal three conditions must be fulfilled:

a. The offense in itself must be *serious*, i.e., something that has been forbidden or commanded by God under pain of losing his friendship; e.g., to tell a lie which would seriously injure someone's reputation would be a mortal sin; to tell an ordinary lie, which does no serious injury, would be a venial sin.

b. The person who commits the sin must *realize what he is doing* and that what he is doing is a serious *offense against God*; e.g., to kill a man deliberately and unjustly would be a mortal sin; to kill a man accidentally would be no sin.

c. There must be *full consent of the will.* A person acting under any circumstance which deprives him of free will would not be guilty of mortal sin.

5. What are the effects of mortal sin?

a. Mortal sin destroys our divine life; hence the word mortal, meaning death dealing.

> *What benefit did you then enjoy? Things you are now ashamed of, all of them tending toward death. But now that you are freed from sin and have become slaves of God, your benefit is sanctification as you tend toward eternal life.*
>
> *The wages of sin is death, but the gift of God is eternal life in Christ Jesus our Lord*–ROM. 6:21–23.

b. Mortal sin makes a man displeasing to God. Nothing one does while in the state of mortal sin can be pleasing to God.

c. Since it is a rejection of God, mortal sin renders the sinner liable to eternal damnation.

6. What is venial sin?

Venial sin is a less serious offense against God. Venial sin is a sin which does not sever our relationship with God, but which does weaken our love for God.

All of us fall short in many respects–JAMES 3:2.

In venial sin, either the offense itself is not a serious matter (e.g., an ordinary lie of excuse, a small theft, a slight disrespect towards God) or else the sinner is not sufficiently aware of the seriousness of his action, or does not give full consent of his will.

7. Can a sin be fully deliberate and yet be only venial?

Yes. Such a sin is called a deliberate venial sin. Deliberate venial sin weakens the will and paves the way for mortal sin. Deliberate venial sin also lessens the intimacy between us and God. Habitual venial sin brings about a state of lukewarmness which is very dangerous.

8. How do we know whether an action is sinful?

Our conscience tells us whether an action is right or wrong, a mortal or a venial sin.

9. How does our conscience know what is right and wrong?

Our conscience is merely our mind judging on moral matters. Therefore, it must be instructed according to the will of God because sin is doing what God forbids. We must learn from Christ, teaching through his Church.

10. How does a person form a good conscience?

Because sin primarily offends God we must first learn what God expects of us in moral behavior. Guidelines are given in many places throughout the pages of Sacred Scripture. Moral theologians under the guidance of the Church have written about moral problems and questions. Once we are aware of the guidelines we are able to make the practical judgment about the goodness or evil of our own personal actions.

Keep in mind that while objectively it would seem a particular action might be mortally wrong, because of subjective influences we might conclude we are free from moral guilt in a particular case.

In case of doubt consult a prudent confessor for advice and counsel.

11. Can mortal sin be forgiven?

Yes. God will forgive any mortal sins and any number of them if the sinner truly repents. When God forgives the sin he not only restores the divine life and the gift of charity, he even restores all the divine life previously possessed.

12. What happens to one who dies in the state of mortal sin?

One who dies in the state of mortal sin will continue to reject God for all eternity. He will never repent, will never turn back to God. He must, therefore, spend eternity in hell.

13. What is hell?

Hell is a state of eternal damnation. When a person, whose destiny is God, has died rejecting God, the person must spend eternity deprived of God, and therefore of all happiness.

Then he will say to those on his left: "Out of my sight, you condemned, into that everlasting fire prepared for the devil and his angels!—MATT. 25:41.

14. Does the all-merciful God send anyone to hell?

Actually, it is not God but the sinner who sends himself to hell. Mortal sin is a rejection of God. Hell is mortal sin carried to its logical and eternal conclusion. God who loves all people certainly desires their salvation and gives them every opportunity to repent and be converted. He alone knows whether anyone actually rejects his merciful overtures.

15. What is purgatory?

Purgatory is a state of purification after death for those who die without repenting of their venial sins. The souls in purgatory possess the divine life and know they are saved; but they do not have the vision of God. They cannot help themselves, but can be helped by the prayers and sacrifices of the faithful on earth and the souls in heaven.

16. What is temptation?

Temptation is an inducement to sin. Deliberate sin, whether mortal or venial, does not "just happen"; it is *preceded* by an inducement to sin, which is called temptation.

17. What are the sources of temptation?

The sources of temptation are three: the world about us, the devil, and our own inclinations to sin. These inclinations are pride, covetousness, lust, anger, gluttony, envy and sloth.

Practice

▲ Since mortal sin is so common and is treated so lightly by the world, we must constantly strive to keep alive in ourselves a real horror of it. We can do this by reflecting frequently on two truths, the Passion and death of our Savior and the fact of hell.

The awful sufferings and death which the Son of God endured were the price God himself paid for the mortal sins of men.

Mortal sin is a rejection of God. A man chooses something that God says he may not have if he wishes to remain a friend of God. If a man dies in such a state of soul God grants him his wish in eternity, namely to be separated from God.

In order to avoid mortal sin we must try to avoid deliberate venial sin. If we are faithful to God in smaller things we shall be faithful to him in serious matters.

We should pray for help from God when we are tempted to sin. If we pray, God will always give us strength to overcome temptation.

In order to avoid sin we must also avoid any person, place or thing which in all probability will lead us into sin. To place ourselves in such an occasion of mortal sin without sufficient reason would be itself a mortal sin.

By prayer and thought try to discover what particular fault in your character you ought to be striving especially to overcome. Work on that fault in your examination of conscience.

† † †

section **37**   **The First Three Commandments**

Another time a man came up to him and said, "Teacher, what good must I do to possess everlasting life?" He answered, "Why do you question me about what is good? There is One who is good. If you wish to enter into life, keep the commandments." "Which ones?" he asked. Jesus replied, "'You shall not kill'; 'You shall not commit adultery'; 'You shall not steal'; 'You shall not bear false witness'; 'Honor your father and your mother'; and 'Love your neighbor as yourself'"—MATT. 19:16–19.

THE GREAT commandment of love requires of us that we act towards God as his children and that we act towards our fellow man as brothers, children of the same Father, members of the Body of Christ.

These two commandments are abstract. To clarify them, God gave us the ten commandments where we find our duties towards God and neighbor set forth in clear terms.

I, the LORD, am your God. You shall not have other gods besides me.

You shall not take the name of the LORD, your God, in vain.

Remember to keep holy the sabbath day.

Honor your father and your mother, that you may have a long life in the land which the Lord, your God, is giving you.

You shall not kill.

You shall not commit adultery.

You shall not steal.

You shall not bear false witness against your neighbor.

You shall not covet your neighbor's house. You shall

*not covet your neighbor's wife, nor his male or female
slave, nor his ox or ass, nor anything else that belongs
to him*—EX. 19:2–16.

If we love God we will keep the first three commandments;
they tell us our duties towards God. If we love ourselves and
our neighbor we will keep the other seven commandments; they
tell us our duties towards ourself and our neighbor.

The ten commandments are not laws which were enacted to
establish order or to test our obedience. They flow from our very
nature as human beings. Because we were created by God and
depend on him completely we must, as intelligent responsible
beings, acknowledge that dependence. We must praise God, love
him, believe him and show reverence for his name. Because each
human being has certain rights which he receives from God, we
must respect those rights.

In studying the ten commandments, therefore, we are studying the laws which tell us how a man must act because he is a
man, how he must act towards God and towards his fellow man.
But, more than that, in studying the ten commandments, we as
children of God, are studying the laws which help us fulfill the
great law of love.

*"You shall love the Lord your God with your whole heart,
with your whole soul, and with all your mind."*

*This is the greatest and first commandment. The
second is like it:*

"You shall love your neighbor as yourself"—MATT.
22:37–39.

* * *

THE FIRST COMMANDMENT: RESPECT GOD

**I, the Lord, am your God.
You shall not have
other gods besides me.**

239

1. What are the positive duties given by the first commandment?

The first commandment binds us to believe in everything which God has revealed, to worship him, to trust him and to love him above all things. In other words, the first commandment commands us to practice faith, hope and charity.

2. How do we practice faith, hope and charity?

We practice faith by believing all the truths which the Church teaches as revealed to us by God, by professing our faith and never under any circumstances denying it.

We practice hope by relying on God's mercy and never doubting that he will forgive our sins if we are truly sorry for them, and that he will give us all the help we need to reach heaven.

We practice charity by keeping all the commandments and doing the works of mercy.

If you love me . . . obey the commands I give you—
JOHN 14:15.

3. How serious are sins against faith?

Sins against faith are most serious, because they strike at the very foundation of our relationship to God.

4. What are the sins against faith?

The sins against faith are:

a. the denial of all or any of the truths which God teaches through the Church,

b. deliberate doubt about any truth of faith,

c. failure to profess the faith when obliged to do so,

d. failure to obtain necessary religious instruction,

e. reading books dangerous to our faith,

f. refusal to accept the authority of the pope as visible head of the Church,

g. the worship of some created thing instead of the true God,

240

h. superstition (this includes astrology, belief in good luck charms, dreams, fortune tellers, etc. Superstition may be a venial sin. But to guide one's life by superstition would certainly be a mortal sin),

i. attendance at spiritualistic seances or the consultation of mediums.

5. What are the sins against hope?

The sins against hope are presumption and despair.

6. How does one sin by presumption?

One sins by presumption by taking for granted that salvation can be obtained by one's own efforts without God's help, or by God's help without one's own cooperation.

7. What is despair?

Despair is a refusal to trust that God will forgive our sins and give us the means of salvation.

8. What are the sins against charity?

All sins are in some way sins against charity. Specific sins against charity are treated under the fifth commandment.

* * *

THE SECOND COMMANDMENT: RESPECT GOD'S NAME

**You shall not take the name
of the Lord, your God, in vain.**

9. What are the positive duties given by the second commandment?

We keep the second commandment by showing reverence to God, and especially to his holy name.

10. What are the sins against the second commandment?

The sins against the second commandment are:

a. blasphemy, i.e., mocking, ridiculing, despising God, his Church, the saints or holy objects (this is one of the most serious of sins);

b. irreverence in using the name of God, Jesus or the saints (this sin is usually venial);

c. cursing, i.e., calling down evil upon another (cursing would be a mortal sin if one were serious; ordinarily one is not);

d. swearing, i.e., calling upon God to witness the truth of what we are saying, when what we are saying is not true or when there is no sufficient reason to call upon God (perjury, i.e., lying while under oath, is a mortal sin);

e. breaking a vow, i.e., a deliberate promise made to God to do something which is particularly pleasing to him (to break a vow would be a mortal or venial sin depending on how one is bound by the vow).

* * *

THE THIRD COMMANDMENT: RESPECT GOD'S DAY

Remember to keep holy the sabbath day.

11. What are the positive duties given by this commandment?

We keep the third commandment by worshipping God in a special way and refraining from unnecessary work on Sunday.

12. Why did the Church change the Lord's Day from the Sabbath to Sunday?

The Church, using the power of binding and loosing which Christ gave to the pope, changed the Lord's Day to Sunday because it was on Sunday (the first day of the week) that Christ rose from the dead and that the Holy Spirit descended upon the apostles.

The bishops of many dioceses have obtained permission from the Pope to anticipate the Sunday masses of obligation on Saturday evenings. This is based on the early biblical notion that one day ends at sundown and the next one begins at dusk.

Attendance at a Saturday evening wedding Mass does not fulfill the Sunday Mass obligation because the wedding liturgy, Scripture lessons and homily are not those of the Sunday Mass. It is our participation in the Sunday liturgy which unites us within the Pilgrim People of God.

13. How are we obliged to worship God on Sundays and Holy Days?

The law of God does not specify the amount of worship required. But there is a Church law which binds us to assist at Mass on Sundays and Holy Days. By observing this law of the Church we are observing also the divine law of worship on the Lord's Day.

14. Is our attendance and participation in the Sunday Mass an obligation?

Yes, we are obliged to attend and participate in the Sunday liturgy unless excused by a serious inconvenience. We would prefer, however, to refer to the Sunday Mass as an opportunity which it truly is. At Mass we meet with and pray with others who share our religious convictions. To be absent from the Sunday Mass would be to miss an opportunity to be with God.

15. Is assistance at Mass all that is required on Sundays and Holy Days?

Assistance at Mass on these days is all that is required under pain of sin. But the spirit of the law requires further worship, a real sanctification of the whole day.

Let the public and private observance of the feasts of the Church, which are in a special way dedicated and consecrated to God, be kept inviolable: and especially the Lord's day which the apostles, under the guidance of the Holy Ghost, substituted for the Sabbath. Now, if the order was given to the Jews, "Six days shall you do work: on the seventh day is the Sabbath, the rest holy

*to the Lord. Every one that shall do any work on this
day shall die:" how will these Christians not fear spiritual
death, who perform servile work on feast-days, and whose
rest on these days is not devoted to religion and piety but
given over to the allurements of the world? Sundays and
Holy Days, then, must be made holy by divine worship,
which gives homage to God and heavenly food to the
soul. Although the Church only commands the faithful
to abstain from servile work and attend Mass and does
not make it obligatory to attend evening devotions, still
she desires this and recommends it repeatedly: moreover, the needs of each one demand it, seeing that all are
bound to win the favor of God if they are to obtain
his benefits*—Enc. on the Sacred Liturgy 150.

16. What kind of work is forbidden on Sunday?

Unnecessary work is the type of work forbidden on Sunday.
Changing social and economic factors have changed the concept
of work. Therefore, it is difficult to give principles with clear-
cut applications to any and all situations.

17. What kind of work is permitted on Sunday?

Such work which is necessary is permitted on Sundays.
Some work is necessary for the common good. For example, it
is necessary for policemen, railroad men, drug store and delica-
tessen workers, etc., to work on Sundays.

Some work is necessary for other reasons; e.g., cooking and
dishwashing in the home, etc. Some work becomes necessary
because of an emergency or in an unusual situation. In the latter
case, if there is any doubt, one should ask one's confessor. Conducting business which is not necessary for the common good is
forbidden on Sunday.

Practice

▲ We cannot love someone we do not know. God has
told us of himself in order that we might love him. Because
we are God's children we know our Father far better than do

244

those who have not the gift of faith. But we can never know God well enough. Our love for our Father should prompt us to seek more and more knowledge of him. We may not be content with the knowledge of our faith gained by reading and study. The better our education the deeper should be our knowledge of the faith. Far too many laymen think that only priests need be concerned with the study of religion. This is a very false. idea. We are all God's children. We should all have a knowledge of our faith commensurate with our age, our intelligence and our education.

▲ Difficulties about matters of faith are not the same as doubts. Difficulties are questions which occur because of an inquiring mind, the need of further knowledge or mistaken information on the point.

† † †

section **38** The Fourth Commandment: Respect Your Parents

My son, take care of your father when he is old; grieve him not as long as he lives. Even if his mind fail, be considerate with him; revile him not in the fullness of your strength. For kindness to a father will not be forgotten, it will serve as a sin offering—it will take lasting root. In time of tribulation it will be recalled to your advantage, like warmth upon frost it will melt away your sins. A blasphemer is he who despises his father; accursed of his Creator, he who angers his mother—SIR. 3:12—16.

WHEN GOD sent his Son into the world he sent him as a member of a family. Jesus chose to have a human mother and a human foster-father and to be subject to them. By so doing he

245

taught us the importance which God places on the family. By his life at Nazareth as a member of the Holy Family Christ has sanctified family life and given us an example of what that life should be. He taught us the dignity of parenthood by the reverence he showed to Mary and Joseph; he saw them as the representatives of his Father.

In the fourth commandment God reminds us that as his children we must respect authority within the family by honoring and obeying our parents. He reminds us, too, that we must respect and obey his other representatives, those who exercise lawful authority over us in the larger family of man, which is the family of God.

* * *

Honor your father and your mother.

1. What are the positive duties of this commandment?

Everyone is obliged by this commandment to obey all lawful authority and to exercise it conscientiously. Parents keep this commandment by providing for the needs of their children, their spiritual as well as their material needs, by giving them affection, protection, discipline, education and good example, by preparing them to live as children of God in this world, and so to attain eternal union with God.

Sons and daughters keep this commandment by obeying, honoring and respecting their parents, and by providing for them in their old age. We must honor them as long as we live.

2. Whom must we obey?

a. Children who are under age and still dependent on their parents must obey them in everything which is not in opposition to the laws of God or the Church.

b. We must obey the Church. Christ the King acts through the pope and through the spiritual ruler of the diocese, the bishop.

*I for my part declare to you, you are "Rock," and on
this rock I will build my church, and the jaws of death
shall not prevail against it. I will entrust to you the
keys of the kingdom of heaven. Whatever you declare
bound on earth shall be bound in heaven; whatever you
declare loosed on earth shall be loosed in heaven*—MATT.
16:18—19.

c. We must obey the civil government. Whether a law binds
us under sin or merely compels our obedience under threat of a
penalty depends on the mind of the law-maker.

3. Does the fourth commandment oblige us to love our country?

Yes. The fourth commandment obliges us to fulfill our
duties as citizens of our country, to respect its laws and institutions, to cooperate for the common good and to defend our country when the cause and the means used are just.

Practice

▲ The right and duty of educating their children belongs to
the parents.

*The family . . . holds directly from the Creator the mission
and hence the right to educate the offspring, a right inalien-
able because inseparably joined to the strict obligation, a
right anterior to any right whatever of civil society and of
the State, and therefore inviolable on the part of any power
on earth*—Enc. on the Christian Education of Youth.

Parents, therefore, may not leave the education entirely to
the school. The school is meant to assist the parents, not
supplant them in this important duty.

▲ Parents have a great responsibility towards their children
in the matter of giving good example. It is idle to suppose that
children will develop right attitudes in regard to respect for law,
the use of money, respect for others, tolerance, etc., if their
parents display the fact that they themselves have un-Christian
attitudes towards these things.

▲ The good or harm which a parent can do by way of example is most evident in the matter of prayer and the sacraments. Parents who are never seen to pray, who miss Mass, or who rarely receive Holy Communion can hardly expect their children to develop good habits in regard to prayer and the sacraments. On the other hand, parents who do pray and teach their children to pray and who receive Holy Communion every time they assist at Mass are giving their children excellent example, and are in a position to encourage their children to do likewise.

▲ One of the duties we have as citizens of our country is that of voting and of doing so intelligently. Nowadays there are organizations which can give us information on candidates for office. A good Christian should take his privilege of voting seriously and exercise it wisely. Remembering that our Lord called us "the salt of the earth," "the light of the world," the good Christian should take an interest in and participate in civic affairs. Only thus can he expect to carry the principles of Christ into civic affairs.

▲ Parents should respect their children's choice of vocation. Parents are frequently wrong in encouraging their children too strongly to follow pursuits which are merely lucrative rather than those which contribute to society, e.g., teaching, nursing, priesthood, or religious life.

† † †

section **39** **The Fifth Commandment: Respect Life**

You have heard the commandment imposed on your forefathers, "You shall not commit murder; every murderer shall be liable to judgment."

What I say to you is: everyone who grows angry with his brother shall be liable to judgment; any man who uses abusive language toward his brother shall be answerable to the Sanhedrin, and if he holds him in contempt he risks the fires of Gehenna. If you bring your gift to the altar and there recall that your brother has anything against you, leave your gift at the altar, go first to be reconciled with your brother, and then come and offer your gift. Lose no time; settle with your opponent while on your way to court with him. Otherwise your opponent may hand you over to the judge, who will hand you over to the guard, who will throw you into prison. I warn you, you will not be released until you have paid the last penny—MATT. 5:21–26.

AS MEMBERS of the family of God we must treat all men as our brothers in Christ; we must assist all men in their journey through life back to the Father. We must, therefore, respect the rights of our fellow men, rights of soul and body. The fifth commandment reminds us that we must practice brotherly love within the family of God and that we must not injure the body or soul of our neighbor. The fifth commandment reminds us, too, that we must acknowledge that our lives as well as those of our neighbor belong to God, and that we must therefore, preserve our own life and health and refrain from risking them rashly or needlessly.

* * *

You shall not kill.

1. How do we keep the fifth commandment?

We keep the fifth commandment by preserving our own life and health and by respecting our neighbor's right to life and health of body and soul.

2. What are the sins against the fifth commandment?

The sins against the fifth commandment are:

a. murder,

249

b. abortion,

c. mercy killing,

d. suicide,

e. mutilation of one's body without a sufficient reason,

f. risking one's life without a sufficient reason,

g. excessive eating and drinking,

h. unjust anger, which leads to hatred, revenge, fighting and quarreling,

i. abuse of the body and mind by drugs or alcohol.

3. Is it ever permitted to take the life of another?

Yes. To kill in legitimate self-defense is not sinful. The state has the right to punish serious crime with the death penalty.

To take part in a just war (one in which the cause and the means are just and in which there is reasonable hope of success) is not against the fifth commandment.

4. Why are abortion and "mercy killing" against the fifth commandment?

Abortion and "mercy killing" are mortal sins against the fifth commandment because in both cases human life is taken unjustly. Abortion is so serious a crime that the Church punishes it by excommunication.

5. How are we obliged to preserve our own life and health?

We are obliged to use every ordinary means in preserving our own life and health. We may not, therefore, risk our life except for a sufficient reason, for example, to rescue another; nor may we allow our body to be mutilated or deprived of an important function unless it be necessary to save the body itself, e.g., an amputation or a hysterectomy in cancer cases.

6. How serious a sin is it to mutilate the body unnecessarily, to deprive it of an important function, or to shorten one's life?

Sterilization, except in the case of legitimate removal of a diseased organ, is a mortal sin because the function of sex is an important function. The use of narcotics, except in licit medical practice, is a mortal sin.

7. What is hatred?

Hatred is wishing evil to another. It is a matter of the will, not the feelings. We are not guilty of sin because we feel an aversion to certain people, as long as we do not encourage or manifest such a feeling. We are obliged to *love* our neighbor, not to like him. Liking is a matter of the feelings and is not always under the control of the will. Nor is it incompatible with supernatural love.

8. Are religious and racial prejudice against the fifth commandment?

Yes. Prejudice is unreasonable and always opposed to charity. To judge and condemn any person because he happens to belong to a certain religious group, nationality or race injures that person. To manifest prejudice in action hurts the feelings of our neighbor, and is therefore a sin against charity. To deny him his rights is a sin against justice as well as charity. This is particularly true in the case of joining an organization which promotes segregation or any other denial of human rights.

9. May we seek revenge or refuse to forgive injuries?

No, we may not. Jesus insisted that our sins will not be forgiven by God unless we forgive our brother's offenses against us.

If you forgive the faults of others, your heavenly Father will forgive you yours. If you do not forgive others, neither will your Father forgive you–MATT. 6:14–15.

10. Why is the use of certain drugs sinful?

Persons may never deprive themselves of consciousness or moral judgment without sufficient reason. Thus to abuse oneself by over indulgence in hallucinatory drugs or alcohol could be a serious sin because of the deadly results of the drugs. Medical science has not yet written the final report on all of the dangers of these newly discovered drugs.

251

11. What is scandal?

Scandal is any evil action or one which has the appearance of evil, which does spiritual harm to another. Bad example is frequently scandalous, since it may easily lead another into the same sin. Bad example given to the young is particularly serious.

*But it would be better if anyone who leads astray one of these simple believers were to be plunged in the sea with a great millstone fastened around his neck—*MARK 9:42.

12. How serious are sins of hatred, scandal, cooperation in sin, and uncharitable words and actions?

The seriousness of such sins is determined by the seriousness of the harm done to our neighbor. Deliberately to wish serious evil to another, to cooperate with him in a serious sin, to give serious scandal or to talk or act against our neighbor in such a way as to injure him seriously is a mortal sin against the fifth commandment.

Practice

▲ In the field of race relations Christians have a great opportunity for giving the world an example of justice and charity. It would be a shocking thing if the behavior of Christians in regard to segregation and other injustices were no different from that of others. We must never forget that our Lord said, "By this will men know that you are my disciples, if you have love one for another."

The Sixth and Ninth Commandments: Respect Sexuality

You must know that your body is a temple of the Holy Spirit, who is within—the Spirit you have received from God. You are not your own. You have been purchased, and at a price. So glorify God in your body—I COR. 6:19—20.

OUR FATHER has given us a world in which human skill and artistry can add to the order and beauty of his creation. But God was not content to allow men to share in his creation merely as workers and artists. He desired to give men and women a share in his fatherhood, a share in the creation of new human beings who are destined to share in the divine life, to be his adopted sons and daughters, to share his happiness for all eternity in heaven. Thus he gave to his children the wonderful power of sex.

The bringing of new life into the world is the first purpose of sex. But this wonderful power in human beings is also something else, something deeply mysterious. It is the means whereby a man and woman with God's blessing give themselves to one another in love, and thereby find their fulfillment in one another and a closer union with God through one another.

Among all the powers that we possess the power of sex is unique. It is the only gift we have which we may not use for our own sake. Our eyes, our ears we use in order to bring the outside world into our mind. Our power of nourishing ourself we use in order to build up our own body. But our power of sex we possess in order that we might give ourselves to another in a union of body and soul which is to last a lifetime.

Love always expresses itself by an attempt to give oneself to the loved one. We give gifts to those we love, the gift of attention,

253

interest, time. We give presents to those we love; the deeper the love the more precious and personal the present. In all this we are seeking ways of giving ourselves to those we love. Our power of sex is in some mysterious way peculiarly, deeply, ourself. The very words, intimate, private, personal, applied to the sexual faculty give evidence of this fact. Thus it is the means whereby husband and wife can give themselves to one another in a love which is fruitful in new human beings, children who are both God's and theirs. The joy and fulfillment to be found in married love are our Father's rewards to his sons and daughters who enter into the vocation of marriage and parenthood.

Sex, therefore, is not merely a means of obtaining pleasure; it is far deeper than that. Still less is it something shameful or sordid. Rather it is something sacred. It is only the misuse of sex that is shameful, all the more shameful because it is the misuse of something sacred. Sex in human beings may never be divorced from love. The misuse of sex is a sin against love, not only against divine love, as is every sin, but against human love as well.

* * *

You shall not commit adultery.
You shall not covet your neighbor's wife.

1. How do we keep the sixth and ninth commandments?

We keep the sixth and ninth commandments by using the power of sex lawfully, according to the plan of God. For married people this means that they use their marriage rights properly, that they freely give the use of those rights to one another, and that they remain faithful to one another.

For unmarried people this means that they do not use the power of sex at all, since its use is lawful only in marriage.

For all, keeping the sixth and ninth commandments means that we cultivate modesty and chastity by guarding our eyes, our ears and our thoughts and imaginations from anything that would lead us into sins against the sixth and ninth commandments.

2. What is the proper use of the sexual power?

The use of the sexual power is the sacred privilege of married couples. It is the means whereby they cooperate with God in procreation and achieve union with one another in body and soul. By its very nature, therefore, the sexual power may be used only in marriage.

3. What are the sins against the sixth and ninth commandments?

Can you not realize that the unholy will not fall heir to the kingdom of God? Do not deceive yourselves: no fornicators, idolators, or adulterers, no sodomites, thieves, misers, or drunkards, no slanderers or robbers will inherit God's kingdom. And such were some of you: but you have been washed, consecrated, justified in the name of our Lord Jesus Christ and in the Spirit of our God–1 COR. 6:9–11 (cf. also GAL. 5:19–24, EPH. 5:5).

Anything which is opposed to the virtue of chastity is a sin against the sixth or ninth commandment.

4. Are demonstrations of affection between unmarried persons against the virtue of chastity?

Demonstrations of affection between unmarried persons are right and good as long as they are true demonstrations of affection and are not the sort of actions which by nature arouse passion.

5. What is the teaching of the Church regarding birth control?

The Church teaches that responsible parenthood is not only legitimate, but necessary. Health problems, both physical and psychological, finances, the population explosion, can be reasons for limiting one's family. If a couple has a legitimate reason for limiting family size, Pope Paul VI teaches that natural family planning methods, since they work in accord with and in cooperation with normal bodily functions, can be morally justified. However, he also teaches that methods of birth control which use a drug or a mechanical device are not justifiable.

Couples with difficulties in this matter should follow the advice of Pope Paul, namely to petition Jesus, who is the ultimate judge or our actions, for help in solving this delicate and serious matter. He also urges them to continue to receive the sacraments of Penance and Holy Communion because they provide the graces needed to strengthen the spiritual lives of the couple.

6. What is natural family planning?

Natural family planning restricts the use of the marriage right to those times of the month when a woman cannot conceive.

During the past few years scientists and doctors have learned how to identify and recognize very reliable signs enabling women to determine more precisely the time of fertility. These natural methods once learned can give peace of mind to persons facing problems in this matter. Further information may be obtained from your instructor, the Family Life Bureau of your Diocese or from the Couple to Couple League of Cincinnati, Ohio, (Box 11084, Zip 45211).

7. Why are thoughts and desires against chastity sinful?

Any deliberate desire to commit a sinful act is in itself sinful. If the act we desire to perform would be a mortal sin, the deliberate desire to commit it would be in itself a mortal sin. Our Lord said,

> *You have heard the commandment, "You shall not commit adultery." What I say to you is: anyone who looks lustfully at a woman has already committed adultery with her in his thoughts*—MATT. 5:27–28.

Thoughts or imaginations of a sexual nature can easily arouse sexual feelings, especially in the young. For an unmarried person, who has no right to the use of sex, to consent to such feelings would be a mortal sin.

8. What is the virtue of modesty?

The virtue of modesty is the virtue which protects chastity by inclining us to guard our senses, so as not to invite temptation and to be considerate in our dress and behavior, so as not to cause temptation to others.

9. Are immodest looks, etc., sinful?

Looks, reading and other such actions which are opposed to the virtue of modesty can be sinful according to the circumstances. If one who has no right to the use of sex were to indulge in such things merely out of curiosity, without consent to any sexual feelings, he would commit a venial sin. To do so with consent to such feelings would be a mortal sin for an unmarried person. In this matter there can be, too, an occasion of serious sin, sometimes even for a married person—the danger of consenting to an unlawful desire for another person. If one, married or unmarried, has a good reason for pursuing a good action which may produce sexual feeling to which he does not consent—e.g., the study of medicine, seeking necessary information—there would be no sin involved.

10. Why is the sixth commandment sometimes called "the difficult commandment"?

Because of the effects of original sin the desire to experience sexual pleasure outside of marriage and unlawfully is easily aroused in us. Our eyes, our ears, our sense of touch, even our imagination can bring us into contact with objects which stimulate the sexual faculty. Yet for unmarried persons, since they have not the right to the use of sex, there can be no deliberate acquiescence in such stimulation, much less a seeking of it, without serious sin.

11. How do we preserve chastity?

We preserve chastity:

by prayer—the habit of prayer, and prayer in time of temptation,

by cultivating devotion to our Blessed Mother,

by the frequent reception of the sacraments of Penance and the Holy Eucharist, by avoiding occasions of sin, such as certain types of books, pictures, entertainments and companions.

Practice

▲ The pagan society in which we live has little regard for the virtue of chastity. Parents and teachers should take special care to inculcate in the young an appreciation of this important virtue. Chastity should be presented not as a repression of the instincts but as a positive virtue which is essential to manliness and womanliness. Above all, they should stress the fact that sex is something good and holy, that there is nothing evil about any part of the body, that the body, good by nature, has been made the temple of the Blessed Trinity. If sex is presented as good and sacred and its importance in marriage explained, it can easily be pointed out why any misuse of sex is a tragic misfortune rather than a daring adventure.

▲ Steady company-keeping between young boys and girls has become an accepted practice in many places. Boys and girls in their teens who are in no position to think of marriage for several years, or who have no thought of marriage at all, see the same person regularly, frequently and exclusively. Besides the obvious disadvantage of such exclusiveness in dating (it narrows the field from which young people can select a partner for marriage) there is another more immediate danger; such steady company-keeping is usually a proximate occasion of mortal sins against chastity. Older couples experience this difficulty; but in their case it is a necessary occasion, and, using the ordinary precautions, they can expect the necessary help from God to keep from sin. Such is not the case with younger boys and girls. In the face of this widespread practice, therefore, even over the protests of their teen-age children, parents have a duty of taking a very determined and strict stand.

† † †

*Then God said: "Let us make man in our image, after our
likeness. Let them have dominion over the fish of the sea,
the birds of the air, and the cattle, and over all the wild
animals and all the creatures that crawl on the ground."*

*God created man in his image; in the divine image he
created him; male and female he created them.*

*God blessed them, saying: "Be fertile and multiply;
fill the earth and subdue it. Have dominion over the fish
of the sea, the birds of the air, and all the living things
that move on the earth." God also said: "See, I give you
every seed-bearing plant all over the earth and every tree
that has seed-bearing fruit on it to be your food; and to
all animals of the land, all the birds of the air, and all the
living creatures that crawl on the ground, I give all the
green plants for food." And so it happened*–GEN.
1:26–30.

OUR LORD taught us to be poor in spirit, not to be attached to nor too desirous of material things.

*What profit would a man show if he were to gain the whole
world and destroy himself in the process? What can a man
offer in exchange for his very self?*–MATT. 16:26.

Material possessions can distract us in our efforts to reach
heaven. On the other hand, the Church tells us that it is good
for men to own things, indeed, that the ownership of some
property can be a positive help on our way to heaven. So
anxious is she that all should be able to own property that she
calls for a better distribution of wealth in the world.

The seventh and tenth commandments regulate the possession
and use of the things God has entrusted to us and to others.

259

There is much injustice in the world today on the part of individuals, groups and governments. Some people are avaricious and greedy. Communist governments deny the right of a person to own productive property. The man who steals, whether he is a pickpocket, an employer or a worker, the Communist state which unjustly deprives a man of what is his, the child who damages property, all these offend against the right order which God has established between his children and the things he has given them for their use.

* * *

You shalt not steal.
You shalt not covet thy neighbor's goods.

1. How do we keep the seventh and tenth commandments?

We keep the seventh and tenth commandments:

by respecting the property of others,
by paying our just debts,
by dealing honestly in business,
by paying a living wage to our employees,
by doing a full day's work for a full day's pay,
by living up to our agreements and contracts,
by returning things we have found.

2. What are the sins against the seventh and tenth commandments?

The sins against the seventh and tenth commandments are:

stealing,
cheating,
vandalism,
acceptance of bribes,
use of false weights and measures,
charging exorbitant prices,
wasting time,
careless work,

violation of contracts and agreements,
envy of another's possessions.

3. How is the seriousness of sins against the seventh commandment determined?

The seriousness of sins against the seventh commandment is determined by the seriousness of the harm done either to the individual or to the community. Ordinarily it is considered serious if the injustice is equivalent to one day's wages for the injured party. A considerable amount taken from even a wealthy person or a corporation would constitute a serious sin against justice.

4. When is there an obligation of making restitution?

Whenever there has been a violation of justice, one is bound to make full restitution. One guilty of injustice is bound in conscience to restore the object unjustly possessed, withheld or destroyed, according to the value it had at the time, together with any natural increase. The sincere intention to restore the value of the goods is necessary before a sin against justice can be forgiven. If one who is guilty of an injustice can no longer find the owner or his heirs, he is obliged to give the stolen goods or their value to the poor or to use them for some charitable cause.

5. What does the Church say about the right to private property?

The Church says that the right to private property is a natural right, one that may not be taken away. This does not mean, however, that a man may do with his property whatever he pleases. It is wrong for him to waste it, misuse it, or to use it in a way that will be harmful to others. Then, too, the good of society may dictate that a man give up the ownership of some particular property, but only when he is justly compensated for his loss.

At the same time a man's superfluous income is not left entirely to his own discretion. We speak of that portion of his income which he does not need in order to live as becomes

261

his station. On the contrary the grave obligations of charity, beneficence and liberality which rest upon the wealthy, are constantly insisted upon in telling words by Holy Scripture and the Fathers of the Church—Enc. of Reconstructing the Social Order 50.

The most serious error of Communism is its atheistic materialism. But it errs, too, and in a serious way, in its denial of the natural right of a man to own property.

6. Is justice between two individuals the only form of justice about which Christians should be concerned?

No! Christians must be concerned about all forms of justice and injustice. A decent and humane social order is vitally necessary if people are to be able to seek God with their whole beings.

> *. . . with respect to the fundamental rights of the person, every type of discrimination, whether social or cultural, whether based on sex, race, color, social condition, language or religion is to be overcome and eradicated as contrary to God's intent. . . .*
>
> *Moreover, although rightful differences exist between men, the equal dignity of persons demands that a more humane and just condition of life be brought about. For excessive economic and social differences between the members of the one human family or population groups cause scandal, and militate against social justice, equity, the dignity of the human person, as well as social and international peace.*
>
> *Human institutions, both private and public, must labor to minister to the dignity and purpose of man. At the same time let them put up a stubborn fight against any kind of slavery, whether social or political, and safeguard the basic rights of man under every political system. Indeed human institutions themselves must be accommodated by degrees to the highest of all realities, spiritual ones, even though meanwhile, a long enough time will be required before they arrive at the desired goal*—Constitution on the Church in the Modern World 29.

7. Why is concern for justice a religious concern?

Concern for justice is a religious concern because it was a concern for Jesus. He came to free men from sin and the effects of sin. Injustice, war, discrimination are all effects of sin. Jesus wants to overcome them. People who are not free because of political, economic or social conditions, people who suffer from war and aggression need to experience the freeing concern and love of Jesus in the actions of the members of Jesus' body, the Church.

Jesus came to unite men and any form of discrimination or injustice separates them.

Jesus came to establish the Kingdom of God here on this earth. The Kingdom will reach completion in the next life, but it has begun now and it embraces every aspect of peoples' lives. It embraces work, politics, education, recreation as well as prayer and religious beliefs.

8. What does the Church say about justice?

In the past eighty years the popes and the bishops have spoken time and time again about social problems. They have outlined the principles of justice against which an individual and a society should judge its norms. A person who truly wishes to live out a baptismal commitment will become familiar with Catholic social teaching as contained in such documents as:

a. Mater et Magrista: Christianity and Social Progress (1961)

b. Pacem in Terris: Peace on Earth (1963), Pope John XXIII

c. Gaudium et Spes: Pastoral Constitution on the Church in the Modern World (1965)

d. Dignitas Humanae: Declaration on Human Freedom (1965), Second Vatican Council

e. Populorum Progressio: On the Development of Peoples (1967), Pope Paul VI.

These, as well as many shorter documents and speeches of the popes and bishops, demonstrate the obligation of Christians to be involved in the search for justice, the right of the Church to speak on these matters and guidelines to help people form their consciences in these matters.

Practice

▲ The Church vindicates the right of workers to join trade unions and urges them to do so and to take an active part in them, not only for the workers' protection but also for the establishment of an economic order characterized by justice, tranquility and order. To this end she encourages associations among employers also, envisioning an order in which these various associations will work together for the good of all.

▲ The ideal wage is one paid with the family in mind. Pope Pius XI said: "The wage paid to the workingman must be sufficient for the support of himself and his family . . . ."

▲ The prevalence of certain unjust practices does not alter the fact that they are sins against justice. Among such practices would be included business deals which are based on the slogan, "Let the buyer beware." To sell a defective article the defects of which are carefully camouflaged is unjust, and therefore un-Christian.

▲ To steal from the government or from a great many people is as sinful as to steal from an individual. The cynical excuse, "everyone does it," is unworthy of a Christian.

† † †

The Eighth Commandment:
Respect the Truth

*All of us fall short in many respects. If a person is without
fault in speech he is a man in the fullest sense because he can
control his entire body. When we put bits into the mouths of
horses to make them obey us, we guide the rest of their
bodies. It is the same with ships: however large they are,
and despite the fact that they are driven by fierce winds,
they are directed by very small rudders on whatever course
the steersman's impulse may select. The tongue is something like that. It is a small member, yet it makes great pre-
tensions.*

*See how tiny the spark is that sets a huge forest ablaze!
The tongue is such a flame. It exists among our members
as a whole universe of malice. The tongue defiles the entire
body. Its flames encircle our course from birth, and its fire
is kindled by hell.*

*Every form of life, four-footed or winged, crawling or
swimming, can be tamed, and has been tamed, by mankind;
the tongue no man can tame. It is a restless evil, full of
deadly poison. We use it to say, "Praised be the Lord and
Father"; then we use it to curse men, though they are made
in the likeness of God. Blessing and curse come out of the
same mouth. This ought not to be, my brothers! Does a
spring gush forth fresh water and foul from the same outlet?
A fig tree, brothers, cannot produce olives, or a grapevine
figs; no more can a brackish source yield fresh water—*
JAMES 3:2–12.

JESUS CHRIST is the way, the truth and the life. Because
he is Truth itself, he detests lying and hypocrisy. Our Lord always dealt gently with sinners; but the lying, hypocritical
Pharisees he sternly denounced time and time again. Christ

expects us to "worship the Father in sincerity and truth," to love the truth as he loves it.

The eighth commandment reminds us that, as members of Christ, we must love truth and refrain from lying, deceit and hypocrisy. Such things come from the devil, "a liar and the father of lies"—JOHN 8:44; they have no place in the family of God.

As members of Christ, we must also be solicitous to protect the good name of others. We must imitate the example which Jesus gave us at the Last Supper, when, with the utmost delicacy, he let Judas know that he was aware of his betrayal, but nevertheless did not name him as the traitor before the other apostles.

* * *

You shalt not bear false witness against your neighbor.

1. How do we keep the eighth commandment?

We keep the eighth commandment by speaking the truth, and by being careful not to injure the good name of others.

2. What are the sins against the eighth commandment?

The sins against the eighth commandment are:

lying,
calumny,
detraction,
revealing certain secrets.

3. What is a lie?

A lie is the expression of something which we know to be untrue, made with the intention to deceive.

4. What kind of sin is it to tell a lie?

To tell a lie is ordinarily a venial sin. If a lie injures someone seriously or is told while under oath (perjury), it is a mortal sin.

266

5. Is it ever permissible to tell a lie?

No, it is never permissible to tell a lie, even to avoid evil or to accomplish good. When there is sufficient reason, however, we may use a mental reservation.

6. What is mental reservation?

A mental reservation is an expression which may be taken two ways. In social and business life there are many commonly used mental reservations; e.g., "Mrs. Smith is not at home," may mean that the lady of the house is actually out, or it may be an accepted polite way of saying that she does not wish to see the caller.

7. What is calumny?

Calumny is lying about someone in such a way as to injure his good name.

8. What is detraction?

Detraction is the unnecessary revelation of something about a person which is true but which injures that person's good name.

9. How serious are the sins of calumny and detraction?

Both calumny and detraction are mortal sins if the statement made about another person is seriously damaging to his reputation. They are venial sins if what is said about the other person is not serious. Gossip when it constitutes calumny or detraction is sinful.

One who has committed either calumny or detraction must make whatever effort is required to restore the good name of the injured person. The resolution to make such restitution is necessary in order to obtain forgiveness of these sins.

10. How serious is the obligation of keeping a secret?

The seriousness of the obligation of keeping a secret is determined by the importance of the secret to the person who confided it.

The secrecy of the confessional may never be violated by the priest for any reason whatsoever, even at the cost of his life.

Practice

▲ Gossip columnists and magazines enjoy such prestige today that we are apt to forget the fact that the unnecessary revelation of the sins and crimes of others is unjustifiable and can be seriously sinful. It is surely out of place for a Christian to read or support a certain type of defamatory magazine which specializes in innuendo, scandal and detraction.

▲ An exaggeration can be a lie. This fact should be remembered not only in social life but in business as well. There is no justification for making exaggerated claims for a product in order to make a sale. A Christian should remember that honesty in speech ought to be one of his hallmarks both in social life and in business dealings.

▲ It is very easy to criticize and complain about others, especially in their absence, to discuss their faults needlessly and pass judgment on their actions. We should, rather, bring out the good points of the person under discussion and defend him as we would ourselves when he is being criticized.

† † †

section **43** **The Commandments of the Church**

I assure you, whatever you declare bound on earth shall be held bound in heaven, and whatever you declare loosed on earth shall be held loosed in heaven—MATT. 18:18.

268

AFTER THE WORSHIP of God, which is her first concern, the Church is concerned with the salvation and sanctification of her members. She remembers, if we sometimes forget, that our Lord insisted on the necessity of penance and mortification. She realizes that penance and other practices which we must observe are necessary for our very salvation. As a wise and practical mother she also realizes that, left to ourselves, we would keep putting off doing these necessary things. Accordingly, she places on her children the obligation of fasting, or worshipping God, of doing at definite times and places that which we might otherwise neglect, to our peril.

The laws of the Church, unlike the laws of God, are subject to change by the Church. She has made them; she can change them; she can modify them; she can grant dispensations from them. The laws of the Church, moreover, are not meant to work an undue hardship on her children. When a Church law becomes a very great burden, much more difficult than intended, we are automatically excused from its observance. The Church is the same gentle Christ whose yoke is sweet and whose burden is light.

In obeying the commandments of the Church it is Christ we are obeying, Christ, who said, "He who hears you, hears me."

1. Where are the commandments of the Church to be found?

The commandments of the Church are to be found in her collection of laws, which is called the "Code of Canon Law."

2. What are the principal commandments of the Church?

The principal commandments of the Church are:

a. to assist at Mass on Sundays and holy days of obligation;

b. to fast and abstain on certain days;

c. to receive Holy Communion during the Easter season;

d. to confess our sins once a year, if we have serious sins;

e. to contribute what is necessary for divine worship, for the maintenance of the Church;

f. to observe the Church's regulations on marriage.

3. What are the holy days of obligation?

The holy days of obligation in the United States are the following feasts:

the Solemnity of Mary—January 1
the Ascension of our Lord—forty days after Easter
the Assumption of our Lady—August 15
All Saints—November 1
the Immaculate Conception—December 8
Christmas—December 25.

4. How serious is the obligation of assisting at Mass on Sundays and holy days of obligation?

We are obliged under pain of mortal sin to assist at Mass on these days.

A serious inconvenience excuses one from this obligation. For example, illness or indisposition which would normally keep one home from work or from a social obligation would constitute a sufficient reason for missing Mass.

5. What are the laws of fast and abstinence?

The laws of fast and abstinence are laws of the Church which oblige us to limit the quality and/or quantity of food we eat on certain days. Fasting limits the quantity of food. Abstinence forbids the eating of meat.

Everyone over 21 but not yet 59 years of age is obliged to fast. On days of fast, only one full meal is allowed. Two other meatless meals, sufficient to maintain strength, may be taken according to one's needs.

Eating between meals is not permitted, but liquids including milk and fruit juices are allowed.

Current Church legislation requires only two days of fasting, Ash Wednesday and Good Friday. It does, however, recommend we pick several other days of our own choice for fasting. The weekdays of Lent are good days for observing this salutary practice.

Everyone over 14 years of age is bound to observe the law of abstinence. Complete abstinence is to be observed on Ash Wednesday and Good Friday. This practice is recommended on all Fridays of the year, but most especially the Fridays of Lent.

Practical Points

1. In some instances one is automatically excused from a law of the Church, e.g., one who has diabetes is excused from fasting. In other cases, where keeping the law would be unusually difficult, there is reason to ask for a dispensation. In such cases it is not lawful to assume that one does not have to keep the law; one must first obtain a dispensation from a priest.

2. It should be remembered that a pastor in making appeals for funds is not asking for money for himself. He is acting as a steward who administers the property of the Church. It is his unpleasant duty to have to ask for money which is needed to keep buildings in repair, etc. If all parishioners (instead of a little better than half of them) contributed according to their means such appeals would not be necessary.

3. The Church has, of necessity, made many laws and regulations concerning marriage. In individual cases when there is need to know the law on some aspect of marriage one should consult a priest.

† † †

**The Final Glory
of the Church**

*Then I saw new heavens and a new earth. The former heavens
and the former earth had passed away, and the sea was no
longer. I also saw a new Jerusalem, the holy city, coming
down out of heaven from God, beautiful as a bride prepared
to meet her husband. I heard a loud voice from the throne
cry out: "This is God's dwelling among men. He shall dwell
with them and they shall be his people and he shall be their
God who is always with them. He shall wipe every tear from
their eyes, and there shall be no more death or mourning,
crying out or pain, for the former world has passed away*—
REV. 21:1–4.

WHEN THE SON of God came into this world he came as a
helpless infant. He lived a life of extreme poverty. He was rejected by the people he came to save. His death on the cross, although actually a triumph, had all the appearances of failure.
And yet Christ, even as he stood in humiliation before the court
which condemned him to death, proclaimed that he was king.
He prophesied that he would return to earth one day, no longer
in poverty and humiliation, but in triumph to judge the living
and the dead.

Belief in the second coming of Christ sustained the early
Church even in the darkest hours, when persecution raged about
it and threatened to overwhelm it. However dark the picture,
the early Christians never forgot that the final victory would be
Christ's.

Today the forces of evil are powerful and well organized.
Men and governments refuse to acknowledge Christ as their king,
openly defy him and persecute and kill his followers. This is to
be expected. Our Lord warned us that such things would happen.

While we spare neither effort nor prayer in extending the kingdom of Christ on this earth, therefore, we, too, should remember that, however powerful the enemy, the final victory will be Christ's. He will return in glory and triumph. His enemies will be forever vanquished; and those who are united to him and share his life will share in his eternal victory.

1. Will the work of the Church ever end?

The Church's work of distributing grace will cease when the world comes to an end; but its work of praising and glorifying God will continue forever in heaven.

2. What will the happiness of heaven be like?

In heaven we shall be happy in a way far greater than any man has ever been happy, even in his happiest moments on earth.

a. There will be no sorrow, no pain, no hardship, no want.

He shall wipe every tear from their eyes, and there shall be no more death or mourning, crying out or pain, for the former world has passed away–REV. 21:4.

Those whom the LORD has ransomed will return and enter Zion singing, crowned with everlasting joy; They will meet with joy and gladness, sorrow and mourning will flee–IS. 35:10.

But the souls of the just are in the hand of God, and no torment shall touch them.

They seemed, in the view of the foolish, to be dead; and their passing away was thought an affliction and their going forth from us, utter destruction.

But they are in peace–WIS. 3:1–3.

b. There will be perfect rest, not the rest of inactivity, but the rest which is the perfect satisfaction of all longing, the rest which the heart finds in the contentment of perfect love.

May the angels take you into paradise: may the martyrs come to welcome you on your way, and lead you into the holy city, Jerusalem. May the choir of angels

welcome you, and with Lazarus, who once was poor,
may you have everlasting rest–RITUAL.

c. There will be final and complete union with God, the
source of all joy and happiness. In this world we can know God
only by faith. In heaven we shall see God as he is, face to face,
and we shall be overwhelmed by his beauty and goodness.

Now we see indistinctly, as in a mirror; then we
shall see face to face. My knowledge is imperfect now;
then I shall know even as I am known–1 COR. 13:12.

d. There will be complete ease and familiarity in our conversation with God. Prayer, which is frequently difficult here on
earth, requiring great application and effort, will be a supreme
joy in heaven. Our conversation with God will be infinitely more
delightful than any we have had, even with those whose company
we have enjoyed most on earth.

e. There will be companionship with all the members of
our Father's great family, the angels and the saints and all those
we have known and loved in this world. There will be no fare-
wells, no separation, no end of the love, peace and joy which
will prevail among the children of God.

Whatever we find pleasant, beautiful or desirable in this
world attracts us because it is a faint reflection of God. We have
moments of exaltation, periods of joy and contentment here
on earth; but they never last. They cannot last long nor satisfy
us for long, because in them we have only the merest reflection of
God. If such hints of the beauty and lovableness of God can delight us here, we can only begin to imagine what happiness will
be ours when we behold the reality, God himself, the inexhaustible source of all happiness.

3. Will the world ever end?

The world as we now know it will end some day. However,
there will be "new heavens and a new earth"–2 PET. 3:13, the
details of which are still veiled in mystery.

4. When will the world end?

Only God knows the day and the hour. Our Lord spoke of the end of the world several times; but because his words are prophecies they are mysterious and are capable now of being interpreted in various ways.

While he was seated on the Mount of Olives, his disciples came up to him privately and said: "Tell us, when will all this occur? What will be the sign of your coming and the end of the world?"

In reply Jesus said to them: "Be on guard! Let no one mislead you. Many will come attempting to impersonate me. 'I am the Messiah!' they will claim, and they will deceive many. You will hear of wars and rumors of wars. Do not be alarmed. Such things are bound to happen, but that is not yet the end. Nation will rise against nation, one kingdom against another. There will be famine and pestilence and earthquakes in many places. These are the early stages of the birth pangs. They will hand you over to torture and kill you. Indeed, you will be hated by all nations on my account. Many will falter then, betraying and hating one another. False prophets will rise in great numbers to mislead many.

Because of the increase of evil, the love of most will grow cold. The man who holds out to the end, however, is the one who will see salvation. This good news of the kingdom will be proclaimed throughout the world as a witness to all the nations. Only after that will the end come"–MATT. 24:3–14.

If anyone tells you at that time, "Look, the Messiah is here,' or "He is there," do not believe it.

False messiahs and false prophets will appear, performing signs and wonders so great as to mislead even the chosen if that were possible. Remember, I have told you all about it beforehand; so if they tell you, "Look, he is in the desert," do not go out there; or "He is in the innermost rooms," do not believe it. As the lightning from the east flashes to the west, so will the coming of the Son of Man be.

Where the carcass lies, there the vultures gather.

Immediately after the stress of that period, "the

*sun will be darkened, the moon will not shed her light,
the stars will fall from the sky, and the hosts of heaven
will be shaken loose." Then the sign of the Son of Man
will appear in the sky, and "all the clans of earth will
strike their breasts" as they see "the Son of Man coming on the clouds of heaven" with power and great glory.
He will dispatch his angels "with a mighty trumpet
blast, and they will assemble his chosen from the four
winds, from one end of the heavens to the other"–*
MATT. 24:23–31.

*Stay awake, therefore! You cannot know the day
your Lord is coming–*MATT. 24:42.

5. How did the early Christians interpret these prophecies?

Some undoubtedly expected the end of the world in their
own lifetime, even though they had been warned by St. Peter·

*Note this first of all: in the last days, mocking, sneering
men who are ruled by their passions will arrive on the
scene.
 They will ask: "Where is that promised coming of
his? Our forefathers have been laid to rest, but everything stays just as it was when the world was created."
. . . This point must not be overlooked, dear friends.
In the Lord's eyes, one day is as a thousand years and
a thousand years are as a day. The Lord does not delay in keeping his promise–though some consider it
"delay." Rather, he shows you generous patience,
since he wants none to perish but all to come to repentance. The day of the Lord will come like a
thief . . . . What we await are new heavens and a
new earth where, according to his promise, the justice of God will reside.
 So, beloved, while waiting for this, make every effort to be found without stain or defilement, and at
peace in his sight . . .
 You are forewarned, beloved brothers. Be on your
guard lest you be led astray by the error of the wicked,
and forfeit the security you enjoy–*2 PET. 3:3–17.

However, even those who did not expect the second coming

of Christ before they died lived in such a way as to be prepared for it. They looked forward with eagerness to the second coming of Christ as the final and glorious fulfillment of all that a Christian should hope for.

6. What will be the great event at the end of the world?

The great event will be the return of Christ to this world. Christ's work on earth will not be finished until he returns in glory to reveal his triumph to all mankind. He himself describes this scene:

> When the Son of Man comes in his glory, escorted by all the angels of heaven, he will sit upon his royal throne, and all the nations will be assembled before him. Then he will separate them into two groups, as a shepherd separates sheep from goats.
>
> The sheep he will place on his right hand, the goats on his left. The king will say to those on his right: "Come. You have my Father's blessing! Inherit the kingdom prepared for you from the creation of the world. For I was hungry and you gave me food, I was thirsty and you gave me drink. I was a stranger and you welcomed me, naked and you clothed me. I was ill and you comforted me, in prison and you came to visit me." Then the just will ask him: "Lord, when did we see you hungry and feed you or see you thirsty and give you drink? When did we welcome you away from home or clothe you in your nakedness? When did we visit you when you were ill or in prison?" The king will answer them: "I assure you, as often as you did it for one of my least brothers, you did it for me."
>
> Then he will say to those on his left: "Out of my sight, you condemned, into that everlasting fire prepared for the devil and his angels! I was hungry and you gave me no food. I was thirsty and you gave me no drink. I was away from home and you gave me no welcome, naked and you gave me no clothing. I was ill and in prison and you did not come to comfort me." Then they in turn will ask: "Lord, when did we see you hungry or thirsty or away from home or naked or ill or in prison and not attend you in your needs?" He will answer them: "I assure you, as often as you

neglected to do it to one of these least ones, you neglected to do it to me." These will go off to eternal punishment and the just to eternal life–MATT. 25:31–46.

7. Will the judgment which Christ makes at the end of the world be a real judgment?

It will not be a real judgment in the sense that Christ will be rendering a decision. At his death each man gives an accounting of his life. Nothing decided at this final accounting will be changed in the last judgment. The damned will still be in hell and the saved in heaven. Christ will announce who has been saved and who has been damned.

8. What happens at our death?

At death we will not go before a judgment seat to hear the Lord pronounce sentence upon us. Rather, by a special illumination, God will let us know whether we are ready for eternal happiness in heaven, whether we must undergo further purification in purgatory, or whether we must spend eternity in hell.

9. What do we mean by the resurrection of the dead?

At the end of the world the bodies of the dead will arise.
St. Paul, speaking of the bodies of the just after the resurrection says:

This corruptible body must be clothed with incorruptibility, this mortal body with immortality–1 COR. 15:53.

The body will be spiritualized, immune to sickness and death. It will be able to move from place to place with the speed of thought. The beauty of the soul will shine forth. The glorified body will be able to pass through solid objects. In a word, it will be beautiful, as Christ's was at the Transfiguration, and will possess all the qualities of Christ's body after the Resurrection.

10. How should we prepare for the second coming of Christ?

Our preparation for the end of the world and the second coming of Christ should be positive rather than negative. Instead of dreading the end of the world and anxiously looking for signs and portents, we should prepare ourselves to meet our Savior by endeavoring to lead a holy life and doing our part in spreading the kingdom of God.

The One who gives this testimony says, "Yes, I am coming soon!" Amen! Come, Lord Jesus!

The grace of the Lord Jesus be with you all.
Amen.

With these words of expectation, St. John ended the Book of Revelation, the last book of the Scriptures.

Conclusion

It is heartening to remember that the final victory will be Christ's and that we shall share in that victory if we remain in union with our Savior. But before the final victory there is much to be done. The Church Militant must constantly strive to conquer the world for Christ. The final victory is assured; but there are other victories possible here and now for the achievement of which God requires our cooperation. There are others, our relatives, friends and acquaintances, who may come to love Christ more, perhaps, even become members of his Mystical Body, provided our example and our efforts are what they should be. Others should be able to see that our lives have been enormously enriched because we have been joined to the Mystical Body of Christ. They should be able to see in our lives evidence of that deepest union with God which comes from prayer. They should be able to see that we live by faith, that we are sustained by hope, that we practice love of God and our neighbor in our daily life.

All the means which will enable us to live up to the great challenge of living the Christian life are at our disposal. God will sustain us in our efforts. No prayer will go unanswered. Aid from our brothers in the great family of God will be forthcoming if we call on the saints in heaven and the souls in purgatory.

The life-giving sacraments are there to give us holiness and strength. We should receive them often. Above all, the great source of grace and love, the Eucharist, is there for our daily use. If we wish to be more deeply united to Christ and our neighbor we should make *daily* Mass and Communion our aim.

Help and encouragement will come to us from association with our fellow-members in the Mystical Body. The more deeply we enter into the life of the parish, the more effective we shall be as Catholics. Above all, we should enter wholeheartedly into the great act of the family of God, the Mass. We should take our part, too, in the parish organizations, and if possible in whatever movement of the lay apostolate is open to us.

Finally, we should remember always the words of Pope Pius XII:

For nothing more glorious, nothing nobler, nothing surely more honorable can be imagined than to belong to the holy, Catholic, apostolic and Roman church, in which we become members of one Body as venerable as it is unique; are guided by one supreme Head; are filled with one divine Spirit; are nourished during our earthly exile by one doctrine and one heavenly Bread, until at last we enter into the one, unending blessedness of heaven–Enc. on the Mystical Body 91.

Nick Vando

Photoshop Elements
Tips, Tricks & Shortcuts

For Windows and Mac

In easy steps is an imprint of In Easy Steps Limited
16 Hamilton Terrace · Holly Walk · Leamington Spa
Warwickshire · United Kingdom · CV32 4LY
www.ineasysteps.com

Notice of Liability
Every effort has been made to ensure that this book contains accurate
and current information. However, In Easy Steps Limited and the
author shall not be liable for any loss or damage suffered by readers
as a result of any information contained herein.

Trademarks
Photoshop® is a registered trademark of Adobe Systems Incorporated.
All other trademarks are acknowledged as belonging to their
respective companies.

In Easy Steps Limited supports The Forest Stewardship Council (FSC),
the leading international forest certification organization. All our titles
that are printed on Greenpeace approved FSC certified paper carry the
FSC logo.

MIX
Paper from
responsible sources
FSC® C020837

Printed and bound in the United Kingdom

ISBN 978-1-84078-904-1

Contents

1 Introducing Elements

Photoshop Elements is a photo-editing program that comprehensively spans the gap between very basic programs and professional-level ones. This chapter introduces the various workspaces and modes of Elements, shows how to access them, and details what can be done with photos in each one.

About Elements

Photoshop Elements is the offspring of the professional-level image-editing program, Photoshop. Photoshop is somewhat unusual in the world of computer software, in that it is widely accepted as being the best program of its type on the market. If professional designers or photographers are using an image-editing program, it will almost certainly be Photoshop. However, two of the potential drawbacks to Photoshop are its cost and its complexity. This is where Elements comes into its own. Adobe (the maker of Photoshop and Elements) has recognized that the majority of digital image users (i.e. the consumer market) want something with the basic power of Photoshop, but with enough user-friendly features to make it easy to use, and for a reasonable price. With the explosion in the digital camera and smartphone market, a product was needed to meet the needs of a new generation of image editors – that product is Photoshop Elements.

Elements contains most of the same powerful editing/color management tools as the full version of Photoshop, and it also includes a number of versatile features for sharing images and for creating artistic projects such as slideshows, cards, calendars and memes for sharing on social media. It also has valuable features, such as the Guided edit and Quick edit modes, where you can quickly apply editing techniques and follow step-by-step processes to achieve a range of creative and artistic effects.

Special effects

One of the great things about using Elements with digital images is that it provides numerous fun and creative options for turning mediocre images into eye-catching works of art. This is achieved through a wide variety of step-by-step activities within Guided edit mode, which have been added to and enhanced in Elements.

Advanced features

In addition to user-friendly features, Elements also has an Expert edit mode where you can use a range of advanced features, including a full set of tools for editing and color adjustments.

Photoshop Elements can be bought online directly from Adobe, as well as from other computer and software sites, or at computer software stores. There are Windows and Mac versions of the program, and these are virtually identical. If Elements is bought from the Adobe website, at www.adobe.com, it can be downloaded and installed directly from there. Otherwise it will be provided on a CD, with a serial number that needs to be entered during installation.

The New icon pictured above indicates a new or enhanced feature introduced with the latest version of Photoshop Elements.

Home Screen

When you first open Elements, you will be presented with the Home Screen. This offers initial advice about working with Elements and also provides options for accessing the different workspaces. The Home Screen appears by default when Elements is opened, and it can also be accessed from the Home Screen button on the bottom Taskbar of either of the Elements modes, the Editor and the Organizer.

Home Screen functions

The Home Screen has a range of options covering tips about using Elements and also for accessing the different modes.

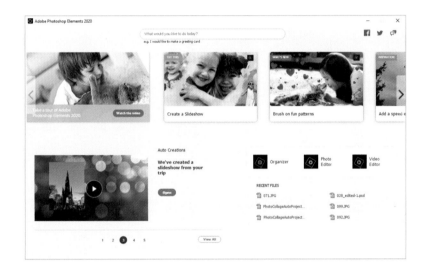

Hot tip

The Home Screen can also be accessed at any time by selecting **Help** > **Home Screen** from the Photo Editor or Organizer Menu bar.

9

① Click on the **Organizer** button to go to the section for organizing and managing photos

② Click on the **Photo Editor** button to go to the section for editing and enhancing photos

③ Click on the **Video Editor** button to open Premiere Elements for working with video (if using Premiere Elements)

Don't forget

Premiere Elements is the companion program for editing digital video. It can be bought separately, or in a two-program bundle with Photoshop Elements.

...cont'd

4 Click on this panel to access the Photoshop Elements help pages, detailing the latest features

5 The top panels can be used to get information about a range of creative photo techniques, such as slideshows and information about using the Home Screen

Create a Slideshow

Get started quickly with the home screen

6 Click on the arrow at the right-hand side of the top panel to view more help options within the Home Screen for creating engaging photo projects

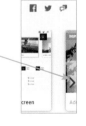

7 Click on the arrow at the left-hand side of the top panel to move back to the previous screen

8 One of the features of Elements is the ability to make Auto Creations. These are artistic slideshows and collages that are automatically created from groups of similar photos. On the Home Screen, Auto Creations are displayed in this panel

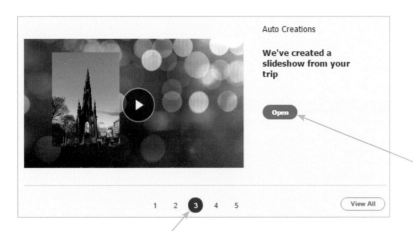

Click on the **Open** button to view an Auto Creation. Click on the **View All** button to see the full range of Auto Creations.

9 Click here to view the available Auto Creations

10 Below the Organizer, Photo Editor and Video Editor buttons, the most recently opened files are displayed. Click on one to open it again in Elements

For more information about Auto Creations, see pages 84-87.

11 Use the Search box at the top of the Home Screen to search for specific photographic techniques, such as changing the colors in a photo or creating a calendar

11

Photo Editor Workspace

From the Home Screen, the Photo Editor workspace can be accessed. This is a combination of the work area (where images are opened and edited), menus, toolbars, toolboxes and panels. At first it can seem a little daunting, but Elements has been designed with three different editing modes to give you as many options as possible for editing your photos.

The components of the Photo Editor (Editor) are:

Menu bar   Editor mode buttons   Panel Bin

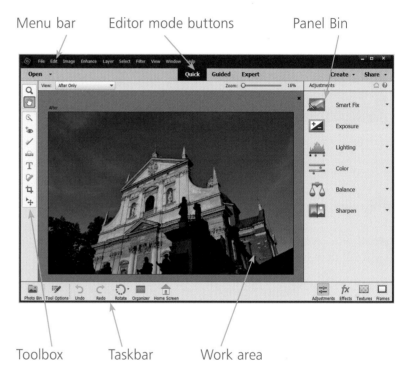

Don't forget

The Elements Organizer can be accessed from any of the Editor modes by clicking on the Organizer button on the Taskbar.

Organizer

Toolbox   Taskbar   Work area

Editor modes

The three different modes in the Photo Editor are accessed from the buttons at the top of the Elements window. They are:

Hot tip

The keyboard shortcut for closing Elements is **Ctrl** + **Q** (**Command** key + **Q** on a Mac).

- **Quick edit mode**. This can be used to perform quick editing options in one step.

- **Guided edit mode**. This can be used to perform a range of editing techniques, following a step-by-step process for each.

- **Expert edit mode**. This can be used for ultimate control over the editing process.

12

...cont'd

Taskbar and Tool Options

The Taskbar is the group of buttons that is available across all three Editor modes, at the bottom left of the Elements window:

One of the options on the Taskbar is Tool Options. This displays the available options for any tool selected from the Toolbox (different tools are available in each of the different Editor modes). See pages 20-21 for details.

Photo Bin

The Photo Bin is another feature that can be accessed from all three Editor modes. The Photo Bin enables you to quickly access all of the images that you have open within the Editor. To use the Photo Bin:

1 Open two or more images. The most recently opened one will be the one that is active in the Editor window

2 All open images are shown here in the Photo Bin

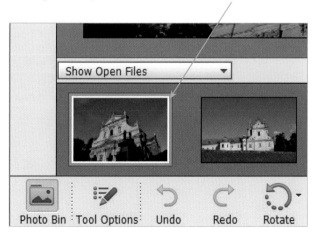

3 Click on an image in the Photo Bin to make that the active one for editing

The items on the Taskbar are, from left to right: show or hide the Photo Bin, show or hide the Tool Options bar, undo the previous actions, redo any undone actions, rotate the active photo, and access the Organizer. In Expert edit mode there is also an option to change the layout.

Images can also be made active for editing by dragging them directly from the Photo Bin and dropping them within the Editor window.

When image editing has begun, this icon appears at its top right-hand corner in the Photo Bin.

Quick Edit Mode

Quick edit mode contains a number of functions that can be selected from panels and applied to an image, without the need to manually apply all of the commands. To do this:

For a more detailed look at Quick edit mode, see pages 88-91.

Some of the options in the Adjustments panel in Quick edit mode (Step 3) have an **Auto** option for applying the effect in a single click.

Move the cursor over one of the thumbnails to view a real-time preview of the effect on the open image. Click on one of the thumbnails to apply the effect.

1 In the Editor, click on the **Quick** button

2 The currently active image is displayed within the Quick edit window. This has the standard Taskbar and Photo Bin,

and a reduced Toolbox. Click here to access the Quick edit panels

3 Select one of the commands to have it applied to the active image. This can be applied either by clicking on one of the thumbnail options or by dragging the appropriate slider at the top of the panel

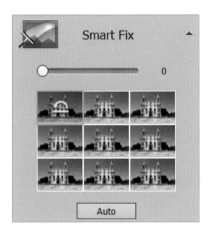

4 Click on these buttons on the Taskbar at the bottom of the Quick edit panel to select **Adjustments**, **Effects**, **Textures** and **Frames** options for adding to photos

Guided Edit Mode

Guided edit mode focuses on common tasks for editing digital images, and shows you how to perform them with a step-by-step process. To use Guided edit mode:

1 In the Editor, click on the **Guided** button

2 The Guided edit window contains a range of categories that can be accessed from buttons at the top of the window. Each category contains Guided edit options. Drag the mouse over each item to view the before and after effect

3 Each item has its own wizard to perform the required task. This will take you through a step-by-step process for undertaking the selected action. Move through the steps to complete the selected Guided edit option

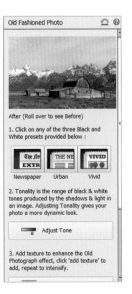

Some new effects have been added to Guided edits in the latest version of Elements.

Guided edit mode is a great place to start if you are new to image editing, or feel unsure about anything to do with it.

Don't forget

Different Guided edits have varying numbers of steps in the required wizards, but the process is similar for all of them.

Expert Edit Mode

Expert edit mode is where you can take full editing control over your photos. It has a range of powerful editing tools so that you can produce subtle and impressive effects. To use Expert edit mode:

Hot tip

Select **Window** > **Tools** from the Menu bar to show or hide the Toolbox.

16

1 In the Editor, click on the **Expert** button

2 The full range of editing tools is available:

Expert edit mode Toolbox   Open panels

Tool Options button

Taskbar Layout button   Expert edit mode panel buttons

Don't forget

When a tool is selected in the Toolbox, the Tool Options bar (above the Taskbar) has various options for the selected tool; see pages 20-21.

The **Layout** button is the one addition on the Taskbar within Expert edit mode, as opposed to Quick and Guided edit modes. Click on the **Layout** button to access options for the display of your open photos within the Editor window.

...cont'd

The Expert edit mode Toolbox

The Toolbox in Expert edit mode contains tools for applying a wide range of editing techniques. Some of the tools have more than one option. To see if a tool has additional options:

1 Move the cursor over the **Toolbox**. Tools that have additional options appear with a small arrow in the top right-hand corner of their icons. Click on a tool to view the options within the Tool Options bar

The tools that have additional options are: Crop, Marquee, Lasso, Quick Selection, Spot Healing Brush, Type, Smart Brush, Eraser, Brush, Clone Stamp, Custom Shape, Blur, and Sponge.

The default Toolbox tools are (keyboard shortcut in brackets):

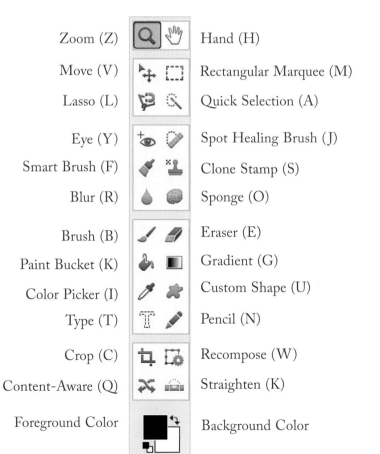

Zoom (Z)   Hand (H)

Move (V)   Rectangular Marquee (M)

Lasso (L)   Quick Selection (A)

Eye (Y)   Spot Healing Brush (J)

Smart Brush (F)   Clone Stamp (S)

Blur (R)   Sponge (O)

Brush (B)   Eraser (E)

Paint Bucket (K)   Gradient (G)

Color Picker (I)   Custom Shape (U)

Type (T)   Pencil (N)

Crop (C)   Recompose (W)

Content-Aware (Q)   Straighten (K)

Foreground Color   Background Color

Keyboard shortcuts can be used by pressing the Shift key and the appropriate letter.

Hold down the Alt key and click on the tools in the Toolbox to scroll through the additional options, if available.

17

...cont'd

Panels

In Expert edit mode, Elements uses panels to group together similar editing functions and provide quick access to certain techniques. The panels can be accessed from the **Window** button on the Expert Menu bar and also from the respective buttons on the right-hand side of the Expert edit mode Taskbar. Click on the **More** button to access the full range of panels:

- **Actions**. This can be used to perform automated actions over a group of images at the same time.

- **Adjustments**. This can be used to add or make editing changes to adjustment layers in the Layers panel.

- **Color Swatches**. This is a panel for selecting colors that can then be applied to parts of an image, or elements that have been added to it.

- **Effects**. This contains special effects and styles that can be applied to an entire image or a selected part of an image. There are also filters that have their own dialog boxes, in which settings can be applied and adjusted. Layer Styles can also be applied to elements within an image.

- **Favorites**. This is where your favorite graphical elements from the Content panel can be stored and retrieved quickly.

- **Filters**. This can be used to add a range of filter effects to an image (see page 92 for details).

- **Graphics**. This contains graphical elements that can be added to images, including backgrounds, frame shapes and text.

- **Histogram**. This displays a graph of the tonal range of the colors in an image. It is useful for assessing the overall exposure of an image, and it changes as an image is edited.

- **History**. This can be used to undo any editing steps that have been performed. Every action is displayed and can be reversed by dragging the slider next to the most recent item.

Hot tip

The panels are opened in the Panel Bin, which is at the right of the Editor window. In Expert edit mode this can be collapsed or expanded by selecting **Window** > **Panel Bin** from the Menu bar.

Hot tip

Some panels can be opened directly with keyboard shortcuts. These are: Effects F6, Graphics F7, Info F8, Histogram F9, History F10, Layers F11 and Navigator F12.

Hot tip

Select **Window** > **Reset Panels** from the Menu bar to revert the panels to their original format. This is useful if you have been working with several panels and want to revert to the default.

...cont'd

- **Info**. This displays information about an image, or a selected element within it, including details about the color in an image or the position of a certain item.

- **Layers**. This enables several layers to be included within an image. This can be useful if you want to add elements to an existing image, such as shapes or text.

- **Navigator**. This can be used to move around an image and magnify certain areas of it.

- **Styles**. This can be used to add styles to the edge of an image, such as a bevel effect.

Working with panels

To work with panels in Expert edit mode:

1 Click on one of the panel buttons on the Taskbar on the previous page to open the related panel

2 If there are additional sections for a panel, click here to view the other options

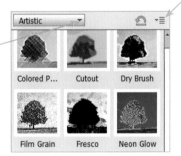

3 Click on the **More** button to view the rest of the available panels

4 The additional panels are grouped together. Click on a tab to access the required panel. Click and drag on a tab to move the panel away from the rest of the group

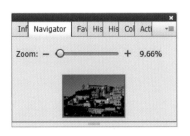

Styles can only be applied to images that have been converted to layers (this can be done when the **Styles** button is selected).

Click here to access the menu for an open panel.

Do not have too many panels open at one time. If you do, the screen will become cluttered and it will be difficult to edit images effectively.

19

Tool Options Bar

When a tool is selected from the Toolbox, in either Expert edit or Quick edit mode, the Tool Options bar is activated on the Taskbar. This provides options for selecting different tools from that category (if there are any), and also settings for the currently selected tool. To use the Tool Options bar:

Use these buttons in the top right-hand corner of the Tool Options bar to, from left to right: access the Help options for the selected tool; access the Tool Options menu; or hide the Tool Options bar (click on a tool to display the Tool Options bar again).

Brush mode has several options for how the brush stroke interacts with the background behind it; e.g. Color Burn, Lighten or Soft Light. These can be used to create artistic effects with the Brush tool and the photo itself.

For a more detailed look at Brush style settings, see pages 164-165.

1 Select a tool from the Toolbox

2 Click here on the Taskbar to hide or show the Tool Options bar

3 The Tool Options bar is positioned above the Taskbar at the bottom of the Elements window

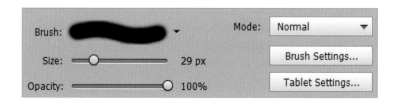

4 Click here to select different tools from the selected category (in this example it is the Brush tool, the Impressionist Brush tool or the Color Replacement tool)

5 For each item there are different settings available; e.g. for the Brush tool there is **Brush** type, **Size** and **Opacity** (how much of the background is visible through the selected brush stroke). There are also options for a wider Brush range, including **Mode:** and **Brush Settings...**

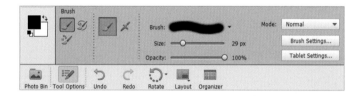

6 Other tools have different settings available from the Tool Options bar. For instance, the **Zoom** tool has options for zooming the currently active image to different magnifications, and also viewing it at specific sizes; e.g. **1:1**, **Fit Screen**, **Fill Screen** and **Print Size**

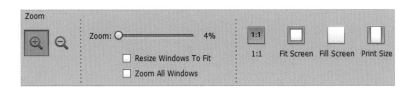

7 The **Type** tool has options for font type, font style, font color, font size, leading (the space between lines of text), bold, italics, underline, strikethrough and also text alignment (left, center or right)

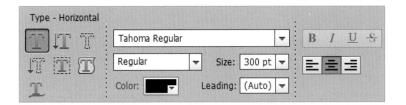

Don't forget

The Type tool also has options for changing the orientation of text and also Warp Text for special effects; see page 152 for details.

8 For the **Marquee** tool and the **Lasso** tool there are options for editing a current selection (add to selection, subtract from selection and intersect with selection) and also for the amount of feathering to be applied. This determines how much around the edge of the selection is slightly blurred, to give a soft-focus effect. The Marquee tool also has an option for setting a specific aspect for the selection; i.e. create it at a fixed ratio or size

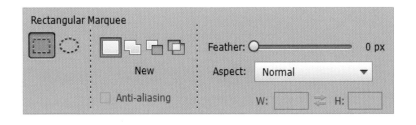

Don't forget

The Marquee and Lasso tools are used to make selections by dragging the tool over the image. This can be symmetrical selections (e.g. Rectangular Marquee) or freehand (e.g. Lasso).

21

Although the Menu bar menus are all available in each of the Editor modes, some of the menu options are not available in Quick edit or Guided edit mode.

Elements does not support the CMYK color model for editing digital images. This could be an issue if you use a commercial printer.

The Mac version of Elements also has a Photoshop Elements menu on the Menu bar. This contains the Preferences options (see next page).

Menu Bar

In the Editor, the Menu bar contains menus that provide all of the functionality for the workings of Elements. Some of these functions can also be achieved through the use of the other components of Elements, such as the Toolbox, the Tool Options bar and the panels. However, the Menu bar is where all of the commands needed for the digital editing process can be accessed in one place.

Menu bar menus

- **File**. This has standard commands for opening, saving and printing images.

- **Edit**. This contains commands for undoing previous operations, and standard copy-and-paste techniques.

- **Image**. This contains commands for altering the size, shape and position of an image. It also contains more advanced functions such as changing the color mode of an image.

- **Enhance**. This contains commands for editing the color elements of an image. It also contains quick-fix options and commands for creating Photomerge effects such as panoramas and combining exposures.

- **Layer**. This contains commands for working with different layers within an image.

- **Select**. This contains commands for working with areas that have been selected within an image, with one of the selection tools in the Toolbox.

- **Filter**. This contains numerous filters that can be used to apply special effects to an image.

- **View**. This contains commands for changing the size at which an image is displayed, and also options for showing or hiding rulers and grid lines.

- **Window**. This contains commands for changing the way multiple images are displayed, and also options for displaying the components of Elements.

- **Help**. This contains the various Help options.

Preferences

A number of preferences can be set within Elements to determine the way the program operates. It is perfectly acceptable to leave all of the default settings as they are, but as you become more familiar with the program you may want to change some of the preference settings. Preferences can be accessed by selecting **Edit** > **Preferences** from the Menu bar (**Adobe Photoshop Elements Editor** > **Preferences** in the Mac version). The available ones are:

- **General**. This contains a variety of options for selecting items, such as shortcut keys.

- **Saving Files**. This determines the way Elements saves files.

- **Performance**. This determines how Elements allocates memory when processing editing tasks.

- **Scratch Disks**. This determines how Elements allocates disk space when processing editing tasks (referred to as "scratch disks"). If you require more memory for editing you can do this by allocating up to four scratch disks. These act as extra areas from which memory can be used during editing.

- **Display & Cursors**. This determines how cursors operate when certain tools are selected.

- **Transparency**. This determines the color or transparency of the background on which an open image resides.

- **Units & Rulers**. This determines the unit of measurement used by items such as rulers.

- **Guides & Grids**. This determines the color and format of any guides and grids that are used.

- **Plug-Ins**. This displays any plug-ins that have been downloaded to enhance image editing with Elements.

- **Adobe Partner Services** and **Update Options**. These can be used to check for related services and determine how updates to Elements are delivered.

- **Type**. This determines how text appears on images.

- **Country/Region Selection**. This is used to select the location from where you are using Elements.

Each preference has its own dialog box in which the specific preference settings can be made.

A scratch disk is an area of temporary storage on the hard drive that can be utilized if the available memory (RAM) has been used up.

Guides and grids can be accessed from the View menu in Editor mode.

Organizer Workspace

The Organizer workspace contains functions for sorting, viewing and finding multiple images. To use the Organizer:

1 In any of the Editor modes, click on the **Organizer** button on the Taskbar

The Organizer has four views, accessed from these buttons:

- Media View   **Media**
- People View   **People**
- Places View   **Places**
- Events View   **Events**

Media View

Media View displays thumbnails of your photos, and also has functions for sorting and finding images:

Albums and Folders   View buttons   Thumbnails

Organizer Taskbar   Keyword (Tag)/Info button

Editor

...cont'd

1 Click on these buttons to apply image-editing effects to a selected image in Media View, or view the Tags and Information panels

For information about using tags and keywords, see pages 48-49.

People View

This view can be used to tag specific people and then view photos with those people in them.

For information about using the Organizer, and its different views, see Chapter 2.

Places View

This view can be used to place photos on a map so that they can be searched for by location.

When you have a group of photos from the same location, add them to Places View so that this can be used to search over your photos.

Events View

This view can be used to group photos according to specific events such as birthdays and vacations.

Create Mode

Create mode is where you can release your artistic flair and start designing items such as photo books and photo collages. It can also be used to create slideshows, and to put your images onto disks. To use Create mode:

Use your 12 best photos when using the Photo Calendar option.

1 In either the Editor or the Organizer, click on the **Create** button

Create ▾

2 Select one of the Create projects. Each project has a wizard that takes you through the Create process. The projects include photo books, greeting cards, photo calendars, photo collages, and covers for CDs/DVDs

Slideshow
Photo Collage
Photo Prints
Photo Book
Greeting Card
Photo Calendar
Prints and Gifts
Instant Movie
Video Story
Video Collage
DVD with Menu
CD Jacket
DVD Jacket
CD/DVD Label

3 The Create wizard takes you through the process so you can display your photos in a variety of creative ways

Create mode projects take longer than normal image-editing functions.

4 For most creations there is a theme that can be applied, to which your own photos can then be added

Click on the **Print** button once a creation has been made, to produce a hard copy.

5 Your photos can be added automatically from the Photo Bin, or you can drag them directly from there onto the creation

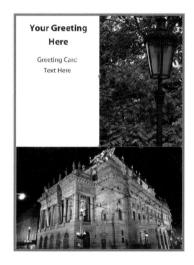

6 Once your photos have been added, a new file is created, to which you can add text, layout designs and graphics. Click on any available text boxes to add text there, click on the **Layouts** button to change the layout of the creation, and click on the **Graphics** button to add a background

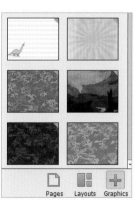

Click on the **Save** button to save a completed creation in a specific file format, and the **Close** button to exit Create mode without saving the project.

7 Click on the **Advanced Mode** button to access the Expert edit mode Toolbox, which can be used to edit the creation in the same way as for a standard photo

Share Mode

Share mode can be used to distribute your images to family and friends in a number of creative ways. To use Share mode:

1 In the Organizer, click on the **Share** button

2 Select one of the Share options, such as sharing to social media sites, sharing via email or creating a DVD or PDF slideshow

The **Share** function can also be accessed from within the Editor, but there are fewer share options available.

28

3 If you are sharing to email, the selected item is added to a wizard that can be used to determine the size and quality of the attachment that you want to send. Click on the **Next** button to move through the wizard

To share an image in an email you need to have an appropriate email app on your computer, and an internet connection.

4 For sharing to social media sites such as Flickr and Twitter, Elements has to initially be

authorized to share content to these sites. Click on the **Authorize** button to give Elements permission to share to the selected app

There is always some risk in giving websites authorization to access your computer.

5 Enter your login details for the selected site and click on the **Authorise app** button (note that the spellings are localized)

You must already have an account with a specific social media site in order to authorize Elements to use it; you cannot create an account during this process.

6 In the Elements window, click on the **Done** button to give Elements permission to share with the selected app

7 Once permission has been given for a social media site, you can share photos to the site by clicking on

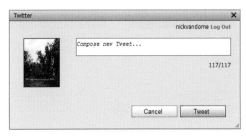

You only have to authorize Elements to use a social media site once. After that, photos can be shared in two clicks from the **Share** menu.

the **Share** button at the top of the Elements window, selecting the required app and entering the necessary information; i.e. a caption

Getting Help

One of the differences between Elements and the full version of Photoshop is the amount of assistance and guidance offered by each program. Since Photoshop is aimed more at the professional end of the market, the level of help is confined largely to the standard help directory, which serves as an online manual. Elements also contains this, but in addition it has the Getting Started option, which is designed to take users through the digital image-editing process as smoothly as possible. The Getting Started option offers general guidance about digital imaging techniques and there are also help items that can be accessed by selecting Help from the Menu bar. These include online help; information on available plug-ins for Elements; tutorials; and support details.

Using the help files

A range of help options can also be accessed from the Home Screen.

1 Select **Photoshop Elements Help** from the **Help** menu and click on an item to display it in the main window. Click on the links at the left-hand side to navigate through each section

The keyboard shortcut for Photoshop Elements Help is F1.

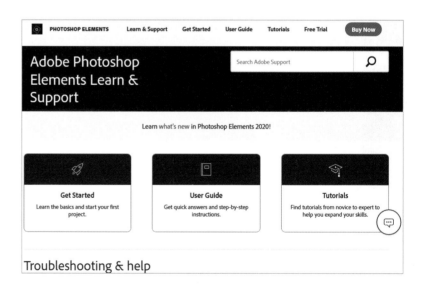

2 Organizing Images

This chapter shows how to download digital images via Elements and how to view and organize them, including using the People, Places and Events views. It shows how you can tag images so that they are easy to find, how to search for items according to a variety of criteria, and how to use albums and folders to organize and manage images in the Organizer.

Obtaining Images

One of the first tasks in Elements is to import images so that you can start editing and sharing them. This can be done from a variety of devices, but the process is similar for all of them. To import images into Elements:

Don't forget

For many digital cameras, the Photo Downloader window will appear automatically once the camera is connected to the computer. However, if this does not happen it will have to be accessed manually, as shown here.

1 Access the **Organizer** by clicking on this button in the Editor

2 Select **File** > **Get Photos and Videos** from the Menu bar and select the type of device from which you want to load images into Elements, or

From Files and Folders...	Ctrl+Shift+G
From Camera or Card Reader...	Ctrl+G
From Scanner...	Ctrl+U
In Bulk...	

Hot tip

Smartphones are widely used for taking digital photos and they can be connected to a computer with a USB cable, for downloading the photos.

3 Click on the **Import** button and select one of the options for obtaining images

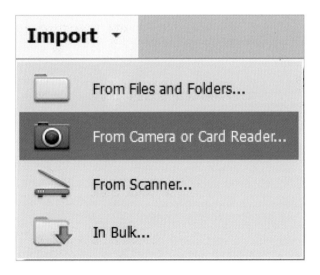

Hot tip

Images can also be imported from existing files and folders on your computer. After this has been done, they will be added to the Organizer's database and you will be able to apply all of its features to the images.

...cont'd

4 If you select **From Camera or Card Reader...**, click the drop-down arrow beside **Get Photos from:** to select a specific device. This can include directly from a digital camera (connected to your computer with a USB cable), a smartphone or a memory card, using a memory card reader

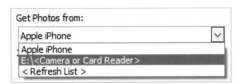

5 The number of files selected to be downloaded are shown under the **Get Photos from:** drop-down box in the Photo Downloader window

6 Click the **Browse...** button to select a destination for the selected images

7 Click the **Get Media** button to download them

Images can also be downloaded from a USB flashdrive. To do this, connect the flashdrive and use the **From Camera or Card Reader...** download option. You will then be able to download the images in the same way as with a camera or memory card reader.

The Delete Options box in the Photo Downloader has options for what happens once you have downloaded your photos. These are: **After Copying, Do Not Delete Originals**; **After Copying, Verify and Delete Originals**; and **After Copying, Delete Originals**. If you do delete the originals from your camera or card reader, make sure you back up the ones that you have just downloaded, to a USB flashdrive or an external hard drive.

...cont'd

8 Click on the **Advanced Dialog** button to access additional options for downloading your images. Here, you can select specific images so that they are not all downloaded at once

Advanced Dialog

The Advanced Dialog Photo Downloader has an option to **Automatically Fix Red Eyes**. Check this box **On** if you want red eye to be removed from photos as they are downloaded.

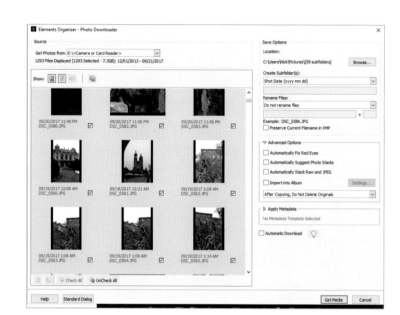

Depending on the number of photos that you have on your camera or memory card, the downloading process may take a few minutes.

9 Click on the **Get Media** button to import the images. They can then be viewed in the Organizer and opened in the Editor

Get Media

Click on the **Minimize** button in Step 9 so that you can get on with other tasks while your photos are being downloaded.

Copying - 3% Completed

From: E:\<Camera or Card Reader>
To: C:\Users\Nick\Pictures\2017 09 18

3%

File 40 of 1293: Copying File...

DSC_0513.JPG

Minimize   Stop

...cont'd

Importing in bulk
Using the Import function, it is also possible to import large numbers of images in one action, with the In Bulk... option:

1 From the Organizer select **Import** > **In Bulk...**

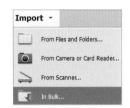

2 In the **Import Media** window, you can select folders to import by checking the box next to them

3 Click here to select a sub-folder

4 Check **Off** the main folder to deselect all sub-folders

5 Click on a specific sub-folder to select it. The main folder is also selected

6 Click on the **Import** button to import the selected folders

By default, the main top-level folder (Pictures) is selected, and so are all of the sub-folders.

Click on this button next to a folder (or sub-folder) to add the folder to a Watch List. This means that when new images are added to this folder on your computer, they will automatically be imported by Elements.

Even though the main folder becomes selected in Step 5, only one sub-folder is selected. This is shown at the top right-hand side of the window.

Media View

Media View is the function within the Organizer that is used to view, find and sort images. When using Media View, images have to be actively added to it so it can then catalog them. Once images have been imported, Media View acts as a window for viewing and sorting your images, no matter where they are located. Media View is the default view when you access the Organizer and can be accessed at any time by clicking on the Media button:

To change the way images are displayed in Media View, select **View** from the Menu bar and check On or Off the **Details** option.

Albums and Folders

Tags and Info panels

Media

Media View can also be used to display video files, audio files, Elements projects and PDF files. To view these, select **View** > **Media Types** from the Menu bar and check On the required items.

Organizer Taskbar

Keyword/Info button

There is also a magnification slider on the Taskbar, which can be used for changing the size at which images are viewed in the main Media View window:

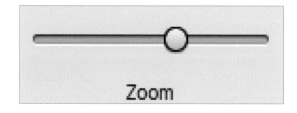

36

...cont'd

Accessing images

To access images within Media View:

1 Click on images to select them individually, or as a group (see second Hot tip)

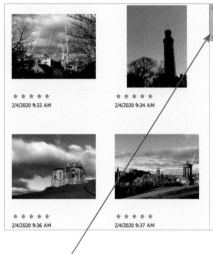

2 Drag the scroll bar to scroll through images within the main window

3 Double-click on an image to view it in the whole Media View window

Hot tip

Select an image in the Organizer and select **View** > **Full Screen** from the Menu bar to view the image at the full size of your monitor.

Hot tip

To select multiple images, drag over the thumbnails, or hold down **Shift** and click on a range of thumbnails to select them all. Alternatively, hold down **Ctrl** (**Command** on a Mac) and click on the thumbnails to select a group of non-consecutive images.

Hot tip

If images were captured with a digital camera, they will appear in Media View in order of the date the image was taken. To make sure this is accurate, set your camera to the correct date and time.

...cont'd

Media View functionality

Media View has a considerable amount of power and functionality in terms of organizing and editing images within the Organizer. This includes the Taskbar and panels for adding tags to images, and viewing information about them:

Media View can be set to watch specific folders on your computer. Whenever images are added to these folders, or edited within them, you will be prompted to add them into the Media View. To specify the folders to be watched, select **File** > **Watch Folders** from the Menu bar and then browse to the folder, or folders, that you want to include.

38

1 The Taskbar is located at the bottom of the main window and contains buttons to, from left to right: show or hide the Albums and Folders panel; undo the previous action; rotate a selected image; add images to a map for Places View; add an event to images for Events View; apply quick editing fixes; access the selected images in the Editor; view the selected images in a slideshow; and access the Home Screen page

2 Select an image in the main Media View window and click on this button to apply instant editing fixes to it (without having to move to the Editor)

3 Click on one of the editing functions in the right-hand panel to apply it to the selected image(s)

When an Instant Fix is applied to a photo, a new photo is automatically created, and this is stored within a **Version Set** with the original photo. See page 41 for more details on Version Sets.

4 Click on this button to view details of selected images in Media View

5 Click on the **Information** tab. Click on these arrows to expand each section

For more details about adding tags to images, see pages 48-49.

6 Access the **General** panel to see information about the image name, size, date taken and where it is saved on your computer. You can edit the name and add a caption here

Hot tip

A caption can also be added to an image by selecting it and selecting **Edit > Add Caption** from the Menu bar.

7 Access the **Metadata** panel to see detailed information about an image that is added by the camera when it is taken

8 Click on this button to view an expanded list of Metadata information

Don't forget

Metadata is information about an image that is stored in the image file itself, in addition to the image that is displayed.

9 Access the **History** panel to view the editing history of the image

Stacks

Since digital cameras and smartphones make it quick, easy and cheap to capture dozens or hundreds of images, it is no surprise that most people are now capturing more images than ever before. One reason for this is that it is increasingly tempting to take several shots of the same subject, just to try to capture the perfect image. The one drawback with this is that when it comes to organizing your images on a computer, it can become time-consuming to work your way through all of your near-identical shots. Media View offers a useful solution to this by allowing you to stack similar images, so that you can view a single thumbnail rather than several. To do this:

You can remove images from a stack by selecting the stack in Media View and selecting
Edit > **Stack** > **Flatten Stack** from the Menu bar. However, this will remove all of the images, apart from the top one, from Media View. This does not remove them from your hard drive, although there is an option to do this too, if you wish.

To revert stacked images to their original state, select the stack and select **Edit** > **Stack** > **Unstack Photos** from the Menu bar.

Only stack similar photos, otherwise you may forget which photos are underneath the stack.

1 Select the images that you want to stack in Media View

2 Select **Edit** > **Stack** > **Stack Selected Photos** from the Menu bar

3 The images are stacked into a single thumbnail, and the existence of the stack is indicated by this icon

4 To view all of the stacked images, click this button

5 Click here to return to the rest of the photos in Media View

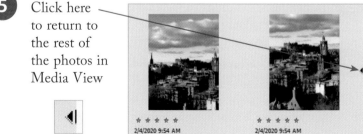

Version Sets

When working with digital images it is commonplace to create several different versions of a single image. This could be to use one for printing and one for use on the web, or because there are elements of an image that you want to edit. Instead of losing track of images that have been edited, it is possible to create stacked thumbnails of edited images, which are known as Version Sets. These can include the original image and all of the edited versions. Version Sets can be created and added to from the Photo Editor and viewed in Media View. To do this:

1 Open an image in the Photo Editor

2 Make editing changes to the image in either Expert edit mode or Quick edit mode

3 Select **File** > **Save As** from the Menu bar

4 Check **On** the **Save in Version Set with Original** box and click **Save**

5 In Media View, the original image and the edited one are grouped together in a stack, and the fact that it is a Version Set is denoted by the icon in the top right-hand corner

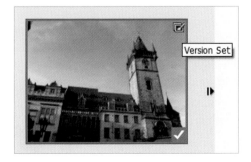

6 To view all of the images in a Version Set, select the set and select **Edit** > **Version Set** > **Expand Items in Version Set** from the Menu bar

The other Version Set menu options include **Flatten Version Set**, and **Revert to Original**. The latter deletes all of the other versions except the original image.

Version Sets are also created if an image has an Instant Fix applied to it in the Organizer.

People View

Shots of people are popular in most types of photography. However, this can result in hundreds or thousands of photos of different people. In Elements there is a feature that enables you to tag people throughout your collections. This is known as People Recognition. To use this:

1 In the Organizer, click on the **People** button, then click on the **Named** button

2 Any named people are shown in the **Named** window

42

3 Click on the **Unnamed** button to view faces that have not already been assigned names

4 Click on one of the thumbnails to add a name

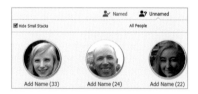

5 Add a name and click on the check mark symbol to apply the name to that group of photos

Adding people directly

To add names manually, directly from a photo:

1 Open a photo at full size in Media View and click on the **Mark Face** button

2 A prompt box appears on the screen. Drag this over the required face, add a name in the **Add Name** box and click on the green check mark to apply the name

Viewing people

To view people who have been tagged with People Recognition:

People Recognition really comes into its own when you have tagged dozens or hundreds of photos. You can then view all of the photos containing a specific person.

1 Click on the **People** button in the main Organizer window

2 Click on the **Named** button. The tagged people's photos are stacked in thumbnails. Click on a thumbnail to view all of the photos of that person (that have been tagged)

Double-click on the thumbnails in the Named window to view the images in a grid. In the grid, double-click on a single image to view it at full size.

Places View

One of the most common reasons for taking photos is when people are on vacation in different and new locations. Within the Organizer it is possible to tag photos to specific locations on a map, so that you can quickly view all of your photos from a certain area. To do this:

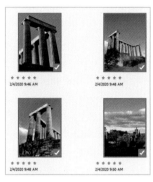

1 In Media View, select all of the photos from a specific location

Hot tip

You can move around the map by clicking and dragging. You can also zoom in and out by right-clicking on the map and selecting the relevant command.

2 On the Taskbar, click on the **Add Location** button

3 Enter a location for the set of photos and click on the **Apply** button

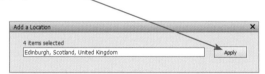

4 To view photos that have been placed on a map, click on the **Places** button in the main Organizer window

Hot tip

Click on the **Unpinned** button at the top of the Places window to view all of the photos that have not had locations added to them. They appear next to the map so that they can be dragged onto a location.

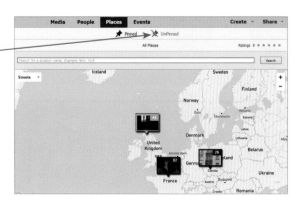

5 Use these controls to move around the map and zoom in and out on it

Hot tip

The map can be viewed as **Map**, **Hybrid**, **Light** or **Dark**. If **Map** is selected, there is also an option for viewing **Terrain**.

6 Click on a set of photos in a location. Click on this button to move through them

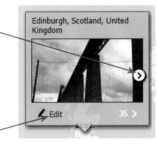

Edinburgh, Scotland, United Kingdom

Edit   35 >

7 Click on the **Edit** button to view the individual photos in the left-hand panel

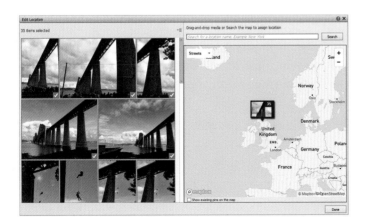

Beware

If a photo with an existing location is selected and the **Add Location** button is clicked, the location for the photo can be changed but it will be removed from the original one.

8 Click on the **Done** button to exit the map

Done

Events View

Photos in the Organizer can also be allocated to specific events such as family celebrations or overseas trips. This is done with Events View. To do this:

46

1 In Media View, select all of the required photos for a specific event

2 On the Taskbar, click on the **Add Event** button

3 In the **Add New Event** panel, add details including name, start and end date, and a description of the event

4 Click on the **Done** button

5 To view photos that have been allocated to an event, click on the **Events** button in the main Organizer window

6 All photos for a specific event are grouped together

...cont'd

7 Double-click on the thumbnail to view all of the photos allocated to the event

Hot tip

Click on the **Suggested** button at the top of the Events window to view groups of photos that Elements thinks may be suitable for new events.

8 Click on the **Back** button to go back to the thumbnail view in Step 6

9 Click on the **Calendar** button on the bottom toolbar to view events from specific dates

Calendar		Clear
	All Years ▼	
Jan	Feb	Mar
Apr	May	Jun
Jul	Aug	Sep
Oct	Nov	Dec

Hot tip

Right-click on an event thumbnail to access a menu with options to edit the event; remove it; set it as a cover photo for the event thumbnail; or view it as a slideshow.

10 Click on the **Add Event** button on the bottom toolbar to create another event in Events View. This is done by dragging photos into the Media Bin and entering the event details as in Step 3

Tagging Images

As your digital image collection begins to grow on your computer, it is increasingly important to be able to keep track of your images and find the ones you want, when you want them. One way of doing this is by assigning specific tags to images. You can then search for images according to the tags that have been added to them. The tagging function is accessed from the Tags panel within Media View in the Organizer. To add tags to images:

Hot tip

When you create a new category you can also choose a new icon.

1 In Media View, click on this button on the Taskbar to show and hide the Tags panel

2 Click here to access the currently available tags

3 Click here to access sub-categories for a particular category

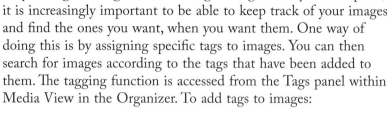

Don't forget

Tags can be created for People, Places and Events. They are also created when items are added to the various sections.

4 Click here to add categories, or sub-categories, of your own choice

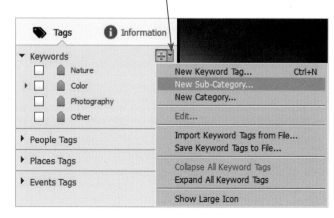

Don't forget

Tags are also referred to as Keywords or Keyword tags.

5 Enter a name for the new category, or sub-category, and click on the **OK** button

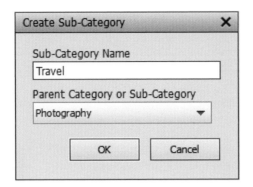

Create Sub-Category ✕

Sub-Category Name

Travel

Parent Category or Sub-Category

Photography ▼

OK   Cancel

6 Select the required images from Media View

7 Drag a tag onto one of the selected images

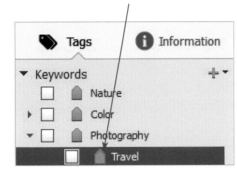

🏷 **Tags**   ⓘ **Information**

▼ Keywords   ✚▾

☐ 🔖 Nature

▸ ☐ 🔖 Color

▾ ☐ 🔖 Photography

☐ 🔖 Travel

8 The tag will be applied to all of the selected images. Each individual image will have the tag added to it

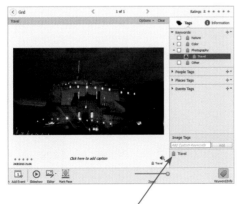

9 The images are tagged with the icon that denotes the main category, rather than the sub-category

Hot tip

Multiple tags can be added to the same image. This gives you greater flexibility when searching for images.

Don't forget

Categories can have several levels of sub-categories. To create additional levels, right-click on a sub-category and select **Create new Sub-Category** from the menu. Give the sub-category a name and ensure that the required item is selected in the **Parent Category or Sub-Category** box.

Don't forget

Tagged images can still be searched for using a sub-category tag, even though they are denoted in Media View by the tag for the main category.

49

Searching for Images

Once images have been tagged, they can then be searched for using those specific tags. To do this:

Using the Search box
Images can be searched for simply by typing keywords into the Search box at the top of the Organizer, in any view:

1 Click on the Search button

2 The Search window contains a Search box at the top of the window and also filter buttons down the left-hand side for conducting specific searches

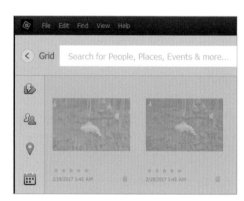

After returning to Grid View in Step 4, click on the **Back** button to return to the main Organizer window. Click on the **Sort By:** box to sort the Search results according to Newest, Oldest, Name or Import Batch.

3 Start typing in the Search box and click on one of the results to view all of the tagged images

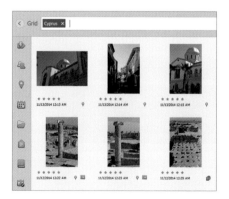

4 Click on the **Grid** button to view the images in the main Organizer window

50

Using search filters

The search filter buttons on the Search page can also be used to find items. To do this:

1 Click on one of the search filter buttons to view the tagged photos, which are displayed according to their tags or categories. Click on one of the thumbnails in the left-hand panel to view the photos within it, displayed in the right-hand panel

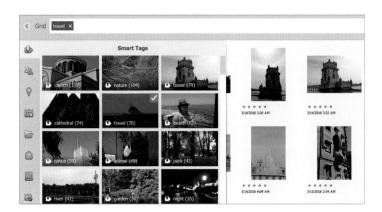

The options for search filters are: Smart Tags; People; Places; Date; Folders; Keywords; Albums; Events; Ratings; and Media Types.

2 For each selection, the filter tag is added in the Search box. Add additional tags to create multiple searches to see all items that have two or more matching tags

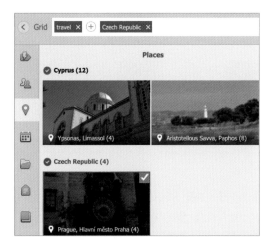

Don't forget

Tags can be viewed for **Keywords**, **People Tags**, **Places Tags** and **Events Tags**.

Hot tip

If you search using a main category, any items that are within that category as a sub-category will be searched for too. If you select a sub-category, this is only what will be searched for.

Don't forget

Roll over a tag next to a photo in Media View to see a description of the Keyword tag.

...cont'd

Searching with tags

Images can also be searched for by using the tags within the Tags panel. To do this:

1 Access the Tags panel from this button

2 Check on a box to view the images that are tagged with that keyword

3 All matching items for a tag are shown together within the Media View window

4 Click on the **All Media** button to return to the rest of the images

Multiple searches

Within the Tags panel it is also possible to define searches for images that have multiple (i.e. two or more) tags attached to them. To do this:

1 Add a tag to an image or images, and click on the tag in the Tags panel to display all of these images (other tags that have been added to them will also be displayed next to the image)

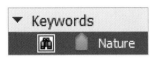

2 Add another tag to the image or images, so that there are at least two attached. Click on both of these in the Tags panel. Only the images containing both tags will be displayed

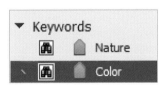

Hot tip

Images that have been tagged within People View, Places View and Events View can also be searched for using the Keywords panel.

Don't forget

If no results are returned for a multiple search, it means that there are no images that contain all of the selected tags.

Don't forget

Two other search options are for **Visual Similarity** and **Duplicate Photos**. These display similar photos that can then be selected and placed in stacks for easier storage. It also enables you to look at similar photos and delete any that you don't want to keep. These options can be accessed by selecting **Find** > **By Visual Searches** from the Organizer Menu bar.

Albums

Albums in Elements are similar to physical photo albums: they are a location into which you can store all of your favorite groups of images. Once they have been stored there, they can easily be found when required. To create albums:

Don't forget

Version Sets and stacks can be added to and viewed in Albums.

Hot tip

Click on the New Album button in Step 1 to view options for collapsing or expanding all of the albums in the panel.

Don't forget

Right-click on an album name to access a menu with options to **Edit**, **Rename** or **Delete** the album.

54

1 In Media View, click here in the Albums panel and select **New Album**

2 Enter a name for the new album and choose a category if required

3 Select the images that you would like included in the new album and drag them into the Content panel

4 Click on the **OK** button

5 The selected images are placed into the new album. Click on an album to view the images within it

Folders

One important factor in storing and searching for photos is the use of folders. Elements can replicate the folder structure that you have on your hard drive and also create new folders and edit existing ones. To work with folders in Elements:

1 The available folders are listed next to the Albums section. Click on a folder to view its contents

2 New folders are created whenever you import photos into Elements using the **Import** > **From Files and Folders...** command

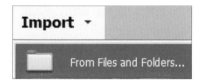

3 In Hierarchy View, right-click on a folder to access the available options for editing it or adding a new folder

Don't forget

Even if you import a single photo, the related folder will be created within Elements, containing the photo.

Hot tip

Right-click within the Hierarchy View to add a new folder. When this is completed it also appears within your file structure on your computer's hard drive.

Auto Curate

Since it is easy to take hundreds or thousands of photos with a digital camera or smartphone, it can become slightly overwhelming in terms of sorting out the best ones. Within the Organizer there is a function that does this for you, by selecting the best range of photos for specific selections. This is known as Auto Curate. To use this:

1 Open the Organizer and select a group of photos, either as an album, a folder or by using a Keyword tag

Auto Curate requires a minimum of 10 photos in a group in order to perform its selection.

2 Check the **Auto Curate** box (above the Keywords and Info panels) **On**

If no selection is made in Step 1, Auto Curate will search over 500 photos to find the best ones.

3 Auto Curate selects what it thinks are the best photos from the group

4 Drag the slider to show more or fewer photos for the Auto Curate selection

Check Off the **Auto Curate** box to return to the original view.

Opening and Saving Images

Once you have captured images with a digital camera, smartphone or a scanner and stored them on your computer, you can open them in any of Elements' Editor modes. There are a number of options for this:

Open command

1 Select **File** > **Open** from the Menu bar, or click on the **Open** button and select an option

2 Select an image from your hard drive and click **Open**

Open As command

This can be used to open a file in a different file format from its original one. To do this:

1 Select **File** > **Open As** from the Menu bar

2 Select an image and select the file format. Click **Open**

Saving images

When saving digital images, it is always a good idea to save them in at least two different file formats, particularly if layered objects such as text and shapes have been added. One of these formats should be the proprietary Photoshop format PSD or PDD. The reason for using this is that it will retain all of the layered information within an image. So, if a text layer has been added, it will still be available for editing once it has been saved and closed.

The other format that an image should be saved in is the one most appropriate for the use to which it is going to be put. Therefore, images that are going to be used on the web should be saved as JPEG, GIF or PNG files, while an image that is going to be used for printing should be saved in another format, such as TIFF. Once images have been saved in these formats, all of the layered information within them becomes flattened into a single layer and it will not be possible to edit these individual layers.

Another option for opening files is the **Open Recently Edited File** command, which is accessed from the File menu. This lists, in order, the files you have opened most recently. Some of these are also listed on the **Open** button's drop-down menu.

A proprietary file format is one that is specific to the program being used. It has greater flexibility when used within the program itself, but cannot be distributed as easily as other images.

The **Save As** command should be used if you want to make a copy of an image with a different file name.

Working with Video

As well as using Elements for viewing and organizing photos, it can also be used in the same way with video. Video can be imported into Elements in a number of ways:

- From a camera that has video-recording capabilities.

- From a digital video camera.

- From a smartphone.

- From video that has been created in the Premiere Elements program. This is a companion program to Elements and is used to manipulate and edit video. It can be bought in a package with Elements, or individually. For more details, see **www.adobe.com/products/premiere-elements/**

To download video into Elements:

Don't forget

Premiere Elements can be bought as a package with Elements, or it can be bought individually.

Beware

Video files are usually much larger in size than photos, and if you have lots of them they will take up a lot of space on your computer.

1 Connect the device containing the video. In the Organizer, click on the **Import** button, select the required device and download in the same way as for photos

Don't forget

To view video clips, double-click on the clip in Media View. The Elements video player will open and play the video clip.

2 The video is downloaded and displayed in the Organizer, in the same way as photos

Don't forget

To find video clips within Elements, select **Find > By Media Type > Video** from the Menu bar, and the video files will be displayed.

3 Video clips are identified by this symbol on their thumbnails in Media View in the Organizer

3 First Digital Steps

This chapter shows how to get up and running with digital image editing, and details some effective editing techniques for improving digital images, such as improving overall color and duplicating items.

Another Auto command on the Enhance menu is Auto Smart Fix. This can be used to automatically edit all of the color balance of an image in one step. This is also available as a panel in Quick edit mode.

Hot tip

The keyboard shortcut for Auto Levels is:
PC: **Shift + Ctrl + L**
Mac: **Shift + Command key + L**

The keyboard shortcut for Auto Contrast is:
PC: **Alt + Shift + Ctrl + L**
Mac: **Alt + Shift + Command key + L**

Hot tip

Two other options for color enhancement in the Toolbox are the Burn tool and the Dodge tool. The Burn tool can be dragged over areas in an image to make them darker, and the Dodge tool can be dragged over areas to make them lighter.

Color Enhancements

Some of the simplest but most effective editing changes that can be made to digital images are color enhancements. These can help to transform a mundane image into a stunning one, and Elements offers a variety of methods for achieving this. Some of these are verging towards the professional end of image editing, while others are done almost automatically by Elements. These are known as Auto adjustments, and some simple manual adjustments can also be made to the brightness and contrast of an image. All of these color enhancement features can be accessed from the Enhance menu on the Menu bar, in both Expert edit and Quick edit modes.

Auto Levels
This automatically adjusts the overall color tone of an image in relation to the lightest and darkest points in the image:

Auto Contrast
This automatically adjusts the contrast of an image:

...cont'd

Auto Color Correction

This automatically adjusts all of the color elements within an image:

Hot tip

The keyboard shortcut for Auto Color Correction is **Shift + Ctrl + B** (**Shift + Command key + B** on a Mac).

Adjusting Brightness/Contrast

This can be used to manually adjust the brightness and contrast in an image:

1 Select **Enhance > Adjust Lighting > Brightness/Contrast** from the Menu bar (in either Expert edit or Quick edit mode)

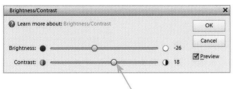

2 Drag the sliders to adjust the image's brightness and contrast

3 Click on the **OK** button

4 The brightness and contrast (and a range of other color-editing functions) can also be adjusted using the panels in Quick edit mode

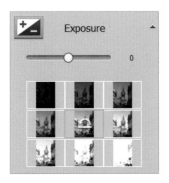

Don't forget

Alter the brightness and contrast by small amounts at a time when you are editing an image. This will help ensure that the end result does not look too unnatural.

Hot tip

Always make sure that the **Preview** box is checked when you are applying color enhancements. This will display the changes as you make them, and before they are applied to the image.

Hot tip

Adjusting shadows can make a significant improvement to an image in which one area is under-exposed and the rest is correctly exposed.

Don't forget

Shadows and highlights can also be adjusted in the Levels panel: **Enhance** > **Adjust Color** > **Levels** from the Menu bar. See pages 118-121 for more details about Levels.

Beware

Some digital cameras have a tendency to create slightly darker images, so adjusting the Shadows/Highlights is always a good option.

...cont'd

Adjusting Shadows/Highlights

One problem that most photographers encounter at some point is when part of an image is exposed correctly, while another part is either over- or under-exposed. If this is corrected using general color correction techniques such as adjusting levels of brightness and contrast, the poorly exposed area may be improved, but at the expense of the area that was correctly exposed initially. To overcome this, the Shadows/Highlights command can be used to adjust particular tonal areas of an image. To do this:

1 Open an image where parts of the image, or all of it, are incorrectly exposed

2 Select **Enhance** > **Adjust Lighting** > **Shadows/ Highlights** from the Menu bar

3 Make the required adjustments by dragging the sliders

4 Click on the **OK** button

5 The poorly exposed areas of the image have been corrected

Cropping

Cropping is a technique that can be used to remove unwanted areas of an image and highlight the main subject. The area to be cropped can only be selected as a rectangle. To crop an image:

1 Select the **Crop** tool from the Toolbox

2 Click and drag on an image to select the area to be cropped. The area that is selected is retained and the area to be cropped appears grayed out

3 Click and drag on these markers to resize the crop area

4 Click on the check mark to accept the changes, or the circle to reject them

...cont'd

Perspective cropping

Due to the way some lenses are constructed on digital cameras, tall buildings can sometimes look distorted (and also at slight angles). This can be amended using the Perspective Crop tool:

1 Open the image to be amended

2 Select the **Perspective Crop** tool from the Crop Tool Options bar

3 Drag the Perspective Crop tool around the required area, in the same way as for a regular crop

4 Drag the top corners of the crop area to specify the dimensions for the selected area (dragging the corners outwards narrows the perspective). Click on the green check mark symbol to apply the perspective crop

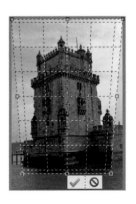

Healing Brush

One of the most popular techniques in digital imaging is removing unwanted items, particularly physical blemishes such as spots and wrinkles. This can be done with the Clone tool but the effects can sometimes be too harsh, as a single area is copied over the affected item. A more subtle effect can be achieved with the Healing Brush and the Spot Healing Brush tools. The Healing Brush can be used to remove blemishes over larger areas such as wrinkles:

1 Open an image with blemishes covering a reasonably large area; i.e. more than a single spot

2 Select the **Healing Brush** tool from the Toolbox and make the required selections in the Tool Options bar

3 Hold down **Alt** and click on an area of the image to load the Healing Brush tool. Drag over the affected area. The cross is the area that is copied beneath the circle. At this point the overall tone is not perfect and looks too pink

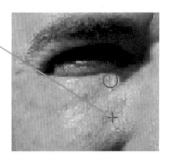

4 Release the mouse, and the Healing Brush blends the affected area with the one that was copied over it. This creates a much more natural skin tone

Hot tip

The Healing Brush tool can be more subtle than the Clone tool, as it blends the copied area together with the area that it is copying. This is particularly effective on images of people, as it preserves the overall skin tone better than the Clone tool does.

Hot tip

The Spot Healing Brush tool can be used to remove items such as small blemishes or spots. Click on this button in the Healing Brush Tool Options bar and drag it over the affected area to remove it.

Hot tip

When dragging over a blemish with the Spot Healing Brush tool, make sure the brush size is larger than the area of the blemish. This will ensure that you can cover the blemish in a single stroke.

Cloning

Cloning is a technique that can be used to copy one area of an image over another. This can be used to cover up small imperfections in an image, such as a dust mark or a spot, and also to copy or remove large items in an image, such as a person.

To clone items:

1 Select the **Clone Stamp** tool from the Toolbox

2 Set the Clone Stamp options in the Tool Options bar

3 Hold down **Alt**, and then click and hold on the image to select a source point from which the cloning will start

4 Drag the cursor to copy everything over which the selection point marker passes

Pattern Cloning

The Pattern Stamp tool can be used to copy a selected pattern over an image, or onto a selected area of an image. To do this:

1 Select the **Pattern Stamp** tool from the Toolbox

2 Click here in the Tool Options bar to access the available patterns

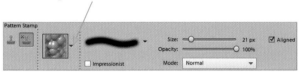

3 Select a pattern for the Pattern Stamp tool

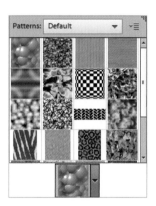

4 Click and drag on an image to copy the selected pattern over it

The Pattern Stamp tool is grouped in the Toolbox with the Clone Stamp tool. It can be selected from the Tool Options panel if the Clone Stamp tool is selected.

Patterns can be added to the Patterns panel by selecting an image, or an area of an image, and selecting **Edit** > **Define Pattern** from the Editor Menu bar. Then, give the pattern a name in the **Pattern Name** dialog box, and click **OK**.

Rotating

Various rotation commands can be applied to images, and also individual layers in layered images. This can be useful for positioning items and also for correcting the orientation of an image that is on its side or upside down.

Rotating a whole image

Don't forget

For more information about working with layers, see Chapter 8.

Hot tip

If an image is only slightly misaligned, then only a small angle value is required in the **Rotate Canvas** dialog box. A figure of 1 or 2 can sometimes be sufficient.

Hot tip

Images can also be rotated using the **Straighten** tool in the Toolbox. To do this, drag the tool on the image to create the required effect.

1 Select **Image** > **Rotate** from the Menu bar

2 Select a rotation option from the menu

3 Select **Custom...** to enter your own value for the amount you want an image rotated

90° Left
90° Right
180°
Custom...
Flip Horizontal
Flip Vertical

Free Rotate Layer
Rotate Layer 90° Left
Rotate Layer 90° Right
Rotate Layer 180°
Flip Layer Horizontal
Flip Layer Vertical

Straighten and Crop Image
Straighten Image

4 Click the **OK** button

Rotating a layer

To rotate separate layers within an image:

1 Open an image that consists of two or more layers. Select one of the layers in the Layers panel

2 Select **Image** > **Rotate** from the Menu bar

3 Select a layer rotation option from the menu

4 The selected layer is rotated independently

Transforming

The Transform commands can be used to resize an image, and to apply some basic distortion techniques. These commands can be accessed by selecting **Image** > **Transform** from the Menu bar.

Free Transform

This enables you to manually alter the size and shape of an image. To do this:

1 Select **Image** > **Transform** > **Free Transform** from the Menu bar

2 Click and drag here to transform the vertical and horizontal size of the image. Hold down **Shift** to transform it in proportion

Click just outside this placeholder and drag left or right to manually rotate an image with the Transform function.

The other options from the Transform menu are Skew, Distort and Perspective. These can be accessed and applied in a similar way to the Free Transform option.

Magnification

In Elements there are a number of ways the magnification at which an image is being viewed can be increased or decreased. This can be useful if you want to zoom in on a particular part of an image for editing purposes, or if you want to view a whole image to see the result of editing effects that have been applied.

View menu

1 Select **View** from the Menu bar and select one of the options from the View menu

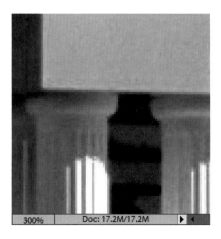

Zoom tool

1 Select the **Zoom** tool from the Toolbox

2 Click once on an image to enlarge it (usually by 100% each time). Hold down **Alt** and click to decrease the magnification

Don't forget

The View menu can be used to display rulers at the top and left of an image, which can be useful for precise measurements and placement. There is also a command for displaying a grid over the top of the whole image.

Hot tip

The keyboard shortcut for zooming in is:
PC: **Ctrl + =**
Mac: **Command key + =**

The keyboard shortcut for zooming out is:
PC: **Ctrl + -**
Mac: **Command key + -**

Hot tip

Click and drag with the Zoom tool over a small area to increase the magnification to the maximum; i.e. 3200%. This can be particularly useful when performing close-up editing tasks, such as removing red eye.

70

...cont'd

Navigator panel

This can be used to move around an image and also magnify certain areas. To use the Navigator panel:

1 Access the **Navigator** panel by selecting **Window** > **Navigator** from the Menu bar

2 Drag this slider to magnify the area of the image within the red rectangle

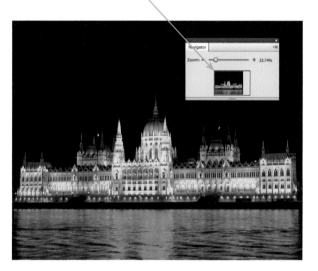

3 Drag the rectangle to change the area of the image that is being magnified

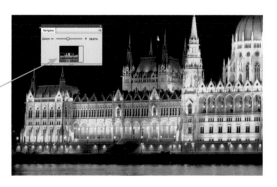

Hot tip

The keyboard shortcut for accessing the Navigator panel is **F12**.

Don't forget

The Navigator panel also has buttons for zooming in and out. These are located at the left and right of the slider.

71

Hot tip

Click on different areas on the thumbnail in the Navigator panel to view these areas in the main Editor window.

Eraser

The Eraser tool can be used to remove areas of an image. In a simple, single-layer image this can just leave a blank hole, which has to be filled with something. The Eraser options are:

- **Eraser**, which can be used to erase part of the background image or a layer within it.

- **Background Eraser**, which can be used to remove an uneven background.

- **Magic Eraser**, which can be used to quickly remove a solid background (see below).

Erasing a background

With the Magic Eraser tool it is possible to delete a colored background in an image. To do this:

1 Open an image with an evenly colored background

2 Select the **Magic Eraser** and make the required selections in the Tool Options bar. Make sure the Contiguous box is not checked

3 Click once on the background. It is removed from the image, regardless of where it occurs

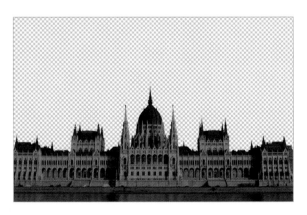

Don't forget

The Background Eraser tool can be used to remove an uneven background. To do this, drag over the background with the Background Eraser tool and, depending on the settings in the Tool Options panel, everything that it is dragged over will be removed.

Don't forget

If the **Contiguous** box is not checked, the background color will be removed wherever it occurs in the image. If the Contiguous box is checked, the background color will only be removed where it touches another area of the same color that is not broken by another element of the image.

4 Quick Wins

This chapter looks at some of the "quick wins" that can be done in Elements, such as removing unwanted objects, changing photos to black and white, and improving hazy photos. It also shows some of the Guided edit and Quick edit options that provide step-by-step actions for creating a range of creative and striking photos. This includes adding items to photos, such as filters and graphics, and creating panoramas.

One-click Subject Selection

Being able to select items within a photo is an excellent option so that you can edit the selection independently from the rest of the image. This usually involves the main subject, or the background, and Elements offers a function where the subject in a photo can be selected with one click. This is available in Expert edit or Quick edit modes:

One-click subject selection is a new feature in the latest version of Elements.

1 Open an image where the main subject is clearly defined against the background

If the background is too similar to the main subject, some of it may be selected at the same time as the subject.

2 Select **Select** > **Subject** from the Menu bar

3 The main subject is selected as indicated by a dotted black-and-white outline

If two or more people are the main subjects in a photo they will all be selected using the command in Step 2.

74

...cont'd

4   Zoom in on the selection to identify any areas that have been missed

5   Select one of the manual selection tools and ensure the **Add** button is selected in the Tool Options bar

For more information about using selection tools, see Chapter 7.

6   Add to the selection as required

7   Editing effects can be made to the selection without affecting the other areas of the image

Click on the **Subtract** button in Step 5 to remove areas from a selection.

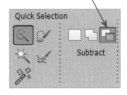

8   Select **Select** > **Inverse** from the Menu bar to invert the selection so that the background is selected. This can then be edited, independently of the main subject; e.g. the background can be deleted, leaving the subject isolated

Quickly Removing Items

One of the most annoying aspects of taking photos is to capture what you think is a perfect image, only to find that there is an unwanted object in the final shot. In Elements, it is possible to delete unwanted items and automatically fill in the area from where these are removed. To do this:

Don't forget

Several different items can be removed from the same photo. To do this, select each one separately and perform the actions from Step 3 onwards.

Hot tip

An object to be removed can also be selected with the one-click subject selection function as shown on pages 74-75.

Hot tip

Unwanted objects in a photo can also be removed using the Object Removal Guided edit. See pages 104-105 for details about how to do this.

1 Open an image that contains an unwanted object

2 Use one of the selection tools to select the unwanted object

3 Select **Edit** > **Fill Selection...** from the Menu bar

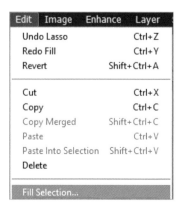

4 Make the selections in the Fill Layer dialog box. Ensure **Content-Aware** is selected

5 Click on the **OK** button

6 The selection is deleted and the area is automatically filled with the background

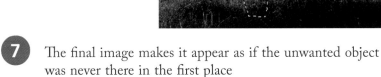

7 The final image makes it appear as if the unwanted object was never there in the first place

Beware

If an area is selected and then deleted it will leave a blank space, filled with either the color palette's background or foreground color.

Beware

If there are too many colors around the selected area, the fill effect may appear inaccurate. If this is the case, try with a slightly different selection area.

Don't forget

Zoom in on the final image to make sure that the background has been filled as accurately as possible.

77

Moving Items in a Photo

Unless you are taking photos under studio conditions, it is probable that you will get some unwanted items in your photos, or the composition may not be exactly as you would like it in terms of the position of the subjects. The answer to this is the Content-Aware editing tool. This can be used to move subjects in a photo and then have the background behind them filled in automatically.

Hot tip

In the Content-Aware Move Options panel, drag the **Healing** slider to specify how the edited area blends with the rest of the image.

1 Open an image with a subject that you want to move

2 Select the **Content-Aware Move** tool from the Toolbox

3 Select the **Move** radio button in the Tool Options bar

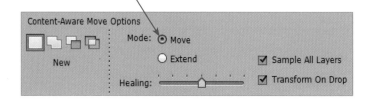

Don't forget

When moving items, it is most effective when the background has a reasonable amount of solid or similar colors.

4 Drag around the subject that you want to move

78

Hot tip

The Content-Aware Move selection area can be moved by using the arrow keys on the keyboard; e.g. left and right, up and down.

5 Drag the subject to a new position

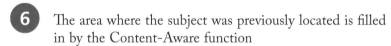

The subject can be positioned anywhere in the photo.

6 The area where the subject was previously located is filled in by the Content-Aware function

The Content-Aware tool can also be used to extend areas within an image. To do this, check on the **Extend** box in the Tool Options bar, drag around the area you want to extend, and then drag the selection into place. The Content-Aware Move tool will automatically fill in the background for the area that is extended.

Opening Closed Eyes

Taking photos of people can be a frustrating business: you think you have captured the perfect shot, only to find that one or more of your subjects has their eyes closed. Thankfully, with Elements these types of photos can be edited by opening any closed eyes in the shot. To do this:

Hot tip

The Open Closed Eyes function can also be accessed by selecting the Eye tool in the Toolbox and clicking on the **Open Closed Eyes** button.

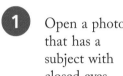 Open a photo that has a subject with closed eyes

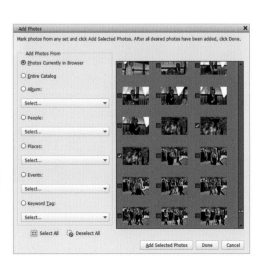

Select **Enhance** > **Open Closed Eyes** from the Menu bar in Expert edit or Quick edit mode

Hot tip

The number of photos being displayed in Step 4 can be filtered by selecting to show items from a specific album, or by People, Places, Events or Keyword tags.

Select a location to choose an image with open eyes for the subject; e.g. the Organizer or from your computer

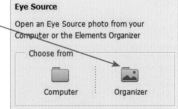

Select the required images and click on the **Add Selected Photos** button

Add Selected Photos

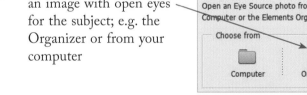

...cont'd

5 Click on the **Done** button

6 The selected images are added to the Eye Source panel

Don't forget

All of the people included in the images selected in Step 4 are included in the Eye Source panel.

7 Click on a suitable image with open eyes for the subject

8 The selection from the Eye Source panel replaces the closed eyes of the subject

NEW

Skin texture can be enhanced by selecting **Enhance** > **Smooth Skin** from the Menu bar. In the Smooth Skin dialog box a circle is placed over a person's face and the skin texture can be enhanced by dragging the **Smoothness** slider. This is a new feature in the latest version of Elements.

9 Click on the **Reset** button to start again, or the **OK** button to apply the change

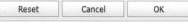

Removing Red Eye

One of the most common problems with photographs of people, whether they are taken digitally or with a film-based camera, is red eye. This is caused when the camera's flash is used, which then reflects in the subject's pupils. This can create the dreaded red-eye effect, where the subject can unintentionally be transformed into a demonic character.

Elements has recognized that removing red eye is one of the top priorities for most amateur photographers, and a specific tool for this purpose has been included in the Toolbox: the Eye tool. This is available in Expert edit or Quick edit modes:

1 Open an image that contains red eye

2 Select the **Zoom** tool from the Toolbox

3 Drag around the affected area until it appears at a suitable magnification. Select the **Eye** tool from the Toolbox

4 Click in the Tool Options bar to select the size of the pupil and the amount by which it will be darkened

5 Click once on the red eye, or drag around the affected area to remove the red eye

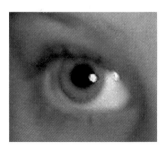

Changing to Black and White

Most digital cameras and scanners are capable of converting color images into black and white at the point of capture. However, it is also possible to use Elements to convert existing color images into black-and-white ones. To do this:

1 Open a color image and select **Enhance > Convert to Black and White** from the Menu bar

2 The Convert to Black and White dialog box has various options for how the image is converted

3 Select the type of black-and-white effect to be applied, depending on the subject in the image

4 Drag these sliders to specify the intensity of the effect to be applied for different elements

5 Click on the **OK** button

6 The image is converted into black and white, according to the settings that have been selected

Hot tip

The keyboard shortcut to access the Convert to Black and White dialog window is **Alt + Ctrl + B** (**Alt + Command key + B** on a Mac).

Hot tip

A similar effect can be achieved by selecting **Enhance > Adjust Color > Remove Color** from the Menu bar.

83

Don't forget

The Guided edits also have an option for turning photos into black and white: **Guided > Black & White > Black and White**.

Auto Creations have been updated in the latest version of Elements and can now be created with B&W Selection, Pattern Brush, Painterly effect and Depth of Field effect.

Hot tip

Auto Creations are created from Events that have been created in Elements, and also from photos that were taken on the same date.

Auto Creations

Organizing and editing photos so that you have a creative and entertaining slideshow to show family and friends can be time-consuming and frustrating. Selected groups of photos can be played as slideshows, but Elements has a more powerful function: Auto Creations.

Auto Creations is an automatic function within Elements that creates artistic slideshows and collages (including transitions between photos and background music). They can be viewed directly from the Home Screen and also deleted or edited, as required. To use Auto Creations:

1 Click on the **Home Screen** button on either the Photo Editor or Organizer bottom Taskbar

2 Auto Creations are displayed in their own panel on the Home Screen

3 Click here to view the top five Auto Creations on the Home Screen

4 Click on the **View All** button to view all of the available Auto Creations

...cont'd

5 Click on the **Trash** icon next to an Auto Creation to delete it

6 On the Home Screen, or in the View All section, click on the **Open** button to view an Auto Creation. If it is a slideshow, it starts playing in its own window

If the Auto Creation is a collage, it will be opened in the Quick Edit section of the Photo Editor – see page 87 for details.

7 Click on the **Back** button to go back to the Organizer

8 Click on these button on the left-hand toolbar to, from top to bottom: add more photos or videos to the Auto Creation and add captions to existing items; change the theme for the Auto Creation; and edit the music being used (see pages 86-87 for more information about editing Auto Creations)

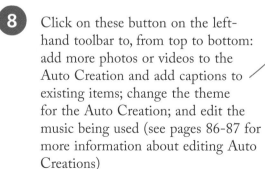

If the Auto Creation has not been saved, you will be prompted to do this when the Back button is clicked in Step 7.

9 Click on these buttons at the top of the window to **Save** an Auto Creation to the Organizer, or **Export** it to a social media site or to a location on your own computer

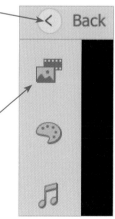

Until an Auto Creation has been saved, it is only available from the Home Screen. Once it has been saved it can also be opened from the Organizer mode.

...cont'd

Editing Slideshow Auto Creations

If an Auto Creation has been opened as a slideshow, it can be edited from within the Slideshow window where it is played, as shown on page 85. To do this:

Hot tip

Click on this button to the right of the caption button in Step 1 to add more photos or videos to the slideshow.

1 Click on the **Media** button and click here to add captions below each photo

Don't forget

Themes are added to the whole slideshow, rather than to individual photos.

2 Click on the **Themes** button to select a background color theme for the slideshow

Beware

If too many different music tracks are added to an Auto Creation slideshow it can make it feel slightly disjointed.

3 Click on the **Audio** button to select music for the slideshow. Click on an item here to add it

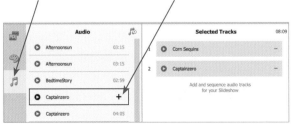

...cont'd

Editing Collage Auto Creations

If an Auto Creation has been opened as a collage, it is opened in the Photo Editor, where it can be edited and then saved as a new project. To do this:

1 Click on the **Open** button next to a collage on the Home Screen

2 The collage opens in Photo Editor mode

3 Click on these buttons to add more photos to the collage, from your computer or the Elements Organizer

4 Click the **Layouts** button on the bottom Taskbar and click on one of the layouts to apply it to the collage

5 Click the **Graphics** button on the bottom Taskbar and click on one of the graphical elements to add it to the collage

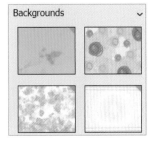

Quick Edit Mode Options

The Quick edit options in Elements offer a number of functions within the one location. This makes it easier to apply a number of techniques at the same time.

Using Quick edit mode

1 Open an image in the Editor and click on the **Quick** button

2 The Quick edit mode has a modified Toolbox with fewer tools, which are displayed here

3 Click on the bottom toolbar to access the Quick edit panel options. The default one is for **Adjustments**

4 Click on the **Adjustments** panel to make the appropriate changes (see pages 90-91)

88

Quick Edit Toolbox

The Quick edit Toolbox has a reduced Toolbox that includes:

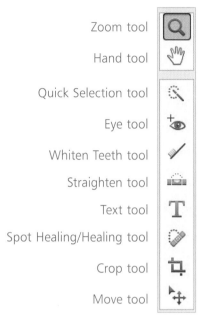

Zoom tool

Hand tool

Quick Selection tool

Eye tool

Whiten Teeth tool

Straighten tool

Text tool

Spot Healing/Healing tool

Crop tool

Move tool

Hot tip

To show or hide the Quick edit Toolbox (and also the Expert edit Toolbox) select **Window** > **Tools** from the Menu bar.

Whitening teeth

One of the tool options in the Quick edit mode Toolbox is for whitening teeth in a photo. To do this:

1 Open a relevant image and click on the **Whiten Teeth** tool, and select a brush size for the tool

2 Drag the Whiten Teeth tool over the teeth

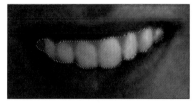

3 The teeth area is selected and whitened in one operation

Beware

The Eye tool is the same as the one in Expert edit mode, which includes the Pet Eye option for removing red eye in photos of pets.

Beware

Do not overdo the teeth-whitening effect, otherwise it will start to look unnatural.

Quick Edit Adjustments

The adjustment panels in the Quick edit section are:

Changes are displayed in the main Quick edit window in real time, as they are being made.

Smart Fix panel

This performs several editing changes in a single operation. Click on the Auto button to have the changes applied automatically, or drag the slider to specify the extent of the editing changes. Click on the thumbnails to apply preset amounts of the change.

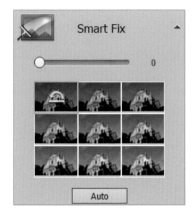

The Exposure panel is a good option for quickly editing photos that are under- or over-exposed; i.e. too dark or too light.

Exposure panel

This provides options for adjusting the lighting and contrast in an image. Drag the sliders to adjust the exposure, or click on one of the thumbnails to apply a preset option.

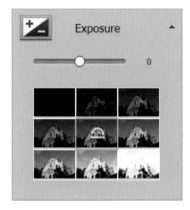

Shadows and highlights can be edited within Expert edit mode:
Enhance > Adjust Lighting > Shadows/ Highlights.

Lighting panel

This provides options for adjusting the lightest and darkest points in an image. This is done by adjusting the shadows, midtones and highlights. Drag the slider to adjust this, or click on one of the thumbnails for an auto option.

...cont'd

Color panel

Click on the Auto button to automatically adjust the hue and saturation of an image, or drag the slider to make manual adjustments. Click on the thumbnails to apply preset amounts.

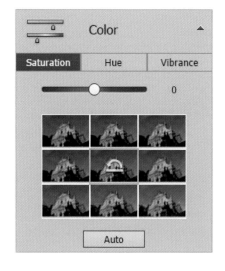

Balance panel

Drag the slider to adjust the warmth of the colors of an image and the color balance. Click on the thumbnails to apply preset amounts.

Sharpen panel

This can be used to apply sharpening to an image to make it clearer: either automatically with the Auto button; with the panel thumbnails; or manually with the slider.

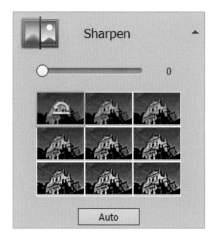

The Balance panel can be used to create some abstract color effects.

Sharpening works by increasing the contrast between adjoining pixels to make the overall image appear more in focus. It can also be accessed by selecting **Enhance** > **Auto Sharpen** or **Enhance** > **Unsharp Mask** from the Expert edit Menu bar. The Unsharp Mask option has a dialog window where the effect can be added as a percentage.

Adding Filters

Filters are an excellent option for adding a range of effects to photos. They can be accessed and applied from the Menu bar in Expert or Quick edit mode, or the toolbar in Expert edit mode:

Don't forget

Each preset option overrides any previous ones that have been selected; they do not build up on top of each other.

1 In Expert edit mode, open the photo to which you want to apply a filter effect, and click on the **Filters** panel button

Filters

Hot tip

The most recently used filter can be reapplied by pressing **Ctrl** + **F** on the keyboard (**Command key** + **F** on a Mac).

2 Click on a filter effect and use the sliders to determine the settings for the filter. Click on the green check mark symbol to apply the filter effect

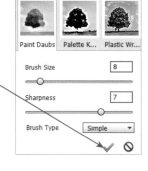

3 Alternatively, in Expert edit or Quick edit mode, click on the **Filter** button on the Menu bar, and select a filter category and sub-category

Hot tip

Use the Unsharp Mask filter to sharpen the focus of a photo. Although this is a filter, it is accessed from **Enhance** > **Unsharp Mask** on the Menu bar. In the **Amount** box, drag the slider to apply the amount of sharpening: a value of 100% or above is effective in most cases.

4 Each category has preset options. Click on one to apply this to the photo

5 Most filters have sliders that can be used to edit the effect that is being applied. After you have made the desired changes, click on the **OK** button

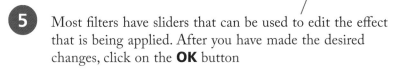

Adding Graphics

In Expert edit mode it is possible to add a wide range of graphical elements to an image. To do this:

1 Click on the **Graphics** panel button

2 At the top of the Graphics panel, click on the **Show All** drop-down menu to select categories and sub-categories

Beware

There are hundreds of graphics that can be used, but try not to add too many to a single image as it may become too cluttered.

3 Graphical shapes can be dragged onto an image, on a new layer, and then resized within the image by clicking on them and dragging the resizing handles

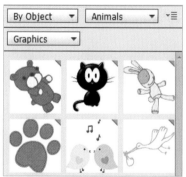

Hot tip

Click on the **Layers** panel button after graphics have been added to see how this affects the construction of the image.

4 Backgrounds can be dragged onto an image as a new layer, and the rest of the content can interact with the background through the application of layer masks or opacity (see pages 146-149)

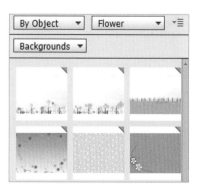

93

Colorizing a Photo

Color is an essential part of a photo, but Elements provides the means to quickly change the colors of a photo. This could be to transform an old black-and-white photo, or change the color elements of an existing color photo. This is known as colorizing the photo and is available in Expert edit or Quick edit modes:

The Colorize option is a new feature in the latest version of Elements.

1 Open an image to which you want to apply the colorize effect

Creating several colorized versions of a photo is a good way to create a colorful artistic sequence of the same shot.

2 Select **Enhance** > **Colorize Photo** from the Menu bar

3 Drag this button to **Auto** and click on one of the preset colorize options to apply it to the photo

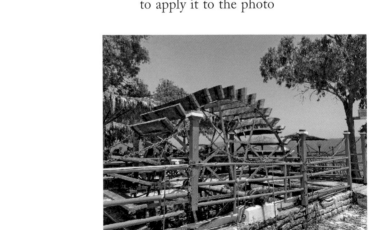

4 Drag this button to **Manual** and click on one of the selection tools below

5 Select an area within the photo so that it can be colorized independently from the rest of the photo

6 Click on the **Droplet Tool** button and click within the selection area to further refine the area to be colorized. This will be the area to which the colorize effect will be applied

Hot tip

Numerous droplets can be added to a selection. Click on one to select it and make it the active droplet; i.e. that is the area to which the colorize effect will be applied.

7 Click on a color within the **Color Palette** to colorize the area specified in the previous step

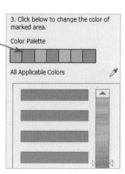

8 Click on the **OK** button to complete the colorization

Using Guided Edit Mode

In Elements, the Guided edit function makes it easier to perform both simple editing functions and also more complex image-editing processes that consist of a number of steps. To use the various functions of Guided edit mode:

Guided edit mode is a great way to become familiar with image editing, and many of your needs will be catered for here. However, once you become confident with this, you may want to expand your horizons and work with some more techniques in Expert edit mode.

96

NEW

Some new effects have been added to Guided edits in the latest version of Elements.

Beware

Save a copy of a photo before you perform a Guided edit on it, to ensure that the original remains the same.

1 Open an image and click on the **Guided** button

Guided

2 Click on the buttons at the top of the Guided edit window to view the different categories

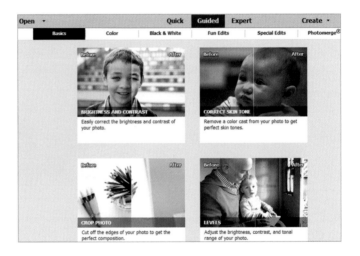

3 Items in each category have a thumbnail image that shows the **Before** and **After** effects for each item. Drag the slider across the thumbnail to view the effect for a greater or lesser amount of the thumbnail

Applying Guided edits

The process for Guided edits is the same regardless of the type of edit that has been selected:

1 Apply the Guided edit effect that has been selected. Different categories have varying numbers of steps; i.e. the Basics category, which is accessed from the toolbar in Step 2 on the previous page, has the fewest number of steps, whereas other options have the type of options shown here

2 Click on the **Next** button once the Guided edits have been completed, to save the final image

3 Specify how you want to save and/or share the final image

4 Click on the **Done** button

For details of some of the Guided edit options, see Chapter 5.

If you do not like an effect that has been applied, click on the **Cancel** button.

97

Click on the **Save** button to save the final image with the same file name, and in the same file format (this overwrites the original). Click on the **Save As** button to save it as a new image with either a new file name or in a new file format, or both.

Photomerge Effects

Within Elements there are a number of Photomerge effects that can be used to combine elements from different photos to create a new image. This can be used to remove items from photos, combine elements from two or more photos, and match the exposure from different photos.

To access the Photomerge options, select **Guided** edit mode and click on the **Photomerge** tab.

The Photomerge options are:

- **Compose**. This can be used to merge a part of one image with the background of another. This is a good option if you want to include people from one photo and transfer them into another photo.

- **Exposure**. This can be used to create a well-exposed photo from a series of photos of the same shot that have different exposures; i.e. one may be over-exposed and another under-exposed. The Photomerge effect combines the photos so that the final one is correctly exposed. This can be done with the **Automatic** option, or the **Manual** one.

- **Faces**. This is an option for combining features of two faces together. This is done by opening photos of two people and then aligning the features of one so that they are merged with the other. This is a fun effect that can be used to combine faces of family members or two friends.

- **Group Shot**. This can be used to add or delete people from group shots. This is done by opening two or more photos of the group. Use the **Pencil** tool to merge a person from one photo into the other, and the **Eraser** tool to delete any areas that you do not want copied to the new photo.

- **Scene Cleaner**. This can be used to remove any unwanted elements in a photo. This is done by using two or more similar photos with elements that you want to remove, then merging the elements that you want to keep into the final photo. This is a good option if a single object has spoilt what is otherwise a good photo.

- **Panorama**. This can be used to create panoramas with two or more photos (see pages 99-100 for details).

For the Exposure Photomerge function, all of the photos used have to be of exactly the same shot, otherwise there will be some overlap in the final image.

The Pencil tool is used for several of the Photomerge options. It is used to draw over an area in a source image that is then merged into the final image.

Creating Panoramas

For anyone who takes landscape pictures, sooner or later the desire to create a panorama occurs. With film-based cameras, this usually involves sticking several photographs together to create the panorama, albeit a rather patchwork one. With digital images, the end result can look a lot more professional, and Elements has a dedicated function for achieving this: the Photomerge Panorama.

When creating a panorama there are a few rules to follow:

- If possible, use a tripod to ensure that your camera stays at the same level for all of the shots.

- Keep the same exposure settings for all images.

- Make sure that there is a reasonable overlap between images (about 20%). Some cameras enable you to align the correct overlap between the images.

- Keep the same distance between yourself and the object you are capturing, otherwise the end result will look out of perspective.

To create a panorama:

Do not include too many images in a panorama, otherwise it could be too large for viewing or printing easily.

Panoramas do not just have to be of landscapes. They can also be used for items such as a row of buildings, or crowds at a sporting event.

66

1 In Expert edit mode, open two or more images and select **Guided** > **Photomerge** > **Photomerge Panorama** from the Menu bar

2 Click on the **Auto Panorama** button to create the panorama automatically from the selected images

In Step 2 there are other options for the style of the panorama.

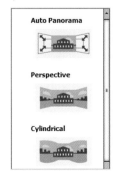

3 Click on the **Create Panorama** button

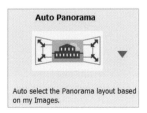

...cont'd

4 The panorama will be created, but with gaps where the images could not be matched. The **Clean Edges** dialog box asks if you would like to fill in the edges of the panorama. Click on the **Yes** button to blend the empty areas with the background

5 Panoramas can usually be improved by applying color correction options such as Brightness/Contrast and Shadows/Highlights. They can also be cropped to make a narrower panorama to highlight the main subject

5 Artistic Effects

This chapter shows how to create stunning effects and features, to give your photos the "wow" factor. This is done in Guided edit mode with numerous templates.

Meme Maker

Memes are graphical images, usually with text added, that are most commonly used for humorous effect on social media. Within the Guided edit mode in Elements it is possible to create your own memes. To do this:

1 Open the image that you want to convert into a meme. Access Guided edit mode and in the **Fun Edits** section, click on the **Meme Maker** button

2 Click on the **Create Meme Template** button to add a border for the meme

Beware

One of the goals of memes is to attract as much attention as possible on social media. However, never put anything rude or offensive in a meme, otherwise you may attract attention for the wrong reasons.

3 The meme border is added to the photo (this can be amended in Step 8)

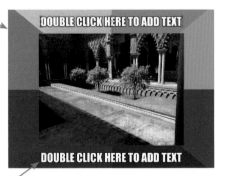

4 Double-click on the pre-inserted text boxes and add the required text for the meme

5 Click on the **Type Tool** button to access the options for formatting the text (drag over the text to select it for formatting)

6 Drag here to resize the photo in the meme, or click on one of the **Flip** buttons to flip the photo vertically or horizontally

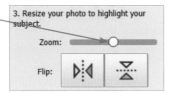

7 Click on the **Effects** button to add effects to the photo (this is an optional feature)

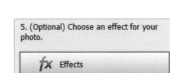

8 Click on these buttons to add a different border to the meme (this is an optional feature)

9 Click on the **Next** button once all of the editing changes have been made

10 Select what to do with the completed meme. This includes saving it within Elements, editing it within either Quick edit or Expert edit mode, or sharing it on a social media site, including Flickr and Twitter

Click on the green check icon to accept text-editing changes, or click on the red circle icon to reject them.

Memes created in Elements can only be shared to a limited range of social media sites from within Elements itself. In order to share them to other sites such as Facebook, click on the **Save As** button in Step 10 and save the image in the JPEG file format. In the Organizer, select the photo and select **Share > Email** from the top toolbar. Email the photo to yourself and then add it to your Facebook page from your smartphone or computer.

Object Removal

Photos frequently have unwanted items in them, whether it is elements such as telegraph poles or cables, or other people in the background. However, there is a Guided edit that can be used to remove these unwanted objects and leave your photos with just the elements that you want. To do this:

The Object Removal Guided edit is a new feature in the latest version of Elements.

1 Open the photo that contains unwanted items

For more information about using selection tools, see Chapter 7.

2 Access Guided edit mode and in the **Basics** section, click on the **Object Removal** button

3 Click on one of the **Selection Tools**

4 Use the selection tool to select an area in a photo to be removed (if the Brush tool is used it creates a red mask)

Once unwanted objects have been removed from a photo it can be cropped to give the main subject even more prominence.

5 If required, click on the **Add** or **Subtract** buttons to increase or decrease the selection area

6 Click on the **Remove Object** button to remove the unwanted item

7 If required, click on the **Spot Healing Brush** button to smooth any small areas with the rest of the photo

For more information about repairing small areas of a photo with the Healing Brush or the Spot Healing Brush, see page 65.

8 Click on the **Next** button to complete the Object Removal effect and save, edit or share it, as shown on page 103

Multi-Photo Text

Creating text from a photo is a great way to produce creative messages or posters. In Elements, text effects can be created from multiple photos, not just one. To do this:

1 Open the image that you want to use as the background for the Multi-Photo Text effect

2 Access Guided edit mode and in the **Fun Edits** section, click on the **Multi-Photo Text** button

3 Click on the **Type Tool** button to add text to the background photo

1. Click the Type Tool button below, and then click your photo and type some text. (Use the tool options along the bottom to adjust the text style.)

T Type Tool

4 Click on the background photo and add the required text. Use the panel below the text to add formatting options

The text on the background has to be a reasonably large size, so the Multi-Photo Text effect can be seen clearly. Depending on the size of the photo being used for the background, aim to use a text size of 800 points, or higher (the maximum is 1296 points). This can be specified here.

If the **Fit** option is selected in Step 5, the text will be expanded proportionally over the background photo; if **Fill** is selected the text will be expanded, and distorted, to fill the whole area of the photo.

5 Click on these buttons to specify how the text fills the background photo

2. (Optional) Choose how you'd like the text to appear on your photo.

Abc   Abc
Fit   Fill

6 Click on the **Create Frames** button to create a frame for each letter

7 Each letter is converted into a frame, into which individual photos can be inserted, and displayed as the shape of each letter

8 Click on a letter to add a photo to it from your computer. Or, click on the **Photo Bin** button to add photos that are currently open in the Photo Bin (photos can be added from your computer from the **Computer** button here too). The selected photos fill the frames in the photo

9 Click on these buttons to add a different background color, or add bevel and shadow effects to the frames (these are optional)

107

Don't forget

After the options in Step 9, save, edit or share the completed photo, as shown on page 103.

Text and Border Overlay

Individual photos can quickly and effectively have both text and a border added to them in Elements. To do this:

1 Open the image to which you want to add a text and border overlay effect

2 Access Guided edit mode and in the **Special Edits** section, click on the **Text and Border Overlay** button

3 Click on the **Select a Border** button and click on a border style for the photo

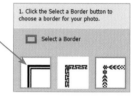

4 Click on the **Add Text Overlay** button to create a text box over the photo's border

5 Click on the **Type Tool** button to add text to the photo. This can be formatted in the Options panel

6 Select a position on the border for the text and click on the **Text Styles** button to add a preset style for the text

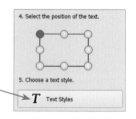

7 The text and border are displayed over the photo. Click on the **Next** button to save, edit or share it, as shown on page 103

Don't forget

By default, the text for the text and border overlay effect is placed in the top left-hand corner of the border. Click on one of the locations on the border in Step 6 to change the position of the text.

Painterly Effect

The Painterly effect is one that creates a border around an image to make it look like it has been painted on a canvas. To do this:

1 Open the image for the Painterly effect

2 Access Guided edit mode and in the **Fun Edits** section, click on the **Painterly** button

3 Click on the **Paint Brush** button and click on the photo to apply the template each time

Don't forget

Texture and Effect are optional for adding to the background.

4 Select a color for the background canvas. Click on the **Select Custom Color** button to select a color other than black or white

5 Select a texture for the background color and an effect for it

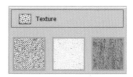

Don't forget

If a texture is added, the **Opacity** slider can be used to determine how much of the textured background is visible.

6 Click on the **Next** button to complete the Painterly effect and save, edit or share it, as shown on page 103

Pattern Brush

Graphical elements are an excellent way to give an extra dimension to a photo, and the Pattern Brush Guided edit provides options for adding a range of graphical patterns. To do this:

The Pattern Brush Guided edit is a new feature in the latest version of Elements.

1 Open the image to which you want to add a pattern

Hot tip

For the Pattern Brush, use a photo where there is plenty of space around the main subject.

2 Access Guided edit mode and in the **Fun Edits** section, click on the **Pattern Brush** button

3 Click on the required pattern

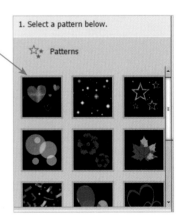

Don't forget

Drag the slider to the right of the pattern options in Step 3 to see the full range available.

4 Check **On** the **Protect Subject** checkbox to ensure that the pattern does not obscure the main subject

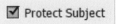

5 Click on the **Fill** button to have the pattern automatically added to the photo

6 Click on the **Paint** button and make selections for the Paint option as required

7 Drag over the area in the photo to which you want the pattern applied

8 Click on the **Next** button to complete the Pattern Brush effect and save, edit or share it, as shown on page 103

The options for painting a pattern over a photo manually include: **Size**, which determines the size of the items within the pattern; **Scatter**, which determines how far apart each item is in the pattern; and **Opacity**, which determines how much of the background shows through the pattern.

Effects Collage

Individual photos can be quickly and effectively turned into impressive collages in Elements. To do this:

1 Open the image that you want to turn into a collage

2 Access Guided edit mode and in the **Fun Edits** section, click on the **Effects Collage** button

3 Select an option for a layout of the collage; e.g. how the photo is split up

4 Select a style for the collage. Click on the down-pointing arrow to access the full range of styles

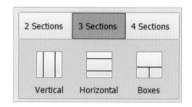

5 Click on the **Next** button to complete the collage and save, edit or share it, as shown on page 103

Hot tip

The option for continuing editing in Expert edit mode (which is accessed on the Save or Share panel as on page 103) is a good way to see the composition of a Guided edit mode image. Click on the **Layers** panel button on the Expert edit mode bottom toolbar to view the layers used to create the image.

6 Beyond Basic Color Editing

This chapter looks at some of the more powerful features for image editing in Elements, so you can take your skills to the next level.

Hue and Saturation

The Hue/Saturation command can be used to edit the color elements of an image. However, it works slightly differently from other commands, such as those for the brightness and contrast. There are three areas that are covered by the Hue/Saturation command: color (hue), color strength (saturation), and lightness. To adjust the hue and saturation of an image:

The keyboard shortcut for accessing the Hue/Saturation dialog window is **Ctrl + U** (**Command key + U** on a Mac).

By altering the hue of an image, some interesting abstract color effects can be created. This can be very effective if you are producing several versions of the same image, such as for an artistic poster.

1 Open an image

2 Select **Enhance > Adjust Color > Adjust Hue/Saturation** from the Menu bar, in either Expert edit or Quick edit modes

3 Drag this slider to adjust the hue of the image; i.e. change the colors in the image

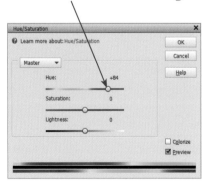

Hue is used to describe the color of a particular pixel or an image.

4 Drag this slider to adjust the saturation; i.e. the intensity of colors in the image

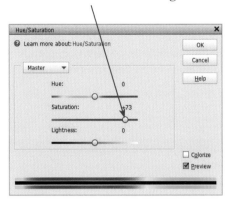

The Lightness option is similar to adjusting image brightness.

5 Check on the **Colorize** box to color the image with the hue of the currently selected foreground color in the Color Picker, which is located at the bottom of the Toolbox

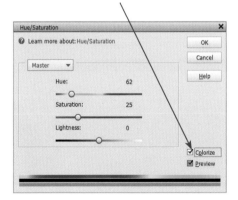

The Colorize option can be used to create some interesting "color wash" effects. Try altering the Hue slider once the Colorize box has been checked On.

6 Click on the **OK** button to apply any changes that have been made

OK

For more on working with color and the Color Picker, see page 166.

Histogram

The Histogram in Elements is a device that displays the tonal range of the pixels in an image, and it can be used for very precise editing of an image. The Histogram (**Window** > **Histogram** in Expert edit mode) is a graph that displays how the pixels in an image are distributed across the image, from the darkest (black) to the lightest (white) points. Another way of considering the Histogram is that it displays the values of an image's highlights, midtones and shadows:

The keyboard shortcut for accessing the Histogram is **F9**.

The Histogram works by looking at the individual color channels of an image (Red, Green, Blue, also known as the RGB color model) or a combination of all three, which is displayed as Luminosity in the **Channel:** box. It can also look at all of the colors in an image.

Image formats such as JPEG are edited in Elements using the RGB color model; i.e. red, green and blue, mixed together to create the colors in the image.

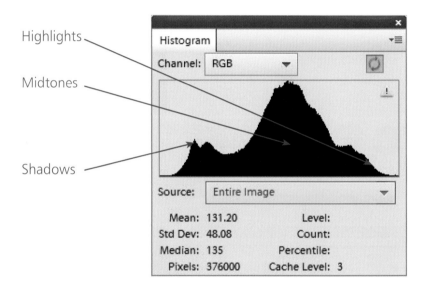

Ideally, the Histogram should show a reasonably consistent range of tonal distribution, indicating an image that has good contrast and detail:

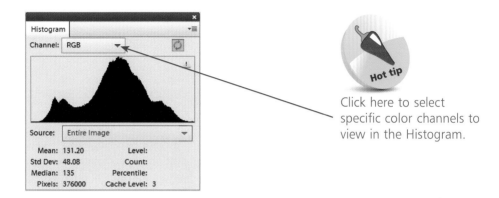

Click here to select specific color channels to view in the Histogram.

However, if the tonal range is bunched at one end of the graph, this indicates that the image is under-exposed or over-exposed:

Over-exposure

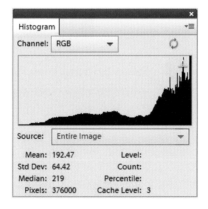

If the Histogram is left open, it will update automatically as editing changes are made to an image. This gives a good idea of how effective the changes are.

Under-exposure

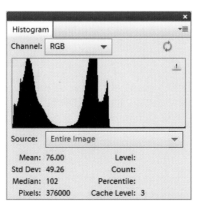

Levels

While the Histogram displays the tonal range of an image, the Levels function can be used to edit this range. Any changes made using the Levels function will then be visible in the Histogram. Levels allows you to redistribute pixels between the darkest and lightest points in an image, and also set these points manually if you want to. To use the Levels function:

Hot tip

The Levels function can be used to adjust the tonal range of a specific area of an image, by first making a selection and then using the Levels dialog box. For more details on selecting areas, see Chapter 7.

Don't forget

In the Levels dialog box, the graph is the same as the one shown in the Histogram.

Don't forget

Image shadows, midtones and highlights can be altered by dragging the markers for the black, midtone and white input points.

1 Open an image

2 Select **Enhance** > **Adjust Lighting** > **Levels** from the Menu bar, in either Expert edit or Quick edit modes

Midtone input point

Black input point

White input point

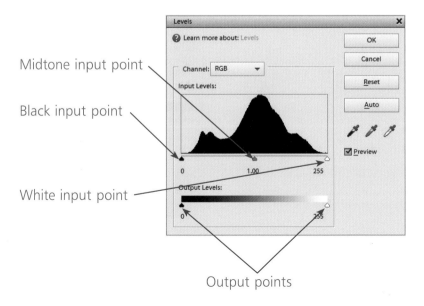

Output points

3 Drag the black point and the white point sliders to, or beyond, the first pixels denoted in the graph to increase the contrast

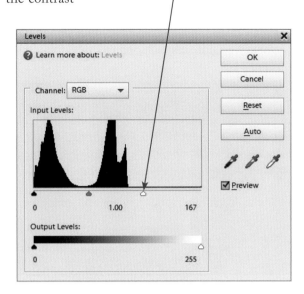

It is worth adjusting an image's black-and-white points before any other editing is performed.

Move the midtone point slider to darken or lighten the midtones in an image.

4 Drag the output sliders towards the middle to decrease the contrast

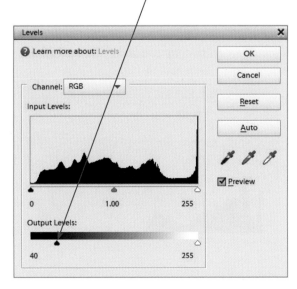

The Auto button in the Levels dialog box produces the same effect as using the **Enhance > Auto Levels** command from the Menu bar.

Adjustments with Levels

Although there is an Auto Levels function within Elements, more accurate editing can be done by using the Levels dialog box:

The Auto Levels option can be accessed by selecting **Enhance** > **Auto Levels** from the Menu bar.

1 Open an image that is either too dark or too light (or requires the midtones to be edited)

The keyboard shortcut for accessing the Levels dialog window is **Ctrl** + **L** (**Command key** + **L** on a Mac).

2 Select **Enhance** > **Adjust Lighting** > **Levels** from the Menu bar

3 If there is no data at one end of the graph, it suggests an image is either too dark or too light (in this instance, too dark). Drag on this button to adjust the image

By default, all of the color channels (RGB for Red, Green and Blue) are edited within Levels. However, click here to select the individual Red, Green and Blue channels so that they can be edited independently.

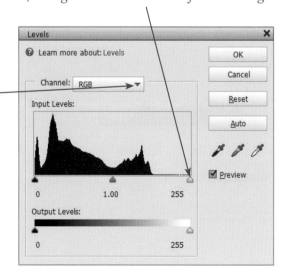

120

4 Drag the button to where the graph starts (or finishes). Ideally, the white and black buttons should be at the right and left of the graph respectively

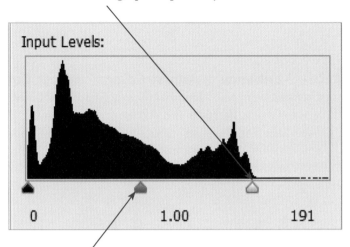

5 Drag on this button to adjust the midtones of an image; i.e. the color in the mid-range between white and black

6 The Levels editing effects are applied to the image

7 Click on the **OK** button to exit the Levels dialog window

Hot tip

Adjusting the midtones manually is similar to using **Enhance** > **Adjust Lighting** > **Shadows/Highlights** from the Menu bar.

121

Don't forget

Levels can also be accessed and applied in Quick edit mode.

Color Curves

If the colors are not ideal in a photo, one option for editing them is with Color Curves. This is done by editing the colors for different elements in the image; e.g. highlights, brightness, contrast and shadows. This can be done with preset options, or you can apply your own settings manually. To use Color Curves:

Don't forget

There is no keyboard shortcut for accessing the Color Curves dialog window.

1 Select **Enhance** > **Adjust Color** > **Adjust Color Curves** from the Menu bar. The Adjust Color Curves window has a **Before** and **After** preview panel at the top of the window, and options for automatic and manual adjustments at the bottom of the window

Don't forget

Color Curves edits the color using the overall color channels in an image. These are the individual Red, Green or Blue channels, or a combination of all three: the RGB channel.

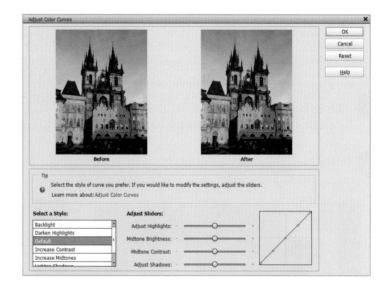

122

Hot tip

To avoid photos where the foreground subject is too dark, use the flash when taking a photo, even when there is bright sunlight behind the subject.

2 Under the **Select a Style:** heading, select the area of color that you want to edit. These include **Backlight** (for images where the foreground subject is too dark), **Darken Highlights**, **Default**, **Increase Contrast**, **Increase Midtones**, **Lighten Shadows** and **Solarize**

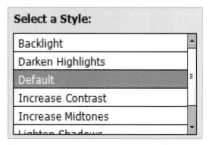

3 For each item selected in Step 2, the appropriate curve adjustments are made automatically (shown on the graph)

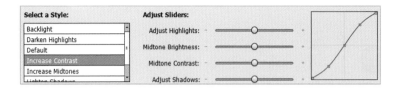

4 Drag the sliders under **Adjust Sliders:** to edit the color elements in the image manually. As you drag the sliders, the graph moves accordingly

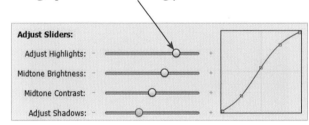

Hot tip

Dragging the sliders in Step 4 is a good way to see how the shape of the Color Curves graph affects the image.

5 The Color Curves editing effects are previewed at the top of the window

Hot tip

Exaggerated colors created with curves can make a striking photo, even if it is not completely realistic.

6 Click on the **OK** button to apply the changes, **Cancel** to remove them, or **Reset** to return to the original image and continue editing it

Remove Color Cast

Even sophisticated digital cameras and smartphone cameras can sometimes misinterpret the lighting conditions of a scene, resulting in an unnatural color in the photo, known as color cast. To remove this:

Don't forget

There is no keyboard shortcut for accessing the Remove Color Cast dialog window.

Don't forget

Color cast is particularly common in indoor shots taken without the flash under artificial lighting. This is known as "white balance", where the camera does not correctly interpret what white should be, and so all of the other colors in the photo are affected too. One way to overcome this is to change your camera's white balance settings if you are taking photos in artificial lighting.

Hot tip

Color cast can be edited manually within Levels. To do this, select one of the individual color channels (Red, Green or Blue) in the Levels dialog window and drag the input sliders accordingly.

1 In Expert edit or Quick edit modes, open the photo affected by color cast

2 Select **Enhance** > **Adjust Color** > **Remove Color Cast** from the Menu bar. Click on an area of the photo that should be black, white or gray. The overall color in the photo will be adjusted accordingly

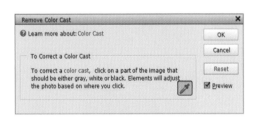

7 Working with Selections

The true power of digital image editing comes into its own when you are able to select areas of an image and edit them independently. This chapter looks at the various ways that selections can be made and edited, using the tools and functions within Elements.

About Selections

One of the most important aspects of image editing is the ability to select areas within an image. This can be used in a number of different ways:

- Selecting an object to apply an editing technique to it (such as changing the brightness or contrast) without affecting the rest of the image.

- Selecting a particular color in an image.

- Selecting an area on which to apply a special effect.

- Selecting an area to remove.

Expert edit mode has several tools that can be used to select items, and there are also a number of editing functions that can be applied to selections.

Two examples of how selections can be used are:

Once a selection has been made, it stays selected even when another tool is activated, to allow further editing to take place.

If a selection is deleted, the space will be filled by the current background color in the Color Picker in the Toolbox.

- Selecting an area within an image and deleting it.

- Selecting an area in an image and adding a color or special effect.

The best way to deselect a selection is to click on it once with one of the selection tools, preferably the one used to make the selection. You can also choose **Select** > **Deselect** from the Menu bar.

Marquee Tools

There are two options for the Marquee tools: the Rectangular Marquee tool and the Elliptical Marquee tool. Both of these can be used to make symmetrical selections. To use the Marquee tools:

1 Select either the **Rectangular** or the **Elliptical Marquee** tool from the Toolbox. Select the required options from the Tool Options bar

2 Make a symmetrical selection with one of the tools by clicking and dragging on an image

Elliptical selection

Rectangular selection

To access additional tools from the Expert edit mode Toolbox, click on a tool and select any grouped tools in the Tool Options bar.

127

To make a selection that is exactly square or round, hold down **Shift** when dragging with the Rectangular Marquee tool or the Elliptical Marquee tool respectively.

Lasso Tools

There are three options for the Lasso tool, which can be used to make freehand selections. To use these:

Lasso tool

Hot tip

When a selection has been completed (i.e. its end point reaches its start point), a small circle will appear at the side of whichever Lasso tool is being used. Click on this point to complete the selection.

1 Select the **Lasso** tool from the Toolbox and select the required options from the Tool Options bar

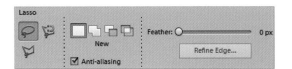

Don't forget

See page 152 for information about Anti-aliasing, which can be accessed in the Tool Options bar.

2 Make a freehand selection by clicking with the mouse and dragging around the object

Polygonal Lasso tool

Beware

With the Lasso tool, do not release the mouse until the selection has been completed.

1 Select the **Polygonal Lasso** tool from the Toolbox and select the required options from the Tool Options bar

2 Make a selection by clicking on specific points around an object, and then dragging to the next point

Don't forget

Making a selection with the Polygonal Lasso tool is like creating a dot-to-dot pattern.

...cont'd

Magnetic Lasso tool

1 Select the **Magnetic Lasso** tool from the Toolbox and select the required options from the Tool Options bar

2 Click once on an image to create the first anchor point

Hot tip

In the Tool Options bar for the Magnetic Lasso tool, the Contrast value determines the amount of contrast there has to be between colors for the selection line to snap to them. A high value detects lines with a high contrast, and vice versa.

3 Make a selection by dragging continuously around an object. The selection line snaps to the closest, strongest edge; i.e. the one with the most contrast. Fastening points are added as the selection is made

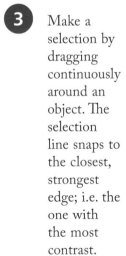

Hot tip

The Frequency setting in the Tool Options bar determines how quickly the fastening points are inserted as a selection is being made. A high value places the fastening points more quickly than a low value.

Magic Wand Tool

The Magic Wand tool can be used to select areas of the same or similar color. To do this:

1 Select the **Magic Wand** tool from the Toolbox and select the required options from the Tool Options bar

2 Click on a color to select all of the adjacent pixels that are the same or similar color, depending on the options selected from the Tool Options bar

Selection Brush Tool

The Selection Brush tool can be used to select areas by using a brush-like stroke. Unlike with the Marquee or Lasso tools, the area selected by the Selection Brush tool is the one directly below where the tool moves. To make a selection with the Selection Brush tool (this is also available in Quick edit mode):

1 Select the **Selection Brush** tool from the Toolbox and select the required options from the Tool Options bar

2 Click and drag to make a selection

3 The selection area is within the borders marked out by the Selection Brush tool

The Selection Brush tool can be used to select an area, or to mask an area. This can be determined in the Selection drop-down box in the Tool Options bar.

The Selection Brush tool is best for selecting large areas that do not have to be too precise. For exact precision, use the Polygonal or Magnetic Lasso tools.

For all of the selection tools, hold down **Shift** to make another selection while retaining the original one.

Quick Selection Tool

The Quick Selection tool can be used to select areas of similar color by drawing over the general area, without having to make a specific selection. To do this:

Don't forget

The Quick Selection tool is also available from the Quick edit mode Toolbox.

Beware

If a very large brush size is used for the Quick Selection tool – e.g. 300 px (pixels) or above – you may select unwanted areas of the image by mistake.

Don't forget

As you drag the Quick Selection tool, it selects whichever areas of color it passes over. As you drag over different areas of color, these will be selected too.

1 Select the **Quick Selection** tool from the Toolbox

2 Select the required options from the Tool Options bar

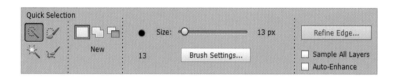

3 Draw over an area, or part of an area, to select all of the similarly colored pixels

Smart Brush Tool

The Smart Brush tool can be used to quickly select large areas in an image (in a similar way to the Quick Selection tool) and then have effects applied automatically to the selected area. To do this:

1 Open the image to which you want to apply changes

2 Select the **Smart Brush** tool from the Toolbox

3 Select the editing effect you want to apply to the area selected by the Smart Brush tool, from the Tool Options bar

4 Select **Brush size** for the Smart Brush tool, from the Tool Options bar

5 Drag the Smart Brush tool over an area of the image. In the left-hand image below, the building has been selected and brightened; in the right-hand image, the sky has been selected and enhanced

Don't forget

Multiple editing effects can be applied with the Smart Brush tool within the same image. This usually requires individually selecting different parts of the image and then selecting the required effect.

133

Don't forget

Some of the other options for the Smart Brush tool include increasing the brightness or contrast, intensifying foliage in a photo, making lips redder, and creating sepia images.

Auto Selections

Instead of having to make precise selections, Elements has a function where selections can be made by dragging around a subject. Elements can then identify the subject and select it.

Once a selection has been made, it can be inverted by choosing **Select > Inverse** from the Menu bar. The keyboard shortcut for inverting a selection is **Shift** + **Ctrl** + **I** (Shift + **Command key** + **I** on a Mac).

1 Open an image and select the **Auto Selection** tool (from the selection tools' subset)

2 Drag the **Auto Selection** tool around the required subject. This creates a rectangular box

3 Release the **Auto Selection** tool to enable it to create the selection

4 Once a selection has been made in this way it can be edited independently from the rest of the image. Also, if the selection is inverted (see first Don't forget tip) the background can be edited and the originally selected subject remains untouched

When a selection has been inverted, the newly selected area can be edited in the same way as for a standard selection in a photo.

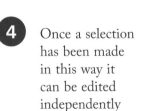

Feathering

Feathering is a technique that can be used to soften the edges of a selection by making them slightly blurry. This can be used if you are pasting a selection into another image, or if you want to soften the edges around a portrait of an individual. To do this:

1 Make a selection

2 Choose **Select** > **Feather** from the Menu bar

3 Enter a **Feather Radius:** value (the number of pixels wide around the radius of the selection that will be blurred). Click on the **OK** button

4 Invert the selection, as shown on the previous page, and delete the background by pressing **Delete** on the keyboard. This will leave the selection around the subject with softened edges

Hot tip

The keyboard shortcut for accessing the Feather Selection dialog window is **Alt** + **Ctrl** + **D** (Alt + **Command key** + **D** on a Mac).

Don't forget

Feathering can also be selected from the Tool Options bar once a Marquee tool is selected, and before the selection has been made.

Hot tip

If required, crop the final image so that the feathered subject is more prominent.

Refining Selections

When making selections it is sometimes difficult to exactly select the area that you want. In Elements it is possible to refine the area of a selection, and also the edges around a selected item. To do this:

The **Refine Selection Brush** option can be used regardless of how the selection was made.

Click inside a selection to add to it; click outside to subtract from it.

Click on the **View** box to select an option for the overlay that covers the current selection, so that you can see exactly what has been selected.

1 In Expert edit or Quick edit mode, make a selection with one of the selection tools

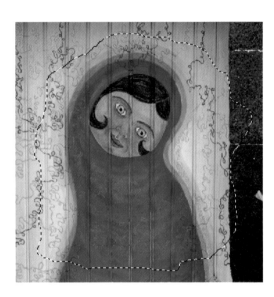

2 Select the **Refine Selection Brush** tool (grouped with the Quick Selection tool)

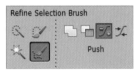

3 Click on this button to add or subtract from the selection with the cursor

4 Click on this button to smooth the edges of the selection by dragging the cursor over it

5 Select a size for the cursor to refine the selection, and the strength for how it snaps to neighboring pixels; the greater the strength, the more the selection will snap to pixels of similar color

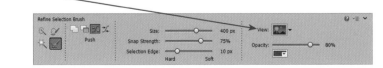

6 Position the cursor inside or outside the selection. It appears as two circles: a smaller one inside a larger one. Use the circles to nudge the selection lines one way or another to refine the selection

Zoom in on a selection for the greatest accuracy in refining it.

Refining edges

It is also possible to add a range of refinements to the edges of a selection, which can be an excellent option for textures such as clothing or animal fur. To do this:

1 Once a selection has been made, click on the **Refine Edge...** button in the Tool Options bar

Refine Edge...

2 Select options here for how much of the edge is detected in terms of being refined. Select **Smart Radius** or enter a manual value for the radius

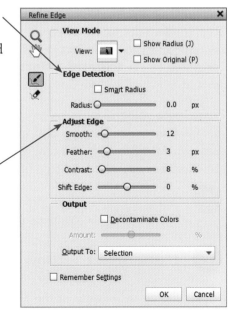

3 Select options here for how the edge is adjusted, using smoothing, feathering, contrast and moving the edge. Click **OK**

The Refine Edge options are particularly useful if you are copying a selection and pasting it into another image that has different textures.

Editing Selections

When you have made a selection you can edit it in a number of ways:

Moving a selection

Make a selection and select the **Move** tool from the Toolbox. Drag the selection to move it to a new location.

Changing the selection area

Make a selection with a selection tool. With the same tool selected, click and drag within the selection area to move it over another part of the image.

Adding to a selection

Make a selection and click on this button in the Tool Options bar. Make another selection to create a single, larger selection. The two selections do not have to intersect.

Intersecting with a selection

To create a selection by intersecting two existing selections, make a selection and click on this button in the Tool Options bar. Make another selection that intersects the first. The intersected area will become the selection.

Expanding a selection

To expand a selection by a specific number of pixels, make a selection and choose **Select** > **Modify** > **Expand** from the Menu bar. In the **Expand Selection** dialog box, enter the amount by which you want the selection expanded.

Growing a selection

The Grow command can be used on a selection when it has been made with the Magic Wand tool, and some of the pixels within the selection have been omitted. To do this:

1 Make a selection with the **Magic Wand** tool and make the required choices from the Tool Options bar

2 Choose **Select** > **Grow** from the Menu bar

Depending on the choices in the Tool Options bar, the omitted pixels will be included in the selection.

Beware

Once an area has been moved and deselected, it cannot then be selected independently again, unless it has been copied and pasted onto a separate layer.

Hot tip

Selections can also be deselected by clicking on **Select** > **Deselect** from the Menu bar, or using **Ctrl** + **D** on the keyboard (**Command key** + **D** on a Mac).

138

8 Layers

Layers provide the means to add numerous elements to an image and edit them independently from one another. This chapter looks at how to use layers to add content to photos.

Layering Images

Layering is a technique that enables you to add additional elements to an image, and place them on separate layers so that they can be edited and manipulated independently from other elements in the image. It is like creating an image using transparent sheets of film: each layer is independent of the others, but when they are combined, a composite image is created. This is an extremely versatile technique for working with digital images.

By using layers, several different elements can be combined to create a composite image:

Original image

Layers should usually be used when you are adding content to an image, as this gives more flexibility for working with the various image elements once they have been added.

Final image
With text, gradient and shapes added (four additional layers have been added).

Text and shapes cannot be added together on the same layer.

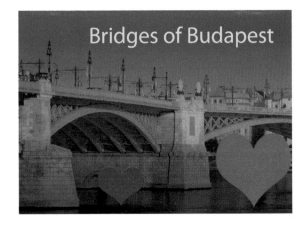

Layers Panel

The use of layers within Elements is done within Expert edit mode and is governed by the Layers panel. When an image is first opened it is shown in the Layers panel as the Background layer. While this remains as the Background layer, it cannot be moved above any other layers. However, it can be converted into a normal layer, in which case it operates in the same way as any other layer. To convert a Background layer into a normal one:

The keyboard shortcut for accessing the Layers panel is **F11**.

1 Click on the **Layers** button on the Taskbar

2 The open image is shown in the Layers panel as the Background

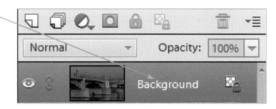

The Background layer can also be converted into a normal one by applying the Background Eraser tool and the Magic Eraser tool.

3 Double-click on the layer. Enter a name for it and click on the **OK** button

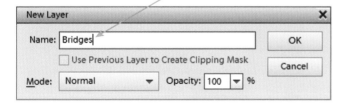

4 The Background layer is converted into a normal layer in the Layers panel

The Layers panel menu can be accessed from the button in the top right-hand corner of the Layers panel.

Adding Layers

New blank layers can be added whenever you want to include new content within an image. This could be part of another image that has been copied and pasted; a whole new image; some text; or an object. To add a new layer:

The keyboard shortcut for adding a new layer is **Shift** + **Ctrl** + **N** (Shift + **Command key** + **N** on a Mac).

1 Click here on the Layers panel

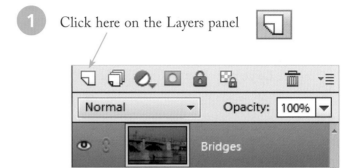

Don't forget

Text is automatically added on a new layer within an image.

2 Double-click on the layer name and overtype to give the layer a new name

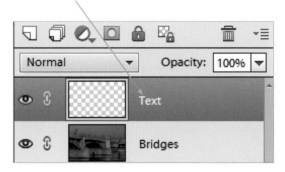

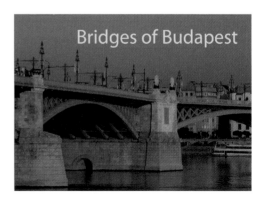

Don't forget

To edit an item on a particular layer, first make sure that the correct layer is selected in the Layers panel. A selected layer is known as the active layer and it is highlighted in the Layers panel with a solid color around it.

3 With the new layer selected in the Layers panel, add content to this layer. This will be visible over the layer, or layers, below it

Bridges of Budapest

Fill and Adjustment Layers

Fill and Adjustment layers can be added to images to give an effect behind or above the main subject. To do this:

1 Open the Layers panel and select a layer. The Fill or Adjustment layer will be placed directly above the selected layer

2 Click here at the bottom of the Layers panel

3 Select one of the Fill or Adjustment options. The Fill options are **Solid Color...**, **Gradient...** or **Pattern...**

143

...cont'd

Fill and Adjustment layers can also be added from the Layer option on the Menu bar.

If you want to edit a Fill or Adjustment layer, double-click on its icon in the Layers panel and then apply the required changes.

If the opacity for a Fill layer is 100%, nothing will be visible beneath that layer.

4 For a Solid Color, Gradient or Pattern Fill, the required Fill is selected from the dialog box and this is added to the selected layer

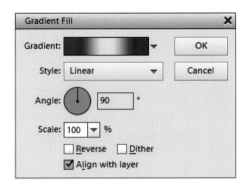

5 For Adjustment options, settings can be applied within the Adjustments panel

6 Once Fill and Adjustment settings have been applied, the effect can be edited by changing the opacity. This is done by dragging this slider, which appears when the **Opacity:** box is clicked On

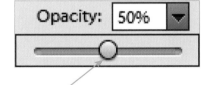

7 The opacity level determines how much of the image is visible through the Fill or Adjustment layer

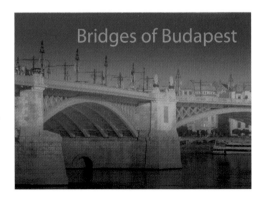

Working with Layers

Moving layers

The order in which layers are arranged in the Layers panel is known as the stacking order. It is possible to change a layer's position in the stacking order, which affects how it is viewed in the composite image. To do this:

1 Click and drag a layer within the Layers panel to change its stacking order

Layers cannot be moved underneath the Background layer, unless it has been renamed.

Hiding layers

Layers can be hidden while you are working on other parts of an image. However, the layer is still part of the composite image – it has not been removed. To hide a layer:

1 Click here so that a line appears through the eye icon, and the layer becomes hidden. Click again to remove the line and reveal the layer

This icon indicates that the layer has a layer mask linked to it. This means that the mask will move with the layer, if it is moved. Click on the icon to unlink the layer mask from the layer (see pages 146-148 for details about layer masks).

Locking layers

Layers can be locked, so that they cannot be edited accidentally while you are working on other parts of an image. To do this:

1 Select a layer and click here so that the padlock is activated. The padlock also appears on the layer itself

Layers can be deleted by selecting them and clicking on the **Trash** icon in the Layers panel. However, this also deletes all of the content on that layer.

145

Layer Masks

Because layers can be separated within an individual image, there is a certain amount of versatility in terms of the ways in which different layers can interact with each other. One of these ways is to create a layer mask. This is a top-level layer, through which an area is removed so that the layer below is revealed. To do this:

Beware

If the Background layer is not renamed as in Step 2, the graphic will be placed directly over the Background layer, rather than being created on a new layer.

Don't forget

When creating the new layer in Step 2, you can also change the opacity and select a different mode, to affect the way the layer interacts with layers below it (if there are any).

Don't forget

Different types of content can be added as the top layer in an image to be used as a layer mask, although whatever is added has to be converted to a normal layer rather than a Background one.

1 Open an image. It will be displayed as the Background in the Layers panel. Double-click on this to select it

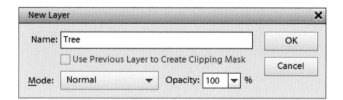

2 Give the layer a new name and click on the **OK** button

3 Click on the **Graphics** button on the Taskbar to access the Graphics panel

4 Use the drop-down menus at the top of the Graphics panel to access different categories and click on a graphic to select it

5 Select a graphic and double-click on it to add it as a layer to the current image. Initially, this is added below the open image. Rename the new layer

Don't forget

If a new layer is not renamed, it will automatically become the Background one.

6 Drag the added layer above the original image (this can also be done by selecting an area in another image, copying it and then pasting it above the existing image)

Beware

The top layer will obscure all layers below it, until either its opacity is reduced or a layer mask is applied.

147

7 The graphic image layer now covers the original one

Hot tip

If numerous layers are used within a single image they can be grouped together within the Layers panel. Select layers within the panel and drag them over this button to create a group of layers that can be managed and edited as a single entity.

...cont'd

If the Brush tool is used to create the layer mask, this is done by drawing over the top layer of the image. As this is done, the layer below will be revealed. Change the level of opacity in the Tool Options bar to change the amount that the layer below shows through the top layer of the image.

The selected layer can also be deleted by pressing the **Delete** key on the keyboard.

Build up an image with several layer masks, to create an artistic effect.

8 Click here to apply a layer mask to the top layer

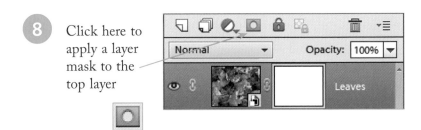

9 Select either one of the **Marquee** tools, the **Lasso** tools, or the **Brush** tool from the Toolbox

10 Select an area on the top layer and delete it, to display the image below it (**Edit** > **Delete** from the Menu bar)

11 In the Layers panel, the area that has been removed is displayed here

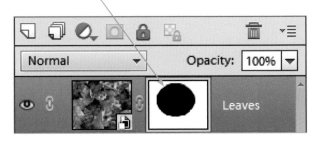

Opacity

The opacity of a layer can be set to determine how much of the layer below is visible through the selected layer. To do this:

1 Select a layer either in the Layers panel or by clicking on the relevant item within an image

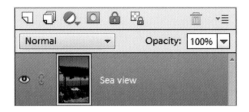

2 Click here and drag the slider that appears below, to achieve the required level of opacity. The greater the amount of opacity, the less transparent the selected layer becomes

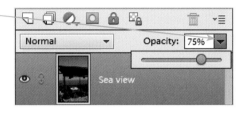

3 The opacity setting determines how much of the background or the layer below is visible through the selected one. This can be used to create some interesting artistic effects, including a watermark effect if the opacity is applied to a single layer with nothing behind it

Hot tip

The background behind an image to which opacity has been applied can be changed within the Preferences section. Select **Edit > Preferences** from the Menu bar (**Adobe Photoshop Elements Editor > Preferences** on a Mac) and then select **Transparency** and edit the items in the Grid Colors box.

Don't forget

Different layers can have different levels of opacity applied to them.

Saving Layers

Once an image has been created using two or more layers, there are two ways in which the composite image can be saved: in a proprietary Photoshop format, in which case individual layers are maintained; or in a general file format, where all of the layers will be merged into a single one. The advantage of the former is that individual elements can still be edited within the image, independently of other items. In general, it is a good practice to save layered images in both a Photoshop and a non-Photoshop format. To save layered images in a Photoshop format:

Hot tip

Before a layer is saved, it is possible to create a composite image consisting of a single layer. To do this, select **Layer** > **Flatten Image** from the Menu bar. To merge the existing layer and the one below it, select **Layer** > **Merge Down** from the Menu bar, and to merge all visible content (excluding any layers that have been hidden) select **Layer** > **Merge Visible**. If layers are flattened, they cannot then be edited independently.

1 Select **File** > **Save As** from the Menu bar

2 Make sure Photoshop (*.PSD, *.PDD) is selected as the format

3 Make sure the **Layers** box is checked On

4 Click on the **Save** button

Beware

Layered images that are saved in the Photoshop PSD/PDD format can increase dramatically in file size, compared with the original image or a layered image that has been flattened.

To save in a non-Photoshop format, select **File** > **Save As** from the Menu bar. Select the file format from the format box (such as JPEG or TIFF) and click on the **Save** button. The Layers box will not be available.

9 Text and Drawing Tools

Elements has options for adding and formatting text, and creating a variety of graphical objects. This chapter looks at how to add and manipulate text and drawing objects.

Adding and Formatting Text

Text can be added to images in Elements and this can be used to create a wide range of items such as cards, brochures and posters. To add text to an image:

Use the Vertical Type tool sparingly, as this is not a natural way for the eye to read text. Use it with small amounts of text, for effect.

1 Select the **Horizontal** or **Vertical Type** tool from the Toolbox

2 Drag on the image with the Type tool to create a text box

3 Make the required formatting selections from the Tool Options bar:

Anti-aliasing is a technique that smoothes out the jagged edges that can sometimes appear with text when viewed on a computer monitor. Anti-aliasing is created by adding pixels to the edges of text, so that it blends more smoothly with the background.

Type tools   Font type   Font size   Color

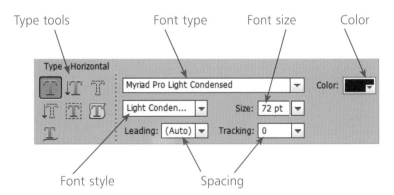

Font style   Spacing

Bold, Italics and Underline   Warp Text

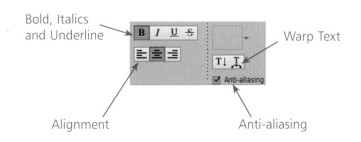

Alignment   Anti-aliasing

152

4 Type the text onto the image. This is automatically placed onto the image as a new layer, at the top of the stacking order in the Layers panel

Each new text box is placed on a new layer.

5 To move the text, select it with the **Move** tool, then click and drag it to a new position

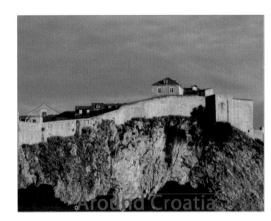

If there are two or more text layers, they can be moved above or below each other in the Layers panel.

153

To format text that has already been entered:

1 Select a **Type** tool and drag it over a piece of text to select it

Around Croatia

Individual words can be selected by double-clicking on them. Text blocks without any returns in the text can be selected by triple-clicking on them. Text blocks containing returns in the text can be selected by quadruple-clicking on them.

2 Make the changes in the Tool Options bar, as shown in Step 3 on the previous page

Around Croatia

3 Click on the green check mark to accept the text entry

Customizing Text

As well as adding standard text, it is also possible to add text to follow a selection, a shape or a custom path. This can be done within Expert edit and Quick edit modes.

Adding text to a selection

To add text to a selection within an image:

In Expert edit mode, select the Move tool and click and drag the text to move it with the selection area.

154

1 Click on the **Type** tool and select the **Text on Selection** tool option

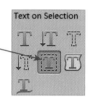

2 Drag over an area of an image to make a selection

Text on Selection text should be reasonably large in size, so that it can be read clearly on the image.

3 Click on the green check mark to accept the selection

4 Click anywhere on the selection and add text. By default, this will be displayed along the outside of the selection

5 Format the text in the same way as with standard text

...cont'd

Adding text to a shape

To add text to a shape within an image:

1 Click on the **Type** tool and select the **Text on Shape** tool option

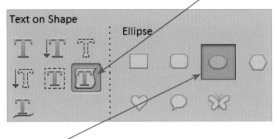

Beware

The butterfly shape is an artistic one, but it can be difficult reading text that is added in this way.

2 Click here in the Tool Options bar to select a shape

3 Drag over an area of an image to create a shape

Hot tip

Once customized text has been added and accepted, it can still be edited in the same way as standard text, by using the Horizontal Type tool and selecting the customized text.

4 Click anywhere on the shape and add text. Click on the green check mark as in Step 3 on the previous page

5 Format the text in the same way as with standard text

Beware

Make sure that there is a good contrast between the text color and the background colors in the image.

...cont'd

Adding text to a custom path

Text can also be added to a custom path that you draw onto an image. To do this:

1 Open the image onto which you want to create text on a custom path

2 Click on the **Type** tool and select the **Text on Path** tool option. Make sure the **Draw** button is also selected

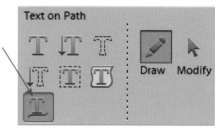

Text on Path

Draw   Modify

3 Draw a custom path on the image

4 Click on the green check mark to accept the text path

5 Click anywhere on the custom path and add text

Always check the spelling when adding text to a custom path, or any other text in an image.

6 Format the text in the same way as with standard text

| Myriad Pro | ▼ | Color: | ▼ |
| Regular | ▼ | 48 pt | ▼ |

Double-click on the text on a text path to select it and edit it, if required.

7 Click on the **Modify** tool in the Tool Options bar. This activates the markers along the custom path

8 Drag the markers to move the position of the custom path

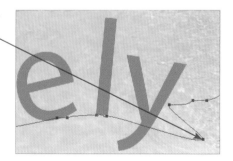

If there is too much text on a custom path it can become jumbled, particularly if you adjust the markers on the path.

9 The custom path can be used to position text in a variety of ways around objects or people

Distorting Text

In addition to producing standard text, it is also possible to create some dramatic effects by distorting text. To do this:

1 Enter plain text and select it by dragging a **Type** tool over it

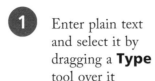

2 Click the **Create Warped Text** button on the Tool Options bar

3 Click here and select one of the options in the Warp Text dialog box. Click on the **OK** button

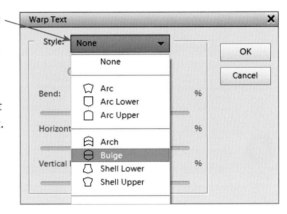

4 The selected effect is applied to the text

Text and Shape Masks

Text masks can be used to reveal an area of an image showing through the text. This can be used to produce eye-catching headings and slogans. To do this:

1 Select the **Horizontal** or **Vertical Type Mask** tool from the Toolbox

2 Click on an image, then enter and format text as you would for normal text. A red mask is applied to the image when the mask text is entered

3 Press **Enter** or click the **Move** tool to border the mask text with dots

...cont'd

Text masks can also be moved around in the original image, using the **Move** tool.

Once a text mask has been copied, it can also be pasted into other types of documents such as Word and desktop publishing documents.

The Cookie Cutter shapes have several different categories that can be selected from the **Shapes** box above the current shapes. The categories include: Animals, Flowers, Music, Nature, Ornaments, Signs, and Talk Bubbles.

4 Select **Edit** > **Copy** from the Menu bar

5 Select **File** > **New** from the Menu bar and create a new file

6 Select **Edit** > **Paste** from the Menu bar to paste the text mask into the new file

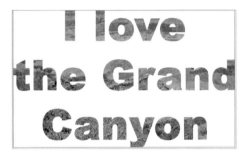

Cookie Cutter masks

A similar effect can be created with shape masks by using the Cookie Cutter tool (grouped with the Crop tool):

1 Select the **Cookie Cutter** tool in the Toolbox and click here to select a particular style in the Tool Options bar

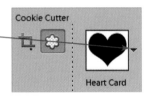

2 Drag on an image to create a cut-out effect

Paint Bucket Tool

The Paint Bucket tool can be used to add a solid color to a selection or an area in an image. To do this:

1 Open the image to which you want to apply the solid color using the Paint Bucket tool

2 Select the **Paint Bucket** tool from the Toolbox (the foreground color is selected by default)

3 Select the **Opacity** and **Tolerance** in the Tool Options bar. The Tolerance determines how much of an image is affected by the Paint Bucket

4 Click once on an area of solid color with the Paint Bucket tool. The color specified in Step 2 will be applied

Don't forget

For more information on working with color, see page 166.

Hot tip

The Paint Bucket tool can also be loaded with a pattern.

161

Hot tip

The higher the tolerance, the greater the area of color applied with the Paint Bucket tool.

Hot tip

Make a selection on an image and then apply the Paint Bucket tool to it, to get the color added exactly where you want.

Gradient Tool

The Gradient tool can be used to add a gradient fill to a selection in an image, or to an entire image. To do this:

Beware

If no selection is made for a gradient fill, the effect will be applied to the entire selected layer.

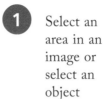 Select an area in an image or select an object

Hot tip

The default Gradient effect in the Tool Options bar is created with the currently selected foreground and background colors within the Toolbox.

2 Select the **Gradient** tool from the Toolbox

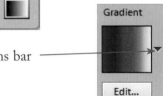

3 Click here in the Tool Options bar to select preset gradient fills

4 Click on a gradient style to apply it as the default

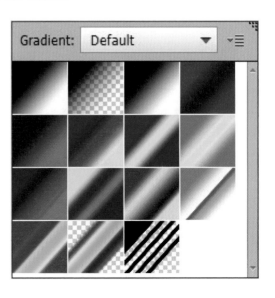

5 Click here in the Tool Options bar to access the **Gradient Editor** dialog box

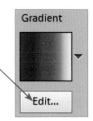

Hot tip

To create a new preset gradient, create it in the Gradient Editor dialog box and click on the **Add to Preset** button, to add it to the list of preset gradients. Click on the gradient's icon to give it a unique name in the **Name** box.

6 Click and drag the sliders to change the amount of a particular color in the gradient

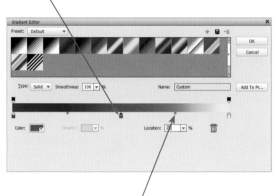

7 Click along here to add a new color marker. Click on the **OK** button

Don't forget

The more color markers that are added in Step 7, the more complex the final gradient will be.

8 Click an icon in the Tool Options bar to select a gradient style

9 Click and drag within the original selection to specify the start and end points of the gradient effect

Don't forget

The amount that the cursor is dragged when adding a gradient determines where the centerpoint of the gradient is located, and also the size of each segment of the gradient.

163

Brush Tool Settings

The Brush tool is very versatile and can be used to create lines of varying thickness and style. There are numerous settings that can be applied, for different styles and effects. To use this:

It is also possible to create your own brush styles, based on part of a photo. To do this, in Expert edit mode make a selection on a photo and select **Edit > Define Brush from Selection** from the Menu bar. Enter a name in the **Brush Name** dialog box and click **OK**. The customized brush is added to the Brush box in Step 3 and can be used to draw on a photo. This operates more like a stamp than a brush. Click once to add the brush image to a photo.

1 Select the **Brush** tool from the Toolbox. The options are shown in the Tool Options bar

2 Click here to select a default brush style

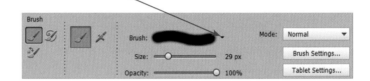

3 Select a brush size and style (hard or rounded edges) or scroll through the **Brush** box to select different brush styles

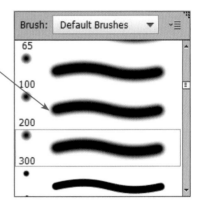

4 Click here to select a different brush type

Change the **Opacity:** setting for the brush in the Tool Options bar to alter the amount of background that is visible behind a brush stroke, including the Define Brush from Selection style, above.

...cont'd

5 Select a size and style for the brush selected in Step 4

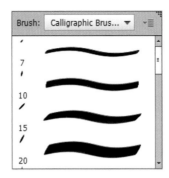

6 Click on the **Brush Settings...** button in Step 2 to make selections for the appearance of the brush

Brush Settings...

7 Drag these sliders to apply the settings for each brush type

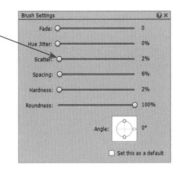

Here are some examples:

- From top to bottom: Default brushes with hard edges, rounded edges and 50% opacity applied.

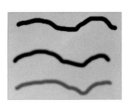

- From top to bottom: Default brushes with **Scatter** applied at 50% and **Hue Jitter** at 50%.

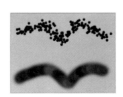

- From top to bottom: The **Calligraphic Brush** and the **Special Effects Brush (Drippy Watercolor)**.

Brush size can also be altered for custom brush styles created with the Define Brush from Selection command (see the first Hot tip on the previous page).

Experiment with small changes initially in Step 7, to get an idea of what each effect looks like. Then build up the effect with a greater percentage, if required.

Do not use too many different brush styles on a single image, as it could become a bit overpowering in terms of design.

165

Beware

Always check the foreground and background colors before you add any colors to an image, to ensure you have the right ones.

Hot tip

Whenever the foreground or background color squares are clicked on, the Color Picker tool is automatically activated. This can be used to select a color from anywhere on the screen.

Don't forget

The Color Swatches panel can be used to access different color panels that can be used to select the foreground and background colors. To do this, select **Window > Color Swatches** from the Menu bar and click on a color to select it.

Working with Color

All of the text and drawing tools make extensive use of color. Elements provides a number of methods for selecting colors, and also for working with them.

Foreground and background colors

At the bottom of the Toolbox there are two colored squares. These represent the currently selected foreground and background colors. The foreground color, which is the most frequently used, is the one that is applied to drawing objects, such as fills and lines, and also text. The background color is used for items such as gradient fills, and for areas that have been removed with the Eraser tool.

Foreground color   Swap foreground and background colors

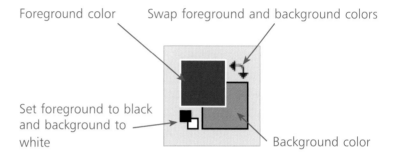

Set foreground to black and background to white

Background color

Color Picker

The Color Picker can be used to select a new color for the foreground or background color. To do this:

1 Click once on the foreground or the background color square, as required

2 In the Color Picker, click to select a color

3 Click on the **OK** button

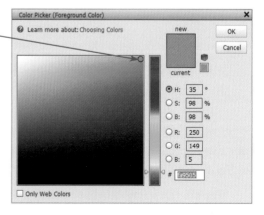

10 Becoming an Elements Expert

This chapter looks at some of the more advanced areas of Elements. These include working with the RAW file format, editing groups of images, and resizing images.

Importing RAW Images

RAW images are those in which the digital data has not been processed in any way, or converted into any specific file format by the camera when they were captured. These produce high-quality images and are usually available on higher-specification digital cameras. However, RAW is becoming more common in consumer digital cameras, and RAW images can be downloaded into Elements in the same way as any other image. Once the RAW images are accessed, the Camera Raw dialog box opens so that a variety of editing functions can be applied to the image. RAW images act as a digital negative and have to be saved into another format before they can be used in the conventional way. To edit RAW images:

The RAW format should be used if you want to make manual changes to an image to achieve the highest possible quality.

RAW images are much larger in file size than the same versions captured as JPEGs.

1 Open a RAW image in the Editor or from the Organizer

2 In the Camera Raw dialog box, editing functions that are usually performed when an image is captured can be made manually

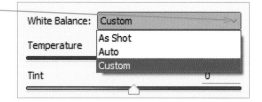

3 Click here to adjust the white balance in the image

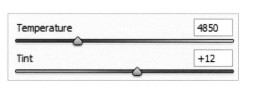

4 Drag these sliders to adjust the color temperature and tint in the image

All images can be opened in RAW by using the **File** > **Open in Camera Raw** command from the Menu bar.

5 Drag these sliders to adjust the exposure, contrast, highlights, shadows, whites and blacks in the image

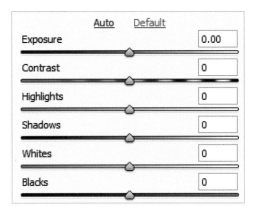

6 Click on the **Detail** tab and drag these sliders to adjust the sharpness and noise in the image

The sharpness of an image refers to the contrast between adjoining pixels, and can contribute to an image appearing more sharply in focus.

169

The noise in an image refers to pixels that have not captured color accurately (mainly in low-level lighting) and can make images look "speckled". **Noise Reduction** in the RAW window can help reduce this, by dragging the available sliders.

7 Click on the **Open Image** button. This opens the image in Expert edit mode, from where it can also be saved as a standard file format such as JPEG

Editing Multiple Images

The rise of digital cameras and smartphones with photographic capabilities means that we are now taking more photos than ever. In terms of editing, this can result in a lot of work if you want to perform similar or identical tasks on a number of images. However, in Elements there is an option for editing multiple files at the same time. This can be with a number of preset options, such as color quick fixes, renaming files and resizing files. To perform editing on multiple files:

The default file format for images taken with most digital cameras and smartphone cameras is JPEG (Joint Photographic Experts Group). However, this can be changed for a group of photos with the Process Multiple Files option.

1 In Expert edit mode, select **File** > **Process Multiple Files** from the Menu bar

2 The **Process Multiple Files** window contains all of the options for selecting and editing multiple files

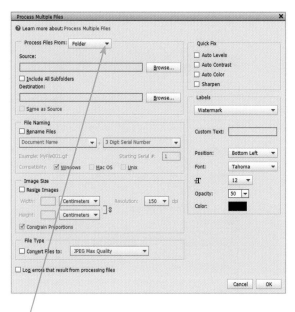

Use the **Opened Files** option in Step 3 to perform a task on specific files, rather than on a whole folder.

3 Click here to select options for the source location of the images to be edited. This can be

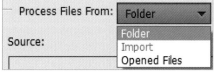

either a folder, images imported from another location, or the currently opened files

...cont'd

4 For the **Folder** option in Step 3, click on the **Browse...** button, navigate to the required folder and click on the **OK** button

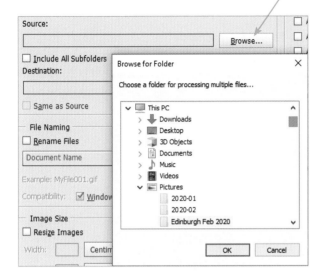

The more images in a folder, the longer it will take to process.

If you select the **Same as Source** option for the source of the processed files, these will overwrite the originals, even if the **Rename Files** option has been selected (it becomes deselected if Same as Source is selected).

5 Select a destination folder in the same way as for selecting the source folder

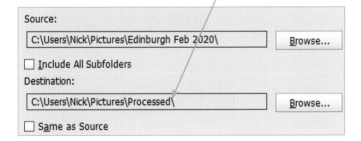

6 Under the **Quick Fix** section, check on any of the fixes that you want applied to all of the images. The options are for **Auto Levels**, **Auto Contrast**, **Auto Color** and **Sharpen**

The Quick Fix options are a good way to edit a group of photos that have been taken under similar lighting conditions.

171

...cont'd

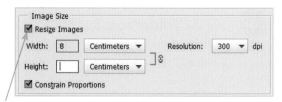

7 Under the **Image Size** section, check **On** the **Resize Images** checkbox and enter the required dimensions and resolution. If **Constrain Proportions** is checked **On**, only one of the **Width** or **Height** boxes has to be completed, as the other one will be adjusted automatically, in proportion

PDF and TIFF file formats generally produce larger file sizes than JPEGs, which is a file format specifically designed to compress file size.

8 Check **On** the **Convert Files to:** button to select an option for converting the files into another file format; e.g. as PDFs or TIFFs

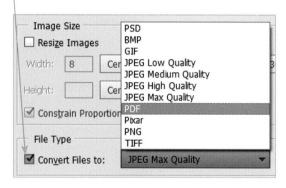

Once all of the required selections have been made for converting the files, click on the **OK** button.

9 Check **On** the **Rename Files** button to rename the batch of files based on a base document name and a sequential identifier

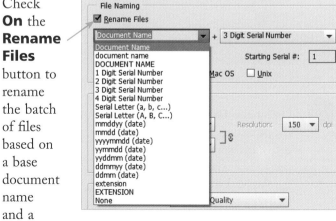

Applying Actions

Within Elements there are a number of preset editing actions that can be applied to images repeatedly, without having to perform all of the separate tasks individually. To do this:

1 In Expert edit mode, open the image to which you want to apply the action

The Actions panel does not have a keyboard shortcut.

2 Select **Window** > **Actions** from the Menu bar. Click here next to an Actions folder to expand it

You cannot create your own actions within Elements.

3 Click on an action to select it

4 Click on this button to perform the action

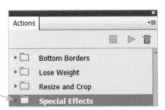

If you have the full version of Photoshop, you can import actions from there. To do this, click on the Actions panel's menu (top-right corner) and select **Load Actions**. Navigate to the Actions folder within the Photoshop program files (**Presets > Actions**) and select an action there. Click on the **Load** button to add it.

5 The action is performed and all of the required editing steps are applied to the image

Viewing File Info

When digital images are taken, they create a considerable amount of related information, also known as metadata. To view this:

1 Open an image in Expert edit or Quick edit mode

2 Select **File** > **File Info** from the Menu bar

3 Click on the **Camera Data** button to view the information (metadata) that was created when the image was captured

4 The Camera Data information includes the **Camera Information** – i.e. the make and model of the camera – and the **Shot Information** – i.e. Focal Length, Exposure, Image Size, Orientation, Resolution and Flash

Camera Information

Make:	Canon
Model:	Canon EOS 350D DIGITAL; S/N: 2630703875
Owner:	
Lens:	

Shot Information

Focal Length:	21.00 mm
Exposure:	1/30 sec; f/4.0; ISO 800; Aperture priority; Pattern metering
Image Size:	3456 x 2304
Orientation:	1 (Normal)
Resolution:	72.00 Pixel per Inch
Flash:	Did not fire

5 Click on the **Basic** button to add your own additional metadata to the image

Basic

Don't forget

The **Shot Information** is created by the camera when a photo is taken.

Beware

Add a **Copyright Status** and a **Copyright Notice** in Step 5 if your photos are going to be published in public, and you are concerned that they may be used by others without your permission.

Save for Web

As digital cameras get more powerful in terms of the size and quality of images that they can capture, one issue is how to use these images on the web or in email: the larger the image, the longer it takes to send in an email or upload to the web. To overcome this, there is an option to save an image specifically for web use. To do this:

1 Open an image in Expert edit or Quick edit mode

2 Select **File > Save for Web** from the Menu bar to open the Save for Web window

3 The size of the original image is shown in the left-hand panel; the new size, in the right-hand panel

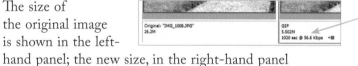

4 Click here to select a file format for the image for the web

5 Enter a new size for the image to reduce the physical size of it; e.g. from 3024 x 3024 pixels to 500 x 500 pixels

6 The size of the image in the right-hand panel is reduced accordingly (in this example, to 208K)

Hot tip

The keyboard shortcut for the Save for Web dialog window is **Alt + Shift + Ctrl + S** (**Alt + Shift + Command key + S** on a Mac).

Don't forget

Next to the image size is an estimate for how long the image will take to download at different download speeds (which can be changed by clicking on the Menu button next to the current speed).

175

Don't forget

Click on the **Save** button to exit the **Save for Web** window.

Image Size

The physical size of a digital image can sometimes be a confusing issue, as it is frequently dealt with under the term "resolution". Unfortunately, resolution can be applied to a number of areas of digital imaging: image resolution, monitor resolution, print size and print resolution.

Image resolution

The resolution of an image is determined by the number of pixels it contains. This is counted as a vertical and a horizontal value; e.g. 4000 x 3000. When multiplied together it gives the overall resolution; i.e. 12,000,000 pixels in this case. This is frequently the headline figure quoted by camera manufacturers; e.g. 12 million pixels (or, more commonly, 12 megapixels). To view the image resolution in Elements:

The keyboard shortcut for the Image Size dialog window is **Alt** + **Ctrl** + **I** (**Alt** + **Command key** + **I** on a Mac).

To view an image at its actual size, or the size at which it will currently be printed, select the **Zoom** tool from the Toolbox and select **1:1** or **Print Size** from the Tool Options bar.

The Resolution figure under the Document Size heading is used to determine the size at which the image will be printed. If this is set to 96 pixels per inch (PPI), then the onscreen size and the printed size should be roughly the same.

1 Select **Image > Resize > Image Size** from the Menu bar

2 The image size is displayed here (in pixels)

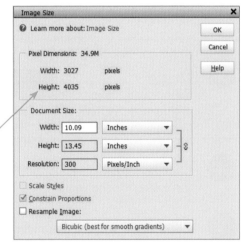

Monitor resolution

Most modern computer monitors display digital images at between 72 and 96 pixels per inch (PPI). This means that every inch of the screen contains approximately this number of pixels. So, for an image being displayed at 100%, the onscreen size will be the number of pixels horizontally divided by 72 (or 96, depending on the monitor), and the same vertically. In the above example, this would mean the image, at actual size, could be viewed at approximately 31 inches by 42 inches (3027/96 and 4035/72) on a monitor. In modern web browsers, this is usually adjusted so that the whole image is accommodated on the viewable screen.

Document size (print resolution)

Pixels in an image are not a set size, which means that images can be printed in a variety of sizes, simply by contracting or expanding the available pixels. This is done by changing the resolution in the Document Size section of the Image Size dialog box. (When dealing with document size, think of this as the size of the printed document.) To set the size at which an image will be printed:

Hot tip

To work out the size at which an image will be printed, divide the pixel dimensions (height and width) by the resolution value under the Document Size heading.

1 Select **Image** > **Resize** > **Image Size** from the Menu bar

2 Change the resolution here (or change the width and height of the document size). Make sure the **Resample Image:** box is not checked (see page 178)

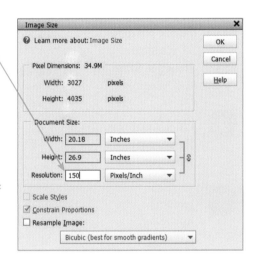

3 By changing one value, the other two are updated too

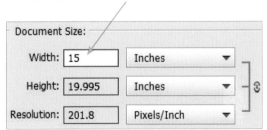

Don't forget

The print resolution determines how many pixels are used in each inch of the printed image (PPI). However, the number of dots used to represent each pixel on the paper is determined by the printer resolution, measured in dots per inch (DPI). So if the print resolution is 72 PPI and the printer resolution is 2880 DPI, each pixel will be represented by 40 colored dots; i.e. 2880 divided by 72.

4 Click on the **OK** button

177

Resampling Images

All digital images can be increased or decreased in size. This involves adding or removing pixels from the image. Decreasing the size of an image is relatively straightforward and involves removing redundant pixels. However, increasing the size of an image involves adding pixels by digital guesswork. To do this, Elements looks at the existing pixels and works out the nearest match for the ones that are to be added. Increasing or decreasing the size of a digital image is known as "resampling".

Resampling

Resampling down decreases the size of the image, and it is more effective than resampling up. To do this:

The process of adding pixels to an image to increase its size is known as "interpolation".

To keep the same resolution for an image, resample it by changing the pixel dimensions' height and width. To keep the same document size (i.e. the size at which it will be printed) resample it by changing the resolution.

1   Select **Image > Resize > Image Size** from the Menu bar

2   Check **On** the **Resample Image:** box

3   Resample the image by changing the pixel dimensions, the height and width, or the resolution

4   Changing any of the values in the Image Size dialog box alters the physical size of the image. Click on the **OK** button

Make sure the **Constrain Proportions** box is checked On if you want the image to be increased or decreased in size proportionally.

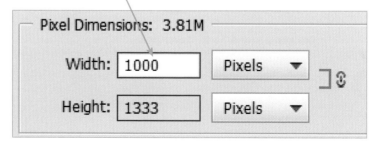

11 Printing Images

This chapter details sizing images and printing them in a variety of formats.

Print Size

Before you start printing images in Elements, it is important to ensure that they are going to be produced at the required size. Since the pixels within an image are not a set size, the printed dimensions of an image can be altered according to your needs. This is done by specifying how many pixels are used within each inch of the image. The more pixels per inch (PPI), then the higher the quality of the printed image, but the smaller in size it will be.

To set the print size of an image (in any of the Editor modes):

The higher the resolution in the Document Size section of the dialog, the greater the quality, but the smaller the size of the printed image.

1 Open an image and select **Image** > **Resize** > **Image Size** from the Menu bar

Hot tip

The output size for a printed image can be worked out by dividing the pixel dimensions (the width and height) by the resolution. So if the width is 2560, the height 1920, and the resolution 300 PPI, the printed image will be approximately 8 inches x 6 inches.

2 Uncheck the **Resample Image:** box. This will ensure that the physical image size (i.e. the number of pixels in the image) remains unchanged when the resolution is changed

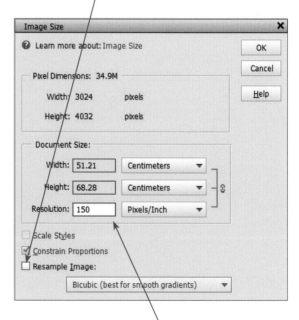

180

Don't forget

As long as the Resample Image box is unchecked, changing the output resolution has no effect on the actual number of pixels in an image.

3 The current resolution and document size (print size) are displayed here

4 Enter a new figure in the **Resolution:** box (here, the resolution has been increased from 150 to 300). This affects the document size; i.e. the size at which the image prints

Document Size:

Width:	25.6	Centimeters ▼
Height:	34.14	Centimeters ▼
Resolution:	300	Pixels/Inch ▼

Viewing print size
In Expert edit mode, images can be viewed at their print size:

1 Click on the Zoom tool

2 In the Tool Options bar, click on the **Print Size** button

3 The image is displayed at the size at which it will be printed. Change the resolution to see how this changes the print size

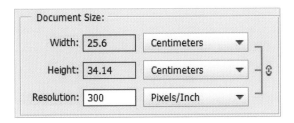

Hot tip

The keyboard shortcut for accessing the Image Size dialog window is **Alt + Ctrl + I** (**Alt + Command key** + **I** on a Mac).

Don't forget

A resolution of 300 pixels per inch (PPI) is a good benchmark for printed images. However, a lower resolution will still produce a good quality and enable the image to be printed at a larger size.

181

Beware

The print size on screen may not be completely accurate, depending on the resolution of your monitor. However, it will still give a reasonably good idea of the size of the printed image.

Print Functions

The print functions in Elements can be accessed from the Menu bar in either the Editor or the Organizer, by selecting **File** > **Print**. Also, all of the print functions can be selected from Create mode. To print to your local printer using this method:

1 Select an image in either the Editor or the Organizer, click on the **Create** button and click on the **Photo Prints** button

2 Click on the **Local Printer** button

3 The main print window displays the default options for how the printed image will appear, and also options for changing the properties of the print

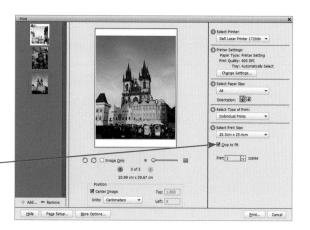

4 Click the **Add...** button to include more images in the current print job, or select an image and click on the **Remove** button to exclude it

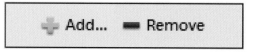

5 Use these options to rotate an image for printing, or change its size or position

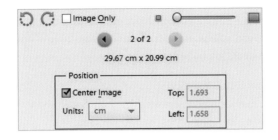

6 Click here to select a destination printer to which you want to send your print

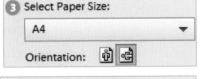

7 Click on the **Change Settings...** button to change the properties for your own local printer

8 Click here to select the paper size for printing

9 Click here to select the print type; i.e. the layout of the image you are printing

10 Click here to select the size at which you want your image to be printed

11 Click on the **Print...** button to print your image with the settings selected above

Hot tip

Check on the **Center Image** box in Step 5 to have the image printed in the center of the page.

Don't forget

The other options for type of print in Step 9 are **Picture Package** and **Contact Sheet**. See pages 184-185 for more details.

183

Print Layouts

Rather than just offering the sole function of printing a single image on a sheet of paper, Elements has two options that can be used when printing images, which can help reduce the number of sheets of paper used.

Picture Package

This can be used to print out copies of different images on a single piece of paper. To do this:

Hot tip

When buying a printer, choose one that has borderless printing. This means that it can print to the very edge of the page.

1 Select an image in either the Editor or the Organizer, click on the **Create** > **Photo Prints** button, and then click on the **Picture Package** button

Don't forget

The Picture Package option is also available if you print photos using **File** > **Print** (or **Ctrl** + **P**; **Command** + **P** on a Mac) from the Menu bar. In the **Prints** dialog window, select **Picture Package** under the **Select Type of Print:** heading.

2 The layout for the Picture Package is displayed in the main print window

184

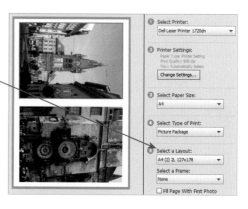

Don't forget

The Picture Package function is useful for printing images in a combination of sizes, such as for family portraits.

3 Under **Select a Layout:**, select how many images you want on a page and if required, select a type of frame for the printed images

...cont'd

Contact sheet

This can be used to create and print thumbnail versions of a large number of images. To do this:

1 Select an image in either the Editor or the Organizer, click on the **Create** > **Photo Prints** button and then click on the **Contact Sheet** button

2 The layout for the contact sheet is displayed in the main Print window

Don't forget

When a contact sheet is created, new thumbnail images are generated. The original images are unaffected.

185

Beware

Do not include too many thumbnails on a contact sheet, otherwise they may be too small to see any detail clearly.

3 Click under **Select Type of Print:** and select the number of columns to be displayed on the contact sheet

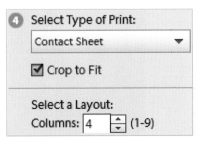

Creating PDF Files

PDF (Portable Document Format) is a file format that is used to maintain the original formatting and style of a document, so that it can be viewed on a variety of different devices and types of computers. In general, it is usually used for documents that contain text and images, such as information pamphlets, magazine features, and chapters from books. However, image files such as JPEGs can also be converted into PDFs, and this can be done within Elements without the need for any other specialist software. To do this:

Don't forget

PDF files are an excellent way to share files so that other people can print them. All that is required is a copy of Adobe Acrobat Reader, which is bundled with most software packages on computers, or can be downloaded from the Adobe website at www.adobe.com

186

1 Open an image and select **File** > **Save As** from the Menu bar

2 Select a destination folder and make sure the format is set to Photoshop PDF, then click **Save**

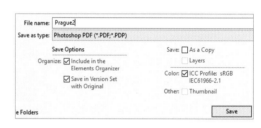

3 The PDF file is created and can be opened in Adobe Acrobat or Elements

Beware

PDF files are generally larger in terms of file size than standard image file formats such as JPEG.

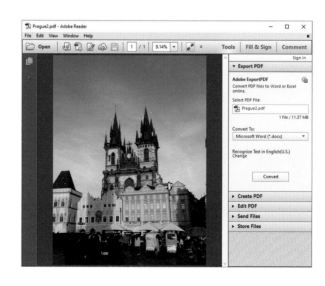

Index